The Ptolemies,
Apogee and Collapse

The Ptolemies, Apogee and Collapse

Ptolemiac Egypt 246–146 BC

John D. Grainger

Pen & Sword
MILITARY

First published in Great Britain in 2023 by
Pen & Sword Military
An imprint of Pen & Sword Books Limited
Yorkshire – Philadelphia

Copyright © John D. Grainger 2023

ISBN 978 1 39909 017 9

The right of John D. Grainger to be identified as
Author of this Work has been asserted by him in accordance
with the Copyright, Designs and Patents Act 1988.

A CIP catalogue record for this book is
available from the British Library

All rights reserved. No part of this book may be reproduced or
transmitted in any form or by any means, electronic or mechanical
including photocopying, recording or by any information storage and
retrieval system, without permission from the Publisher in writing.

Typeset by Mac Style
Printed in the UK by CPI Group (UK) Ltd, Croydon, CR0 4YY.

Pen & Sword Books Limited incorporates the imprints of After
the Battle, Atlas, Archaeology, Aviation, Discovery, Family History,
Fiction, History, Maritime, Military, Military Classics, Politics,
Select, Transport, True Crime, Air World, Frontline Publishing, Leo
Cooper, Remember When, Seaforth Publishing, The Praetorian Press,
Wharncliffe Local History, Wharncliffe Transport, Wharncliffe True
Crime and White Owl.

For a complete list of Pen & Sword titles please contact

PEN & SWORD BOOKS LIMITED
47 Church Street, Barnsley, South Yorkshire, S70 2AS, England
E-mail: enquiries@pen-and-sword.co.uk
Website: www.pen-and-sword.co.uk
or
PEN AND SWORD BOOKS
1950 Lawrence Rd, Havertown, PA 19083, USA
E-mail: Uspen-and-sword@casematepublishers.com
Website: www.penandswordbooks.com

Contents

Maps		vii
Introduction: Ptolemy III's Inheritance and Problems		ix
Chapter 1	The Third Syrian War	1
Chapter 2	The Ptolemaic Kingdom as a Superpower	19
Chapter 3	Ptolemy III and Egypt	34
Chapter 4	Court Crisis and a New War	49
Chapter 5	The Fourth Syrian War	59
Chapter 6	An Accumulation of Problems	71
Chapter 7	Rebellion and Court Coups	85
Chapter 8	Egypt Beset: the Fifth Syrian War	98
Chapter 9	Ptolemy V	117
Chapter 10	Approaching the Sixth Syrian War	130
Chapter 11	The Ptolemaic Disaster: The Sixth Syrian War	145
Chapter 12	The Aftermath of War: Division and Rebellion	167
Chapter 13	Ptolemy VI at Peace	182
Chapter 14	Victory and Death: The Seventh Syrian War	194
Conclusion		212
Appendix I: The Ptolemaic Descent		215
Bibliography		216
Notes		220
Index		235

Maps

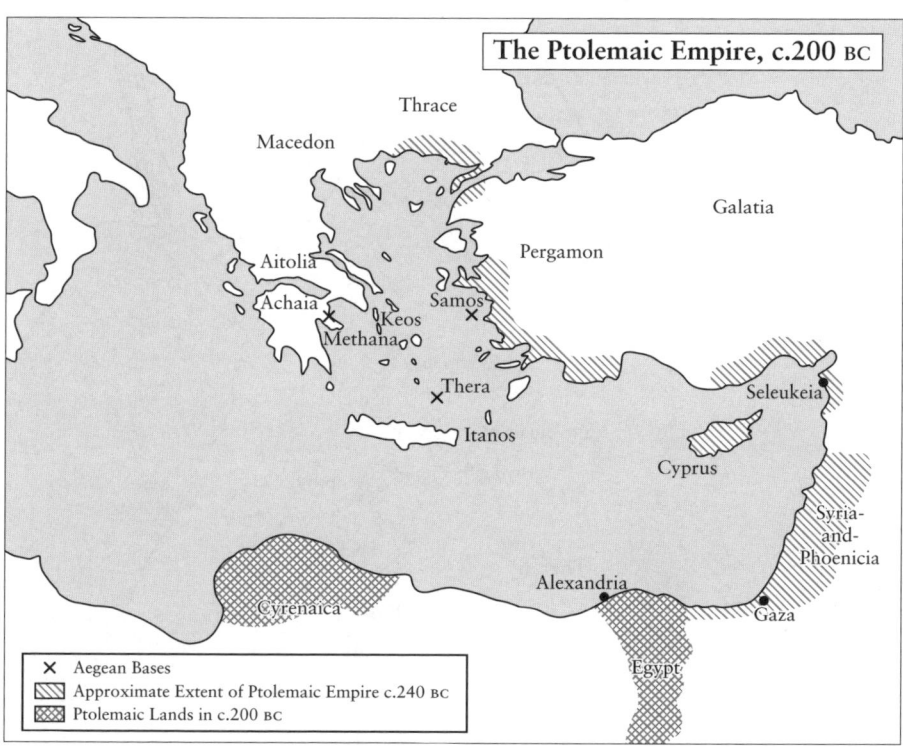

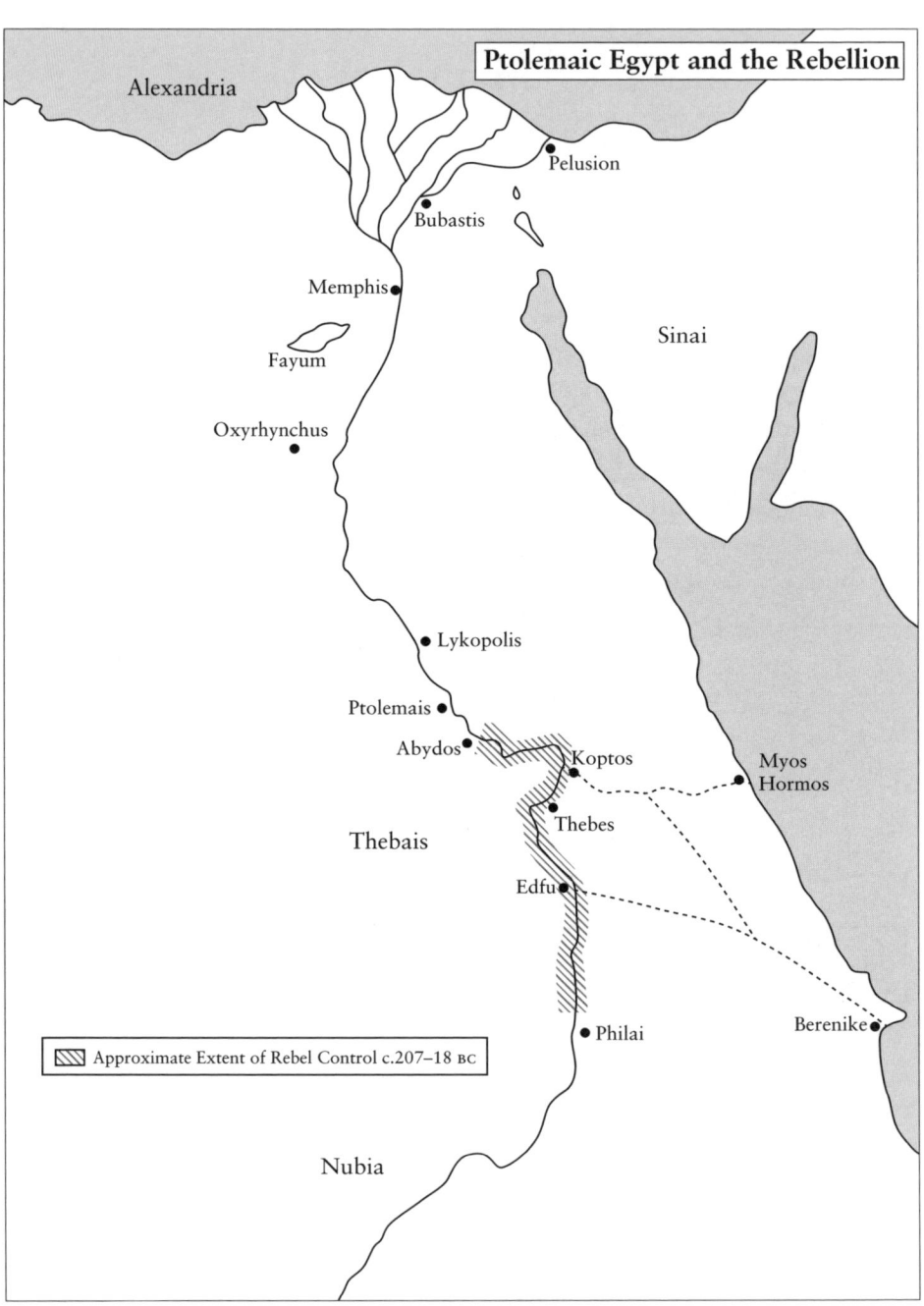

Introduction: Ptolemy III's Inheritance and Problems

On the death of Ptolemy II in late January 246 BC, his eldest son became king as Ptolemy III. He was already in his late 30s, having been born soon after 285 BC, when his parents married. He had little or no direct experience of government, other than whatever tutoring of him his father had done. He was, it seems, close to his father, perhaps because his elder brother, Ptolemy 'the Son', had died while operating as a king in Ephesos; Ptolemy II could not afford to lose another son. He was, therefore, keen to keep his heir close, and was also sensible enough to ensure that his heir was properly educated and included in the discussions of affairs. What the old king could not do was in any way compensate for his son's privileged upbringing; he had been born the son of the king, had lived in an exceedingly wealthy, even decadent, court, surrounded by servants willing to provide all things he wanted, under a king who had scarcely stirred from the palace for long periods, though certainly working hard at the necessary duties. The later evidence suggests that the example of such diligence wore off after some years, and the pleasures of wealth and decadence took over. The new king had received an even more pampered upbringing than his father, who practised diligence all his life; Ptolemy III was a copy of the old man only for a time.[1]

Ptolemy III was the third of the family to rule. His grandfather had chosen Egypt as his satrapy during the arguments following the death of Alexander, and had defended the land with determination and success. He had extended his rule over a large part of the lands around the eastern Mediterranean – Cyrenaica, Syria and Phoenicia, the coast of Asia Minor, Aegean islands. He had participated in most of the coalitions which were formed to bring down the kingdom of Antigonos I, and to suppress the ambitions of his son Demetrios I; he had in the process first allied with, and then quarrelled with, Seleukos, who complained that Ptolemy, his friend, had deprived him of his proper share in the division of Antigonos' lands.

x   The Ptolemies, Apogee and Collapse

Ptolemy I's son, Ptolemy II Philadelphos, was one of the most spectacular kings of his time, though the spectacle hid much failure. He had extended and then lost an empire in the Aegean, but had acquired one in the lands of the Red Sea and Nubia. He had fought Seleukos' successor, Antiochos I, twice, without success, and Antigonos Gonatas, Demetrios' son, again without success. For a king who rarely shifted from the palace, and then only into nearby Egypt (the '*chora*'), he had indulged in a lot of warfare: in a reign of thirty-seven years (283–246 BC) he was at war for eighteen of them. He had a large professional army, a militia, and the largest navy in the Mediterranean, and yet he lost control of the Aegean islands and failed to regain Cyrenaica. His major achievement had perhaps been to extend his power into Africa and along the Red Sea, and to devise a rigorous taxation system for Egypt and its empire, which left a large part of his Egyptian subjects in poverty and seeking ways to evade his taxes.

A result of the reign of Ptolemy II was that his successor had several immediate problems to solve on his accession. He was betrothed to Berenike, the daughter of Magas, the king of Cyrenaica who had died in 250 BC. She was (apparently) beleaguered in the acropolis in Cyrene after her father's death, and the kingdom she might claim to have inherited had disintegrated. Probably some of the disintegration was the result of Ptolemaic intrigues, aimed at undermining the republican regime which had been attempting to govern since Magas' death, and promoting the unification of Egypt with Cyrenaica and the marriage of Ptolemy III with Berenike. This is a confused period of Cyrenaican history, of which we know all too little, and which lasted for four or five years, but soon after Ptolemy III's accession in Egypt the problem was solved, at least to the satisfaction of Ptolemy. Berenike married her king and went to live in Alexandria.[2] There was no attempt to re-install her as a ruler in Cyrenaica. Instead the whole province was taken over by Ptolemy, and its several cities became semi-independent – or at least autonomous – though under effective Ptolemaic suzerainty.

Exactly how this was done is quite unclear, but it was probably a combination of Ptolemaic pressure and the new determination of the wealthiest Cyrenaicans who formed themselves into ruling oligarchies in order to defeat the insurrectionary democracy. Once the leaders of an attempted radical revolution, the professional revolutionaries Ekdelos and

Damophilos,[3] had been expelled, and Berenike, who could have headed an independence movement, was removed to Alexandria, the conflict died away. The governments of the cities were in oligarchic hands, or perhaps a democracy of the middle class, and they were all frowned over by distant Ptolemaic power. No doubt the memory of the disorders between 250 and 246 BC was sufficient to deter any more revolutions for some time, or to persuade the most violent of the democrats to leave.

This acquisition was not only a considerable extension of Ptolemaic territory, where he inherited the influence of Magas in diplomatic contacts with the western Mediterranean powers, but was also a marked success against the Antigonid enemy in Macedon and Greece. The dead Demetrios the Fair would automatically have looked to his half-brother Antigonos Gonatas for support if he had ruled long enough and come under serious pressure from Ptolemy. There can be little doubt that in encouraging Demetrios to take up the offer of marriage at Cyrene, Antigonos had such a political connection in mind. It was Demetrios' death which opened the way for the Ptolemaic coup. But Macedonian kings bore in mind the advantages of gaining control of Cyrenaica for themselves.

This was a major political triumph for Ptolemy III, something which had escaped both his father and his grandfather. It also freed him from any threat from that direction. One of the players in the conflict in the province had been Demetrios the Fair, from the Macedonian royal family of the Antigonids. His murder, at Berenike's hands, had effectively ended any pretence of influence of the Antigonid family, though it did not extinguish Antigonid interest. Once Berenike was removed and Demetrios eliminated, the future of the cities of the province depended on Ptolemaic control, and perhaps investment – the development of the country was expensive. The province was to be quiet for several more decades.

The region had been a fertile source of recruits for the Ptolemaic army under Magas, and this continued for the next forty years. Stalwart efforts have been made to produce figures based on the study of papyri and inscriptions to give some idea of the relative strength of recruiting from various parts of the Mediterranean; however, this can only give an imprecise and quite inaccurate count of the numbers, but some idea of the proportions of recruits from the several sections of the Mediterranean lands can be deduced. So, for what it is worth, for the third century BC it seems as though the Ptolemaic kings could rely on recruiting about ten per cent of their mercenaries from Cyrenaica. This percentage collapsed after the beginning of the great revolt of 205 BC and the defeat by Antiochos III in the Fifth Syrian War in 198 BC.[4]

For the moment, therefore, Ptolemy III had begun his reign well. Another problem, however, was the threat from the Seleukid kingdom, firmly established in Asia Minor, Babylonia and the East, and, most pertinently, in North Syria. With Ptolemy II's death early in 246 BC, the peace of 253 with Antiochos II ceased to have effect, so there was the immediate possibility of a new Syrian war, though it did not happen for some months. The delay was probably due to Antiochos II's own final illness, so that when the new war did begin it was on Ptolemy III's initiative.

Ptolemy III himself can be assumed to have been busy for several months establishing his authority in Egypt, and in securing Berenike and Cyrenaica. But the threat from the north was no doubt a factor in his mind while dealing with Cyrenaica, since one of the preceding Syrian Wars had involved attempted simultaneous joint attacks from both Syria and Cyrenaica, when Magas married Apama, the daughter of Seleukos I; this was one good reason to solve the Cyrenaican issue first and quickly.

Then there was the problem of Macedon and Greece. Ptolemy II's power in the region had foundered as a result of failures and defeats in the Kremonidean War (267–261 BC) and the Second Syrian War (260–253 BC), but Ptolemy III did inherit a fairly strong position in the region, from which a revival might be possible. He was firm friends with Rhodes, based on mutually beneficial economic interests. He held a good part of the coastal region of Lykia and Karia in southwestern Asia Minor with garrisons and subservient cities. He had a major naval base at Samos. In the Aegean he held bases at Itanos in Crete, the island of Thera, and the town of Methana – 'a little Gibraltar' – on the Argolid peninsula, providing a well-policed maritime route across the Aegean to Greece. He may also have inherited the base at Keos developed during the recent war, but it seems likely that it had been given up.

His father had fought Antigonos Gonatas before and during the Kremonidean War, and this was an undeclared conflict which was liable to break out into active hostility at any time. No peace treaty ever was agreed between these monarchies. Antigonos was involved in 246 BC in recovering Corinth from the widow of his cousin Alexander, while Ptolemy II had subsidized the adventurer Aratos of Sikyon in his ambitions in the same area.⁵

One of the defeats Ptolemy II had suffered was to lose control of the Island League of the Kyklades, but that league, so far as it still existed, was now in some way under Rhodian influence; given the close relations between Ptolemaic Egypt and Rhodes, this might be seen as Rhodes acting as Ptolemy's agent in the area.⁶

Beyond the eastern Mediterranean, Ptolemy had other matters to concern him. One was the situation in the Red Sea. His father had invested large resources in developing trade between Egypt and the southern end of the Red Sea, first of all to acquire elephants for his armed forces in order to compete with the Indian elephants acquired by the Seleukid kings. Ships from Egypt were also able to intercept part of the trade in incenses from the south of Arabia and to tap into the trade in Indian goods, including silks, cottons and spices, which reached southern Arabia in Indian and Arab ships. This had been achieved at a great cost to the government. A canal had been cleared to link the Nile with the Red Sea; roads had been constructed between the Nile in Upper Egypt and the new ports which were constructed on the Red Sea coast; specialized ships to carry the captured elephants had been developed and built; large numbers of sailors and soldiers had been employed in hunting for the elephants and in manning the ships. The investment had been enormous. Ptolemy III had to decide whether to continue this work, for the cost of maintaining it was also high. And the elephants which were captured were smaller than the Indian ones, and could not face them in battle.

The new king presided over an empire of disparate populations. In his new province of Cyrenaica the dominant group were Greeks, many of whom were descended from immigrants who had arrived four centuries before (as it happened, the first group came from Thera, now a Ptolemaic naval base). This history was one of the sources of the strong sentiment for independence the region had always displayed. It had been threatened by Persians, had submitted to Alexander, but at a distance, had fought Ptolemy I several times, and accepted a quasi-independent condition under Magas, Ptolemy I's stepson, who eventually made himself a quasi-independent king. This was a country which needed careful handling, hence the concession of autonomy to the cities, which helped divide the country, making it easier to dominate. It was also the home of Libyan tribes, pastoralists living on the desert edge, who may or may not be hostile, and who infiltrated into the Greek regions.

Syria-and-Phoenicia were much more complex. The province stretched from the city of Gaza, on the border with Egypt, to the Eleutheros River in northern Phoenicia, and from the coast of the Mediterranean eastwards to an indefinite boundary in the Syrian/Arabian desert. Phoenicians, Jews, Philistines, Nabataeans, Aramaeans, Arabs, Ituraeans, all these and more inhabited their own parts of the country, which was sprinkled with the new Greek and Macedonian immigrants. Each of these peoples had their own territory, their own particular history, and increasingly their own languages. The whole country was governed by a Greek-speaking governor-general and an administration appointed by Ptolemy. These were men who were descended from, or were themselves, immigrants from various parts of the Mediterranean, imposed on the well-settled native population. There is no indication that any of these administrators appointed from outside spoke the language of any of the Syrians – other than the Greeks and Macedonians who had settled there, of course. The Syrian communities tended to collect around their own national central temples – of Dushares, Yahweh, and so on, partly as a means of holding on to their tribal individuality.

There was enough combustible material here to demand careful governance, as the future would show. That there is no indication of uprisings, riots, and rebellions in Syria in the Ptolemaic period could be put down to that careful governance, but it is more likely due to Syria having enjoyed a period of peace since about 300 BC, after several decades of intermittent warfare and invasions from outside. The benefits of that peace were emphasized every now and again, when a 'Syrian War' broke out between the Ptolemaic and Seleukid empires. There had been two of these wars in this period of peace, but neither had impinged seriously on Syria, though Ptolemy I and II had fortified the northern frontier as a precaution – the Seleukid king maintained a claim to 'Syria-and-Phoenicia'. But perhaps the most telling item of information which marks Syrian attitudes to Ptolemaic rule is that Syria was the source of relatively few recruits either to the Ptolemaic army or to the kingdom's administration. Syria, having suffered centuries of unpleasantness from Assyrians, Babylonians, Persians, and Macedonians, kept its collective head down.

A more enthusiastic participant in the Ptolemaic state was Cyprus. The island prospered under the Ptolemies, sent considerable numbers of young men into the army, and still more into the navy. It was, along with Phoenicia, the place where Ptolemy's ships were built, having the wood and material resources for the work, as well as skilled shipbuilders; it also held a large garrison of mercenaries. In Ptolemy I's time it was often governed by a member of the Ptolemaic family, but by the time of Ptolemy III the governors were appointed from members of the Greek Egyptian aristocracy, usually experienced soldiers. The island was generally content under their rule, though this is more an impression from the absence of records than anything else. It had certainly not been involved in any of the international conflicts for at least forty years.

The population of the island was mixed. The majority of the population was Greek, descended from a Mycenaean-period immigration, but part of the land was inhabited by Phoenicians, who took a full part in the administration and yet retained their individuality as Phoenicians; the inhabitants did form a much-better-integrated population than that of either Syria or Cyrenaica.

The Ptolemaic possessions along the coasts of southern and western Asia Minor fluctuated in extent regularly with the balance of power in the area between Seleukids and Ptolemies. This was an area where the cities, all autonomous, looked to the immediate advantage, switching allegiance from king to king and into independence as opportunity and advantage offered. If threatened, they usually did not resist. Some were subject to Ptolemaic or Seleukid governors; those under Ptolemaic control were harshly taxed, and did not hesitate to complain. One city, Termessos, had been given to Ptolemy son of Lysimachos, a stepson of Ptolemy I, as a principality, and his descendants ruled it for three more generations. (He was also the son of the King Lysimachos who had ruled Asia Minor as a kingdom; his presence could be seen as a deliberate Ptolemaic provocation.) These cities were all subject to the fluctuating powers of their greater neighbours; like the Syrians they knew when to keep mum and wait.

The main Ptolemaic possession was Egypt. Here there was little in the way of integration of the various elements of the population. The Greeks and Macedonians and Karians did integrate as 'Greeks', though some continued to identify themselves as from those lands, but they had little alternative, in the presence of the vastly greater population of Egyptians, but to band together and become Greek. The division between 'Greeks' and Egyptians remained stark throughout the period of Ptolemaic rule (and after). The Greeks did not learn Egyptian, though the men took Egyptian women as wives and concubines; the Egyptians perforce learned at least some Greek so as to communicate with their rulers, though in the villages it is probable that only a few learned much of the language, the majority remaining monolingual in Egyptian. There were some other distinct groups in the country as well, Jews in particular, a considerable number of whom lived in Alexandria. There were Phoenicians (some of whom had moved to Egypt well before Ptolemy's time), Nabataeans, Syrians, Libyans, and Nubians, but, apart from the Jews, the numbers were relatively small.

Relations between the Greek rulers and their Egyptian subjects were, therefore, less than cordial. The almost complete lack of integration fostered a mutual dislike. Connections were mainly channelled through the Egyptian temples and their priests, who were pleased to accept gifts and privileges from the rulers, but displayed little loyalty to the kings. Above all, the heavy taxation regime kept the Egyptian population in poverty, while the Greek population in Egypt generally prospered, in part because many of them were employed in the administration and so were paid out of the product of those taxes; the settlers had been allocated estates of good land which kept them in comfort often living on the work of Egyptian peasants. The contrast in living styles and personal wealth was visible above all to the Egyptians.

The reign of Ptolemy II had been a time when new taxes were devised and new and more productive ways of enforcing older taxes worked out. The Egyptians, through long practice over thousands of years of oppressive governments, had devised ways of evading or avoiding those taxes. Greek-Egyptian relations were thus in a state of generalized hostility on the part of the latter, and some complacency among the former. But a change of king was always upsetting, and not only in international relations. There is no sign that in 246 BC, in his first year, Ptolemy III was aware of this Egyptian hostility – indeed, he no doubt accepted it as normal, and thus disregarded it. But his concentration on international problems and his marital opportunity evidently led then to his neglect of his own kingdom. The latter proved to be a fatal weakness in the former.

Chapter 1

The Third Syrian War

Ptolemy III was an unlikely conqueror, and in fact did little more in that line than his father, preferring much of the time to remain in his palace, or in Alexandria; however, in the one campaign he undertook personally he was undeniably successful. He was perhaps distracted from his nuptials in 246 BC by two items of news, to only one of which he reacted. In the Aegean a detachment of the Ptolemaic fleet, based at one of the Ptolemaic islands, came out to cruise in the western part of the sea. It encountered the main Macedonian fleet under Antigonos Gonatas himself, which was probably heading for Corinth, where the king was concerned to recover the city from Nikaia, the widow of Alexander, his nephew; she had seized the city after Alexander's death and appeared to be intending to rule it as her own principality.

The two fleets met off the island of Andros, probably by accident. Andros was certainly a strategic location for Antigonos in the conflict over Corinth, and a Ptolemaic fleet there would be able to interrupt Antigonid communications between Macedon and the Peloponnese and Attika. As usual in this period the details of what happened, and why, are unclear, except that the result was another sea victory for Antigonos. The Ptolemaic commander appears to have been a man called Sophron of Ephesos, who was not the overall naval commander in the region. That office may have belonged to another of the survivors of the battle, a man called Ptolemy Andromachou, supposedly Ptolemy III's half-brother, though his name shows that his father was called Andromachos; he could be the son of one of Ptolemy II's many mistresses. (His parentage is in fact not known, other than the name of his father; it would be best to abandon any theory of his relationship to the king.) He may have been the overall commander in the Aegean but the uncertainty is manifest in the number of speculatives in this passage.

The defeat the Ptolemaic fleet suffered – no more than a detachment against the main Antigonid fleet – was hardly surprising, and of more importance to Antigonos than to Ptolemy. The result, therefore, was similarly of little note for Ptolemy, simply a confirmation of Antigonid seapower in the north Aegean; if the meeting was accidental, as it probably was, it was of minor interest; neither king was interested in pursuing it to a full-scale war. Antigonos secured his communications, at least temporarily, while there was no change in the Ptolemaic situation, which was more concerned with the eastern Aegean than the west.[1] At Itanos in Crete, the city voted to honour King Ptolemy and Queen Berenike with a 'sacred enclosure'; this may perhaps be a reaction to the defeat, or an affirmation of loyalty, a declaration of which would bring benefits to the citizens, and a reminder to Ptolemy to continue protecting the city.[2]

The second item of news was of much more immediate interest to the Ptolemaic government. In July 246 BC Antiochos II died.[3] This event was far more important than the Battle of Andros, and probably overshadowed any notice Ptolemy took of the naval defeat. Antiochos had showed no reaction to the death of Ptolemy II six months before, even though Ptolemy III was preoccupied with settling himself in power, gaining control of Cyrenaica, and getting married. It may be that Antiochos had been ill for some time, though it also seems that his death was unexpected; any ill-health was perhaps kept secret. He had moved to Ephesos a year or two before, returning to his first wife, Laodike, and abandoning his Ptolemaic wife, Berenike ('I'), at Antioch. She had been a prize in the peace treaty of 253 BC, reluctantly conceded by Ptolemy II, for her delivery was a clear indication of the Ptolemaic defeat in the preceding war, and her husband might be able to mount a claim to the Ptolemaic throne, or any children might do so. Berenike had produced a son, Antiochos, in about 250 BC, but by continuing in regular correspondence with her father, who had sent supplies of Nile water to her, supposed to encourage pregnancy, it appeared that she was more of a Ptolemaic agent in the Seleukid court than a loyal Seleukid wife. Her child was being assumed in Ptolemaic circles to be the heir to Antiochos II's throne.

Antiochos II's return to his first wife was a clear sign that the interpretation of the baby as Antiochos II's successor was nonsense. He already had two sons by Laodike, of whom the eldest, Seleukos, was about twenty years of age, certainly old enough to succeed as king without dispute; the second, Antiochos, was some years younger; both were healthy and capable. In Seleukid eyes, there was no question but that Seleukos was the heir, and when the old king died, Seleukos took the title at once (Seleukos II).[4] Here, therefore, was another problem for Ptolemy III, one which was brought to him by his own, or his father's, unwarranted assumptions about his nephew's status. He evidently assumed that the child would automatically succeed, though that is difficult to believe. Berenike, who was the main driver in this situation, and whose status would depend on her son being recognized as king, was in control of the main administrative centres of the Seleukid kingdom, at Antioch and Seleukeia in Syria, and so in the best situation for making a coup. She controlled Antioch from the palace and was able to order Seleukid ships at Seleukeia-in-Pieria to sail to Egypt with her news. Such activity will have certainly persuaded many in Syria and nearby that she was in control more widely.[5]

The assumption of the child's succession was certainly spread, at least in the Ptolemaic regions. In Kildara in Karia, a fairly out of the way place, the news of Antiochos II's death induced the Ptolemaic governor in that region to announce that Antiochos, the son of Antiochos and Berenike, was now king.[6] This was more significant than the unimportance of the city (or the bad condition of the stone) might suggest. The governor was Tlepolemos son of Atrapates, a major political figure in the Ptolemaic government, Olympic victor in 256, and priest of Alexander and the deified Ptolemies in 247/246 BC – the most prestigious priesthood in Egypt.[7] If such a man, in such a position, and with strong Alexandrian connections, was responsible for proclaiming Antiochos as the new Seleukid king, this was clearly official Ptolemaic policy. He can only have made the proclamation if he knew this, or was obeying an order from Ptolemy himself. There is, however, no other indication that any other city did the same, which may only mean that no other city had time to record it epigraphically. Ptolemy III's own reaction does indicate that it was official policy.

Laodike and Seleukos, who were in Ephesos when Antiochos died, had the advantage of being on the spot; Seleukos' succession was a fact throughout Asia Minor before Berenike in Antioch heard of her husband's death. Nevertheless she had her infant son proclaimed as the new King Antiochos, though her authority was geographically limited to Seleukid Syria. The news was sent to her brother by a small Seleukid naval force from Seleukeia-in-Pieria. Berenike's proclamation was accepted in Syria, where she had obvious support and control of some forces, but the news that Seleukos was king also arrived, and from later events, this evidently caused divisions in the citizenry, and a revival of loyalty to the main Seleukid line.

Berenike sent a force into Kilikia, where the royal treasury at Soloi was appropriated. The governor of the region, Aribazos, attempted to combat this, but failed when two of the citizens rallied the rest, and they came out against him; this permitted Berenike's man to remove the treasure. Aribazos escaped into the hills where he was killed by some of the hillmen, who sent his head to Antioch; they were clearly in possession of the facts of the situation. Berenike, in her son's name, had therefore secured control of north Syria and Kilikia, a crucial area for dominating the whole kingdom.[8]

Ptolemy reacted cautiously, which suggests he was taken by surprise, but perhaps believing in the authority claimed by his sister. He first sent a small group of his own ships to investigate. These vessels will have come from Cyprus, or one of the Phoenician cities, or Alexandria; since the orders came from the king, it may be that Alexandria had been the base of the ships involved – and Berenike had already sent her messenger ships there also. Ptolemy had evidently then decided to investigate in person, and came up from Alexandria with a squadron of ships, halting at Poseideion, a small town and port on the coast between Laodikeia and Seleukeia, Seleukid territory. Meanwhile a Ptolemaic commander called Andriskos had used the smaller force to capture a city, though which one is not known; it was not Seleukeia, but may have been one of the Kilikian towns.

Ptolemy's purpose was evidently to provide support for his sister and her usurper-son. He was being careful, seeking to discover the exact situation before committing himself. He was evidently anxious to avoid a new Syrian War, yet was also seeking to support his sister in her pretensions, which in the event were to prove contradictory aspirations. All this took place without Ptolemy receiving any more information about the condition of affairs within Syria, other than what his sister had told him in her original message, and what Andriskos could provide. At Poseideion, Ptolemy could presumably obtain more information, but he evidently waited for some time before moving on; the official version was that he was waiting for the reception at Seleukeia to be organized. The whole situation has all the hallmarks of improvisations by various officials and that the confusion and the contradictions gradually increased. Ptolemy showed sense in pausing before moving further.

Meanwhile in Antioch the opposition to Berenike's activities had gathered strength, perhaps increasingly angered by the princess's assumption of authority. Two citizens, Ikadion and Gennaios, Seleukid loyalists, may have been contacted by a messenger from Queen Laodike at Ephesos – but Laodike is cast by some sources as the evil genius in these events, and this may be only a later assumption; more likely, they acted on their own initiative when they heard that Seleukos had been proclaimed king in Asia Minor. They gathered an armed force and turned on Berenike; in their first attack they succeeded in killing the child Antiochos, who had to have been their primary target. This in theory cut the ground out from under Berenike's pretensions, but she escaped, or was allowed to get away. The thinking by the assassins may have been that if she could get to Ptolemy still alive then a war might still be avoided; on the other hand, Berenike is much more likely to have sought a war for revenge after the killing of the son.

The activities at sea of Andriskos, whatever they were, and the arrival of Ptolemy and his fleet at Poseideion may then have compelled the assassins to go further, assuming that if Berenike was eliminated, Ptolemy would give up and leave. If so, they were mistaken. It is highly likely that Berenike refused to go any further away than Daphne, still close to Antioch. She was accompanied there by her maids and by a force of Galatian guards. Subsequent events suggest that she had considerable support in Antioch and Seleukeia, though this was perhaps only what might be called acquiescent support, based on a perception that she seemed to be in control. The death of the boy Antiochos would probably reduce this support, but was probably not yet announced.

Ptolemy, at Poseideion, and in ignorance of what was happening in Antioch, announced that he was in Syria to visit his sister, and arrangements were made for a ceremonial landing and reception at Seleukeia. In Antioch the assassins decided that they had to eliminate Berenike before Ptolemy arrived. Her death would destroy any support she had accumulated, and that support would probably go to Seleukos, rather than Ptolemy. The Galatian guard was persuaded to turn on her; she died, along with three of her maids, but the result of the attack remained confused and uncertain.

It was explained that she had been wounded, and was confined to bed, where in fact one of her maids pretended to be her. The death of the child was also being concealed by her and by the assassins, each for their own reasons.

Ptolemy's explanation that he was visiting his sister allowed him to land at Seleukeia, where he received a gratifyingly enthusiastic civic welcome. That the Ptolemaic king was landing at the name city of Seleukos I, Ptolemy I's nemesis, was an extraordinary enough event; that he received a welcome by the citizens can only be explained by the political confusion in the Seleukid kingdom at the time. The story that he was aiming to visit his sister, and that he arrived with only a small guard, implied that it was some species of state visit of the informal type. His stated reason for arriving precluded him from being accompanied by a sizeable force, so he could enter Seleukid territory with his personal guard only; it was not an invasion. He brought his ships into the harbour, and this in effect, if not in obvious intention, gave him control of the city whenever he chose to assert it. He went up to Antioch where he at last learned what had happened, and that both Berenike and Antiochos were dead. He had received another enthusiastic civic reception from a variety of officials from 'satraps and the other officers and priests, the bands of magistrates', so the news of the deaths had evidently been most efficiently concealed.

Ptolemy's first purpose, he had said, was to visit his sister; his second, whether announced or not, had been to support her in her seizure of power, and to ensure that his nephew's rights to the throne were enforced and respected. He must have realized, when the news of their deaths emerged, that the enthusiasm of the satraps and all the rest who had greeted him would quickly evaporate. The welcome had been no doubt promoted by Berenike's supporters only, while curiosity to see a foreign king in these particular cities may have attracted others. The activities of Ikadion and Gennaios had demonstrated all too clearly that there were citizens who opposed her and so opposed Ptolemy's project as well.

Ptolemy succeeded in continuing the concealment of the deaths for a time, and no doubt used the pause to bring in more forces and to secure his occupation of the two cities, above all by garrisoning their acropoleis. This apparently gave him immediate military superiority in Syria and Kilikia, which Berenike had already largely acquired. This was a defensible geographical and military position, with the Taurus Mountains to the north, the Mediterranean to the west controlled by his ships from Cyprus, and the Euphrates River on the east. But he would need a larger force than the marines and sailors of a squadron of ships if he was to be able to defend his gains.

It is just about possible to call this a military campaign since it is clear that Ptolemaic forces were the instrument by which Ptolemy III gained control of Syria and Kilikia. But to do so is to rather stretch the meaning of a 'campaign' going well away from what it usually means in a military context. It was, rather, a continuation, an intended consolidation of the *coup d'état* conducted by Berenike; the military 'campaign' was what soldiers sometimes call a 'promenade', little more than the occupation of enemy territory during which minimal opposition is found. With Antioch and Seleukeia in Ptolemaic control, and at least part of Kilikia also, the morale of Seleukid partisans can only have been much reduced. There were other cities enough in the region, fortified, and garrisoned to some extent, but they appear to have made no resistance. It seems likely that the root of Seleukid confusion was the failure of Antiochos II to publicly name his successor, together with the Ptolemaic propaganda about Antiochos the child, and the assumption that Berenike was governing. The general population, kept in ignorance, subject to lies and rumours, reacted to whoever could show authority; in Syria this was first Berenike, then Ptolemy.[9]

The Ptolemaic forces were built up. Some could come from Cyprus, but one record shows that he had, at least eventually, 'a force of infantry and cavalry and elephants from' Africa, along with his fleet. With such a force he secured, besides Antioch and Seleukeia, the Seleukid elephant corps at Apameia, a more effective force than his own.[10] The death of Berenike and her son became known during this expanding occupation, and Ptolemy may have been accepted as king, or at least as the man giving the orders.

Ptolemy could claim a great success, and went on, in the usual fashion of Ptolemaic propaganda, to claim more than he held, by announcing that he had been accepted as king in the eastern provinces of the Seleukid empire, and as far as Baktria or India.[11] The problem with all these claims is that there is no other evidence for them. Babylonia, with extensions eastwards, shows no evidence of Ptolemaic control, which would certainly have been recorded by the Babylonian 'Astronomical Diarist', and indeed the diarist did pay close attention to the royal authority, and records the presence of three of Antiochos II's children, Seleukos, Antiochos and their sister Laodike in the city in 245 BC, presumably to bolster their local support.[12] And without control of Babylonia there could be no Ptolemaic presence further east. Ptolemy did appoint a satrap for Mesopotamia, the land stretching east of the Euphrates as far as the Tigris and the Zagros Mountains; this was Xanthippos, of a prominent aristocratic family of Alexandria.

It is at times assumed that Ptolemy himself went on this campaign, but there is no evidence for this. How far east Xanthippos went in occupying his satrapy, if at all, is not known, though there was probably little to prevent him from marching as far as the Tigris; but if he did so with only a small force, he was very likely to be attacked, and it is highly unlikely he had a force of any size with him: it may well be that he had only a nominal appointment. The state of a Ptolemaic occupation in Syria, no matter how effective it was, would hardly have been felt in Mesopotamia when the population, and the officials, had time to understand what was happening; Babylonia had long been staunchly loyal to the Seleukids. A satrap was also appointed for Kilikia, a man called Antiochos, another prominent Alexandrian, though how much of Kilikia he controlled is not clear.

The reception in Alexandria of the news of Ptolemy's successes in Syria was no doubt enthusiastic, but we have no description of it. The only reaction we have is by Ptolemy's bride, Berenike, daughter of Magas. She is described, in a poem by Kallimachos, as dedicating a lock of her hair in the temple of Arsinoe II at Zephyrion next to Alexandria (built by the *nauarchos* – admiral – Kallikrates thirty years before). She had much to pray for. As a murderess she was obviously in need of constant royal protection, and her new husband was absent on a military campaign which was clearly dangerous. Plenty of symbols were recruited here – the popular Arsinoe II, Aphrodite (joined with Arsinoe at the temple); Kallimachos was a Cyrenian whom she had probably known at home as she grew up. She was being identified as the king's 'sister', a euphemism for wife, but also a reminiscence of the marriage of Ptolemy II and Arsinoe II, which was being boosted by the government. The death of Berenike in Syria, who might well have become Ptolemy III's wife had she not married Antiochos II, may well have been something of a relief; the two women were in some sort of competition; it will have been recalled that Arsinoe II had been a widow when she replaced Arsinoe I; the parallel was too exact for comfort.¹³ Berenike I was surely missed in the government circles.

In Syria all the appearances were of the annexation of Syria to the Ptolemaic kingdom, but Ptolemy was busier at gathering loot than establishing a competent administration. He might appoint satraps (though not in Syria), but he had to employ as his other officials those who had remained in office from the Seleukid regime. They had run the system under Antiochos II, and these were the 'officials' who had greeted Ptolemy in his initial advance and occupation. They had little reason to be loyal to Ptolemy, and as soon as his occupation stalled, they would withdraw such support as they had provided. He stayed in Syria over the winter of 246/245 BC, no doubt wondering what to do next. If he really aimed to secure control over the East as far as 'India', he would need to bring up much larger forces than he had already done, or secure the allegiance of the Seleukid soldiers, which might be possible with a mercenary army but was unlikely with the citizens or the settlers. His real target should have been Asia Minor, where his competitors could gather a substantial army. With an active Seleukid king in Asia Minor he faced severe competition. Most in Asia Minor would be automatically loyal to the Seleukid king against Ptolemy, and Ptolemy could not guarantee that his control of Syria and Kilikia would last, and so would provoke some scepticism. He had occupied only two parts of the Seleukid Empire, despite his extravagant claims. He would need to fight much harder and longer to validate those claims than he had done so far. And there is no sign that he was a serious warrior, nor that he had sufficient forces to extend his rule as far as the Taurus Mountains or the Euphrates.

The excuse he needed to leave the campaign and go home came in 245 BC when a rebellion developed in Egypt. The size, composition, and purpose of the rebellion (called a *seditio* in the sources), is little known. It seems to have been an uprising by oppressed peasants who had been driven to this by the constant heavy taxation which had increased since the 'Revenue Laws' of Ptolemy II a dozen years earlier, a condition aggravated by an unusually low Nile flood, and by spotting the opportunity provided by the absence of the king in Syria, and the consequent slackening of the governmental regime. The long-standing *dioiketes* (financial controller or senior minister) Apollonios disappears in 245 BC; he may have died, or he may have been dismissed as a result of the uprising, as a scapegoat. Ptolemy had with him in Syria a number of his Egyptian administrators, such as Xanthippos and Antiochos, and a good proportion of the army, with which he had extended his occupation as far as the Euphrates and perhaps beyond. This military contingent would need to be expanded as the threat to his conquests from Seleukos II grew. In Egypt this concentration of military strength far away may well have been another of the triggers for the uprising. Ptolemy was paying the price in this uprising for his expedition. He could perhaps understand now why his father very rarely left Egypt.

Ptolemy III was now in a difficult situation. He must have come to realize that to maintain control of his conquests would be increasingly difficult, and to extend them would be even more so, and probably impossible, but if he did not expand, the Seleukid reply would soon arrive. Either solution in Syria would require heavy garrisons of Ptolemaic troops holding down an increasingly hostile country. The only chance of success had been to support Berenike and her son as rulers, and to convince the politically important people of Syria, that is the Greeks and Macedonians, if not of the whole Seleukid empire, that Antiochos the child was their rightful king. This was now no longer possible, if it ever had been, given the immediate competition out of Asia Minor, and the staunch opposition from Babylonia. Alternatively, he could convert Syria into a Ptolemaic protectorate, or perhaps a series of autonomous cities under Ptolemaic supervision, as he had instituted in Cyrenaica. Such alternatives probably occurred to Ptolemy and his advisers, but all of them – except rule by Berenike, now no longer possible, since the news of her death had come out – were dependent on achieving a peace with Seleukos II, and this was, as they must have realized, out of the question. The alternative was that the Ptolemaic forces would have to hold on virtually indefinitely in Syria, and fight off every Seleukid offensive.

So when news of the rebellion in Egypt arrived, Ptolemy could use it as an excuse to return to Alexandria, where he was able to put down the rising without much difficulty.[14] But the low Nile brought hunger and famine to the whole country, and grain supplies had to be brought in from Cyprus, Syria-and-Phoenicia, 'and many other lands at great cost'.[15] He will probably have taken back to Egypt some of the troops which were in Syria, at least his personal bodyguard, but he was now involved in a major war there. If he continued to hold onto his conquests, he would need to reinforce his forces there. That is, Ptolemy III had quickly, within a year of his accession, come up against the same problem which had caused Ptolemy II's defeats in the Kremonidean and Second Syrian wars: the strictly limited military manpower available to Ptolemaic Egypt; given the existence of active discontent, and the need to garrison Syria, it was even more limited than before.

The armed forces consisted of three, or four, elements. The fourth was the navy, which can be set aside in this particular inventory. The land forces consisted of mercenaries, which were professional soldiers available to serve wherever the government insisted, but they were expensive and not necessarily loyal; the second were the cleruchs, immigrants, often ex-mercenaries, who were allocated moderate-sized estates on condition that they mustered into the army in emergencies, though they could not be held in service for very long, and were not available for distant long-term expeditions; they did however have a substantial stake in the Ptolemaic system, a good basis for loyalty; and, third, the *machimoi*, armed Egyptians, who were used particularly as a local police force in rural Egypt; they had been employed as soldiers by Ptolemy I, but not since the Battle of Gaza in 312 BC; no doubt because of their doubtful allegiance to the dynasty. (Egyptians did serve in the Ptolemaic navy, however.) Of these, only the mercenaries were available to fight in Syria. The war there would enlarge and would proceed at least for some time – years at least, and would soon exert great pressure on Egypt, on its manpower and its finances. The Ptolemaic Empire had once more run up against its limits, serving and fighting in Syria took it beyond these limits into an over-extension which Ptolemy II had successfully avoided by using only small forces in his wars, and depending on his navy.[16]

Ptolemy returned to Egypt in 245 BC, summoned by the rebellion. He took with him the accumulated loot of north Syria. This would include the contents of the Seleukid treasury (including that seized by Berenike from Soloi, reputed to be 1,500 talents). He claimed to have 'liberated' 2,500 statues and sacred objects of Egyptian origin from foreign imprisonment. They had been removed by earlier invaders, though how and where he found them is not known. If anywhere they would have been in Babylonia or Assyria or Persia, but the Assyrian cities had been comprehensively destroyed, and he never reached the other places; one must conclude that the claim was pure propaganda, indeed a lie, no doubt as part of the campaign to quieten the Egyptian rebels; some would no doubt be delivered to the Egyptian temples, with much fanfare. Nobody ever counted them, of course. He would claim to have rescued captive gods, so shaming the rebels. But the loot otherwise is said to have been valued at 40,000 talents, if one can believe that.[17] The rebellion was fairly easily suppressed and, indeed, some historians argue it away, while others exaggerate it, so vague are the references to it. It certainly did not last long, and the suspicion must arise that Ptolemy III saw the uselessness of continuing to stay in Syria and used the rebellion as an excuse to leave.

It was at this time, if not earlier, that Ptolemy's naval detachment under Sophron was defeated off Andros. The other named survivor, Ptolemy Andromachou, returned to Ephesos. The precise position of this man is not described, any more than is that of Sophron, but it would seem that Ptolemy was in charge in some way in Ephesos, which had been recovered from Seleukid rule under his command. Ephesos had shifted between Seleukid and Ptolemaic control more than once in the past generation, and had been the home of Laodike and Antiochos II until recently. It would seem therefore that the city had been taken by Ptolemy Andromachou and Sophron from the Seleukids since Antiochos' death, perhaps in the confusion occasioned by Antiochos' death without naming a successor. So it seems likely that there were factions in the city favouring both empires. The garrison was at least in part composed of Thracian mercenaries. Ptolemy Andromachou had earlier campaigned in Thrace, where he captured Ainos for Ptolemy, and had perhaps recruited these mercenaries in the process; all part, no doubt, of the Syrian War. But back in Ephesos his mercenaries killed him, and Sophron found himself threatened by Laodike, who is credited (by Phylarchos, so some scepticism is required) with murdering Sophron's mistress. The actual result appears to have been that Ephesos was recovered by Laodike for Seleukos II against Ptolemaic intrigues, and held at least for a time; again this is part of the Syrian War. That is to say, the war in Syria was accompanied by a conflict in Asia and Thrace.[18]

This war among the Aegean cities is part of a conflict of intrigues, as by Laodike at Ephesos, and partly a naval war, which is implied by the Ptolemaic capture of Ainos and the Battle of Andros. The Battle of Andros was possibly tangential to this conflict, but it seems more likely to be an accidental collision; it is unlikely to have had relevance for the Syrian war. Antigonos was too busy in Corinth to involve himself in Asia, at least at that moment; Ainos was often included in the Macedonian kingdom, but it was probably autonomous at the time, and under Thracian control when taken by Ptolemy.

From 245 BC onwards therefore there were two areas of warfare, the eastern Aegean/Asia Minor, and Syria/Kilikia. The recovery for Ptolemy III of the city of Ephesos by Ptolemy Andromachou was followed by the latter's capture of Ainos in Thrace, and probably of Maroneia nearby – the two cities are grouped together in 242 BC under the governorship of the Spartan soldier Hippomedon, though Maroneia was governed by another man for a time. Soon after he returned to Ephesos, Ptolemy Andromachou was killed by his Thracian mercenaries, leading to the recovery of Ephesos by the Seleukids. Ptolemy III pulled out of Syria in the early part of 245 BC, leaving garrisons in the cities. Seleukos II at this time, and perhaps as a result of the recovery of Ephesos and the news that Ptolemy was leaving Syria, collected a fleet from the Aegean ports he still controlled, and set out to take advantage of Ptolemy's retreat. It must have seemed an ideal opportunity for a campaign of recovery in Syria. He sailed along the Anatolian coast, but was caught in a storm – perhaps he was sailing in the spring, which is notoriously stormy in the Mediterranean. His fleet was wrecked, with great loss amongst his sailors and troops. He himself survived, just.[19]

Seleukos recovered on land. He is recorded in Babylon in 245 BC and later in that year he had gathered more forces in Asia Minor, though he had lost his fleet, and now he attacked Ptolemy III's position in Syria, attacking from the north, through the Taurus passes. The cities in Syria succumbed as readily to him as they had to Ptolemy, except Seleukeia-in-Pieria, which Ptolemy had garrisoned extra strongly. How long this took is not recorded, but one must allow at least a year and perhaps two for the process of campaigning and recapture. There will have been fighting to drive out Ptolemy's forces. An inscription from Smyrna dated to the wartime period, perhaps 242 BC, records his crossing into Seleukis (north Syria) – that is, it had already happened before the epigraphic note had been composed.[20] Antioch was his by 244 BC, for, though he was beaten in a small battle, he returned to the city, which was therefore already his, and he was able to mint coins there.[21] By driving right across Seleukis to seize

Antioch, which must be one of the first places he captured, Seleukos cut off the Ptolemaic forces on the Euphrates and in Mesopotamia, whose route of retreat will have been due south into the Orontes Valley. This victory was marked by the founding of a new city, Kallinikon ('victorious') where the Balikh River joins the Euphrates.[22] Xanthippos, the supposed Ptolemaic governor of Mesopotamia, vanished, as did his soldiers.

In the Aegean the acquisition of the Thracian towns was followed, or accompanied, by the seizure of the Seleukid position on the Hellespont, the Gallipoli Peninsula and at least one point on the Asian coast, a place which was renamed Ptolemais. There seems to have been no attempt to expand on that position; the main purpose, no doubt, had been to gain control of both sides of the Hellespont waterway. Several Aegean islands now came under either Ptolemaic control or strong Ptolemaic influence; Samos (briefly seized by Timarchos from Miletos), was recovered; Lesbos and Samothrake, already contacted by Ptolemy II, were dominated, the latter by Hippomedon's control of its Thracian *peraia* (territory) at Ainos and Maroneia. Ptolemy received an honorific decree from the city of Samothrake.[23]

This brought Ptolemaic power once more close to Macedon, which Antigonos Gonatas, given the earlier hostilities between the dynasties, and the result of the Battle of Andros, could only see as a threat. Ptolemy III renewed contacts with the Akhaian League in the Peloponnese, which had seized Corinth in 243, soon after Antigonos had himself recovered it from Nikaia. This destroyed Antigonos' position in the south, though he maintained control of Attika and kept his contacts with the dictators of several of the Peloponnesian cities. Ptolemy encouraged Aratos of Sikyon, the prime mover of Akhaian expansion, and Ptolemy was elected as a *hegemon* of the league for 243 BC, an honorary position in the circumstances, but a clear sign of the Akhaian international alignment, as well as that of Ptolemy. Antigonos could only see this as an insult, salting the wound of his loss of Corinth.[24] At least Ptolemy did not commit more than money to this Greek policy, for at the same time his forces were suffering repeated defeats at the hands of Seleukos in Syria. The wide range of Ptolemaic activity is shown, however – in Greece, in the north Aegean, in Ionia, in Lykia, and in Syria, as well as suppressing the Egyptian rising.

By 244 BC Seleukos had recovered most of Syria and all of Mesopotamia but Ptolemy's forces were holding on in some parts, including the city of

Seleukeia-in-Pieria. In the Aegean, Ptolemy's fleet had ranged north to the Hellespont and had driven out any Seleukid presence in that area. The local cities along the Hellespont either succumbed to that fleet, or quickly adapted their policies to the arrival of the new political situation, but the fleet did not go far beyond the Hellespont: control of the Hellespont was sufficient. No attempt seems to have been made to establish Ptolemaic authority in the Thracian interior; the city of Kypsela, which had been taken by Antiochos II a few years before, now reverted to independence under a tyrant called Adaios.[25] The naval defeat at Andros had probably made the Ptolemaic forces extra cautious, and essentially confined them to the eastern Aegean. That is, within a couple of years Ptolemy's conquest of Syria – if the occupation can be called a conquest – had been largely erased and a stalemate had developed in the west.

By that time also, however, the two kings had invested a major amount of time, resources, and prestige in the war and had no wish to stop. It is likely that the Seleukids were angry enough to aim to drive out the Ptolemies from all north Syria, in particular from Seleukid-in-Pieria, the half of the kingdom, and the place where the first kings were interred; similarly the killing of Berenike and Antiochos fuelled Ptolemy's anger equally.

By 243 BC the war turned upon the control and possession of the city of Seleukeia. This was the first city founded in Syria by Seleukos I, his window onto the Mediterranean, with a capacious artificial harbour, walls climbing the overlooking hills, and a temple (in the Doric style) in which the urns holding the ashes of the first two Seleukid kings were held. As a symbol of dynastic prestige and identity this would be hard to beat, and, of course, this was why Ptolemy held on to it, and why Seleukos continued the war for it. Apart from that city the war was essentially over by 243 BC; it went on for two more years because Ptolemy wanted to hold Seleukeia as a symbol of his conquest.

Also, in the background, was a constant, permanent, Seleukid resentment at Ptolemy I's original seizure of Syria-and-Phoenicia in 301 BC, that long-standing grievance, which was now exacerbated by Ptolemy's holding Seleukeia, and probably a number of other cities in Asia Minor. The war which had begun with a near-peaceful occupation of Seleukid Syria by the Ptolemaic forces, had then developed into a serious military conflict as Seleukid counter-attacks came; the two armies were now fighting each other without a clear victory in view for either of them. A lengthy stalemate was in prospect; it was unlikely to end easily.

Some diplomacy was involved. Arados on its island had perforce accepted Ptolemaic suzerainty in 246 BC, faced by the overwhelming strength of the Ptolemaic fleet on its maritime doorstep, and its coins were minted to the Ptolemaic standard for the next two years.[26] By 243 or 242 BC, Seleukos had struck a new deal with the city, whereby he accepted it as autonomous and returned the city's *peraia* territory to it; in exchange the city shifted its allegiance once more.[27] One must admire the city's conduct; it seems clear that throughout the Hellenistic period its overall and constant aim was always to recover its full independence, and it operated to advance towards that goal whenever an opportunity arose. It was now as near independence as it ever got for the next century and a half, and it held that position for two or three decades; but this was contingent on Seleukid weakness; as Seleukid strength returned, Arados' autonomy was reduced.

Seleukos, with his seaward flank thus secured, and perhaps with the use of Arados' fleet, invaded Ptolemaic territories in Syria-and-Phoenicia, south of the Eleutheros River. Only two items of information are recorded for this campaign, but they are indicative of an early Ptolemaic defeat and then recovery. The city of Orthosia, the first fortified place Seleukos reached on crossing the Eleutheros River, was captured.[28] This would indicate that Seleukos' aim was to advance along the coast road, between the sea and the Lebanon Mountains, possibly hoping that the Phoenician cities along that road would succumb to a diplomatic offensive, backed up by some force, like that which brought around Arados. But by this time, Ptolemy will have had time enough to install strong garrisons in the Phoenician cities and there is no sign that the Seleukid advance had any effect beyond Orthosia. The other item is a report in Eusebios (and so very late) that Seleukos captured or fought in the area of, Damascus.[29] This is an achievement also credited to Antiochos II in the previous war and again later to Antiochos III, so Eusebios may simply be assuming that the Seleukid king fighting in Syria would attack that city. It has to be said that capture by Seleukos II seems most unlikely when the difficulties of approaching the city are understood; whatever happened it is quite evident that he really got no further south than Orthosia, and that city was then retaken by the Ptolemaic army.

If he did capture, or campaign in the area of, Damascus, he was certainly unable to hold the city. When Orthosia was retaken by Ptolemy's forces, Seleukos' problems in his wider kingdom became so pressing that he at last agreed to make peace. In 246 BC, perhaps on the news of the Ptolemaic capture of Syria, the satrapy of Parthia, already detached into quasi-independence by its rebellious satrap Andragoras, was invaded by a coalition of nomad groups from the north called the Parni and headed by Arsakes, the first of the Parthian dynasty. So the satrapy, which gave its name to the invaders, moved into full independence and enmity.[30] This in turn severed some of the land connections between Baktria in the east and the main Seleukid kingdom, and the satraps there became hereditary as Diodotos I and II, to be succeeded by independent kings. Parts of Iran were also less than submissive.

A second reason compelled Seleukos to make peace. In Asia Minor, Seleukos' younger brother, Antiochos, had been left in nominal charge while Seleukos fought in Syria, supervised by his mother Laodike. By 241 BC, perhaps after a period of argument and dispute between the brothers, Antiochos claimed the kingship for himself, thereby initiating a civil war. (Laodike is sometimes blamed for this, Antiochos being assumed to be her favourite son, but she was blamed for far too many Seleukid disasters, including the death of her husband, for this to be credible.) One must suspect some Ptolemaic intrigues here, but there is no evidence; the blame is laid on Laodike's influence, but by 241 BC Antiochos had been ruling autonomously in Asia Minor for five years, and was now about twenty years old; he had probably become used to exercising power, and the prospect of peace in Syria would indicate that this was about to end with Seleukos' return. Hence his declaration of independence and his acceptance of a crown.

Seleukos, beset on all sides by the disintegration of his kingdom, took the sensible decision, and made peace with his main enemy Ptolemy, in order to be free to recover control at home. The peace terms are nowhere detailed, but they certainly included relinquishing Seleukeia-in-Pieria to Ptolemaic control, though Seleukos did retain the rest of Syria and Mesopotamia. Many of the cities along the Asian coast had fallen to Ptolemy and were retained. Kilikia, at least the coastal area of Rough Kilikia, remained to Ptolemy also. One source says the peace was to last ten years, but this is not attested anywhere else, nor was such a limit placed on any other peace treaty of these dynasties, and there is no sign that either Seleukos or Ptolemy expected it to end in 231 BC; it was presumably to last during the lifetimes of both kings, in the usual way, and would expire on the death of one of them.

So it could be claimed by Ptolemy that he had gained a victory. It had been costly, not only for Seleukos, but also for Ptolemy, whose kingdom had simultaneously been extended even further than ever before, and had been revealed to be fragile in its central territory, Egypt. It was once again, overextended; its extension had only taken place because its opponent was temporarily weakened.

The peace terms left an even more powerful legacy of dislike between the dynasties, not only in the dispute over Syria-and-Phoenicia, which was so old by now as to seem familiar, but now the Ptolemaic occupation of Seleukeia. Here were Seleukid grievances which would in future lead inevitably to a further war – a grievance which would last until the dynasty recovered its kingdom. For Ptolemy this was clearly well in the future, and could be ignored. But two lessons seem to have been learned: handing out Ptolemaic princesses as brides to enemy kings was dangerous; as a practice it was abandoned for another eighty years; and Syria-and-Phoenicia was vulnerable, and would need to be defended.

This was a peculiar war in the sequence of Syrian Wars, which usually involved a battle or two. It was clearly improvised on the spot by Ptolemy III when he heard that Antiochos II was dead and his sister had seized the moment to proclaim her infant son as the new Seleukid king. As a result, he arrived in northern Syria with inadequate forces, complicated by the fact that his sister and her son were both dead and so he was campaigning for a lie. He clearly attempted to campaign with minimum forces, just as his father had done, but his father had not attempted to conquer large areas (and that practice had only lead on to long wars, and ultimate defeat). His aim, moreover, had been only to capture a city or establish a base. The result of Ptolemy III's war was the extension of the Ptolemaic kingdom over a series of cities from Seleukeia-in-Pieria to Ainos in Thrace, none of which were of particular value, and defending which stretched Ptolemaic resources beyond their limits.

Chapter 2

The Ptolemaic Kingdom as a Superpower

Ptolemy III, with minimal personal effort, merely a cruise from Alexandria to Seleukeia, and a stroll to Antioch, had secured notable extensions to the empire he had inherited, which placed him as the dominant power in the eastern Mediterranean. The Seleukid Empire had been deprived of one of its most important cities, Seleukeia-in-Pieria, and a huge quantity of loot had been taken to Egypt. The Seleukids had been shut out of contact with the sea along most of the Mediterranean coast except Smooth Kilikia, so that its only remaining large port was Laodikeia-ad-Mare, and out of the whole of the Aegean coast. It was also mired in a civil war between royal brothers, and had suffered rebellion, invasion, and amputation of its eastern territories. Then, almost as a bonus, two years after the end of the Third Syrian War, Antigonos Gonatas, the other prime enemy of Ptolemaic Egypt, died (in 239 BC), and his successor became involved in troubles on Macedon's northern frontier, a problem which recurred whenever a king of Macedon died. From the viewpoint of Alexandria, politically and internationally, everything looked fine.

By 243 BC Ptolemy had adopted the epithet Euergetes, 'benevolent, generous', and he and his wife were worshipped along with his grandfather and father and their wives, as *theoi euergetai* (benevolent gods).[1] No doubt this was essentially another propaganda gesture to soften the blow of the violent suppression of the rising in 245 BC, and to emphasize the reception of the Syrian loot, some of which went to the temples; the emergency purchase of grain to relieve the famine is also in the background of the choice of title.

There is some sign that, as the famine had developed while Ptolemy was in Syria, it was Berenike who organized the relief measures.[2] Along with a few other items in the sources, the picture emerges of a woman capable of making, and willing to make, independent political decisions, and of being able to argue against her husband. He was, unusually for a

Ptolemy, monogamous (so far as we know), and this suggests a harmonious marital partnership, perhaps like that of the Philadelphoi rather than the bigamous Ptolemy I, and without the extensive philandering of Ptolemy II. The loyalty of her husband would, of course, give Berenike considerable strength in the royal household.

Ptolemy relaxed. He was recorded as an avid dice player.[3] He had been most uxorious in the first years of their marriage, and Berenike gave birth to six children in its first seven or eight years, at least five of which lived and thrived; the last child, Berenike, died in 238 BC, after which there were no more.[4]

Apart from Berenike, whose role in government was actually quite limited (on one occasion scolding Ptolemy, and on another deciding the question of a woman's inheritance – in the woman's favour[5]), we do not know the names of any of the other advisers and heads of department in this reign. The *dioiketes* Apollonios who had been in office in the latter part of the reign of Ptolemy II disappears from the record in 245 BC, either dying or retiring; other possibilities are that his death was the trigger for the rebellion, or that he was dismissed as a scapegoat as part of the reaction to the peasant uprising and the famine. He must have been in part responsible as the most prominent member of the government which had imposed the heavy taxation, though Ptolemy III's decision to go to war was probably the main reason. He was taken by surprise by the famine, so any dismissal thus might be justified, or it might be a case of casting blame on others to deflect it from the king. His successor in office, if any, is not known.

The absence of references to high officials in the reign of Ptolemy III would suggest that they were less influential than Apollonios had been under his father, and much less so than the several men who later served under Ptolemy IV. This in turn would suggest that the king was a more determined controller of the government than Ptolemy II had been in his last years, or than Ptolemy IV ever was. This may be seen as a reassertion of royal authority. The high officials who operated under Ptolemy IV were certainly important in the earlier reign, when they emerged as important men, but they turned out to be a ruthless crew, and Ptolemy III must bear some responsibility for promoting them so that they could their seize power under his son.

The Ptolemaic aristocracy was clearly vulnerable to persuasive and ruthless officials usurping royal power. Their absence from the records under Ptolemy III suggests that he himself had the ruthless qualities required. His evident partnership with his wife in government might show that she, as a couple of stories imply, was a major influence in insisting on his conduct of business. The story of his addiction to dice, for example, ends with her telling him off for neglecting some legal business.

And yet the names of some probable officials of the court in Ptolemy III's reign can be suggested, even if they do not appear to have exercised much independent power. In 222 BC, at the accession of Ptolemy IV, Sosibios emerged as a very powerful figure in the court and the government. He was the son of another Sosibios, son of Dioskorides, who had come from Taras in southern Italy, and who rose to be chief of the royal guard under Ptolemy II. (He may have been a refugee from the wars of Pyrrhos and Agathokles of Syracuse, in which Taras changed hands several times; or perhaps from the Roman seizure of the city in 272 BC.) The first Sosibios served as priest of Alexander and the Deified Ptolemies in 234/233 BC, the highest priesthood in Alexandria, and was thus high enough in affairs to be a royal adviser and official; he was also an Olympic victor, an achievement which he shared with Berenike and her husband and other Ptolemaic chiefs.[6]

Closer to Ptolemy was probably his brother Lysimachos, though he scarcely appears in the records until his death.[7] Since he did survive all through the reign of Ptolemy III, there was probably no dissent between them; his relationship with the king will have given him instant access, and a personal importance even if he did not hold any office, or even if he did not choose to exercise that influence. This would similarly apply to Ptolemy's eldest son Magas, who was trusted with an independent military command in the last year of the king's life.

Other relations were Archagathos and Agathokles, the children of the Syracusan King Agathokles and his last wife Theoxene, a daughter of Berenike, the wife of Ptolemy I, by her first husband. Theoxene left Syracuse just before Agathokles' death, persuaded to leave by the dying king, in order to save them from the mob violence he expected when he died, which happened in 289 BC.[8] They went to Egypt and Cyrene (Magas was her brother). It seems reasonable to assume that Agathokles' action here was only partly to preserve the lives of his sons, and as much to present Ptolemy I with the opportunity of reinstating them in Syracuse, a prospective offer he did not take up. They must be counted as possible pretenders to the Syracusan throne for the rest of their lives, and even as possible challengers for the Ptolemaic throne. There was a daughter also, another Theoxene. Either she or her mother appear to have become involved in the plot of Arsinoe I against Ptolemy II and was banished along with Arsinoe to Koptos.[9]

One of the sons, Archagathos, was given a post as *epistates* (governor) by Magas, his uncle.[10] This was apparently a post on the Libyan frontier, by no means the unimportant position it is sometimes portrayed as. That frontier was active in 274 BC when Magas took his expedition against Egypt, and supervising it will have required attention and the trust of Magas. We do not know when or how long he held that post – he was in his 20s in 274 BC, therefore possibly he was given the post after the 274 episode. We do not know what other posts he was given, but he was probably dead by the time Ptolemy III succeeded. There is also an inscription in Alexandria which mentions him.

Theoxene II, his sister, married an unknown man, perhaps called Theogenes, and they had at least one son, called Agathokles after his grandfather. Like Sosibios, he suddenly appears in the sources at the time of the death of Ptolemy III, in an influential position, and this would suggest that he had also been prominent earlier in that reign. He married Oenanthe, a migrant from Samos, whose status is not known. She has been described as an *hetaera* (courtesan), though this is only a guess, and they had a daughter, Agatha. She later married Agathokles, and had a son, also Agathokles; she then apparently changed her daughter's name to Agathokleia, perhaps to emphasize her (now) royal connections. The royal link brought either or both of the Agathoklean men to prominence and he rose to royal office or an adviser under Ptolemy III.[11]

The governor of Karia in 246 BC who assumed that Berenike's son Antiochos was the new king of the Seleukid kingdom, Tlepolemos son of Atrapates, was the priest of Alexander and the Deified Ptolemies in 247/246, and again in 246/245 BC, so spanning the death of Ptolemy II and the accession of Ptolemy III. He had been reappointed after Ptolemy II's death – presumably official appointments ceased on a king's death – and had then served for a second year.[12] This may be because of the difficulties caused by the succession of a new king, and/or by the absence of the king from Alexandria. This is the first case of reiteration of the priesthood since it had been founded, and it was reiterated in the next two years (245/244 and 244/243 BC) when the post was held by Archelaos son of Damas.[13] Tlepolemos had gone on to be governor of Lykia (where at Kildara he is recorded as proclaiming Antiochos son of Berenike I as king of the Seleukid kingdom. Certainly one can assume that Tlepolemos was a royal adviser, and probably Archelaos also. The priesthood was a post awarded as a prize to prominent men of the Ptolemaic aristocracy, and to be appointed was to put one's family in that position definitively (very similar to the office of consul at Rome in this respect); it was perhaps a way of creating a hereditary set of aristocratic families, and thus a set of wealthy people who would always act in support of the monarchy.

Ptolemy's success in the Third Syrian War, together with the suppression of the Egyptian rising, left him supreme at home and overseas, but this lasted only for a fairly short time. On the one hand, the internal condition of Egypt was quiet, though the memory of the rising no doubt periodically rattled nerves. The taxation system, which was in part the cause of the rising, continued to screw wealth out of the poor for the benefit of the rich – and the royal court is included in that set. The warning which the rising provided was clearly not taken. Probably the blame was put on the low Nile, and perhaps Apollonios.

The exploration of the Red Sea lands continued. Agatharchides of Knidos, who wrote on the subject in the next century, remarked that Ptolemy III was enthusiastic about the elephant hunts. And it was he whose inscription was placed at Adulis, in the southern part of the Red Sea, boasting of his conquests in the Third Syrian War with some considerable exaggeration, if not actual lies.[14] It is evident that the trade which was developed in Ptolemy II's time continued under his son. Ptolemy III sent one of his courtiers, Simmias, on an exploratory expedition, whose report is referred to with approval by Agatharchides.

The expense of all this must have been considerable. The extension of the empire into the northern Aegean, the holding of many extra cities along the Asia Minor coast, and Seleukeia-in-Pieria, will have required using more forces than before 246 BC as garrisons. It is in Ptolemy III's reign that the defensive system in the Bekaa Valley, the 'Lines of Chalcis', were developed; they had to be built, and, again, garrisoned. The Navy had to be maintained, all the more importantly now that the empire was so much larger; and in fact there is some indication that this work languished. By continuing the expensive elephant hunts, capturing animals of little use against the Indian elephants of the Seleukids, he was again spending more on essentially useless display – as he did also in his palace. This was all another aspect of the thoughtlessness of the regime, where the rising of 245 BC was ignored. No doubt the taxation revenue held up, but another low Nile might well stimulate another rising.

The international situation in the eastern Mediterranean remained difficult. The very fact that the Ptolemaic state was in the position of a superpower in the region's political system, meant that Ptolemy III had to pay heed to everything that happened between India and Gibraltar, just in case it should, or might, impact on his position. His aim, so far as we can tell, was simply to maintain his superior position; he showed no further aggressive intentions, which did not mean he remained at peace and inactive.

In the western Mediterranean, Rome had finally concluded its long war with Carthage in the same year that Ptolemy made peace with the Seleukid king.[15] A Roman embassy to Ptolemy III in 241 BC is mentioned in one late source; it is not noted anywhere else, but, if it actually existed, it was probably to compliment him on his victory, and it would have been polite to reply similarly. The defeated city of Carthage dissolved into civil war, the Mercenary War, just as the defeated Seleukid kingdom collapsed as it entered its own 'War of the Brothers' (or 'Fraternal War'). The civil wars lasted about the same length of time, until 237 BC, and the two earlier victors both took advantage of their victims' predicament, Rome to seize Sardinia, Ptolemy to interfere in Seleukid affairs. But Rome was almost as weary as its defeated enemy and chose, after seizing Sardinia, to concentrate on its internal affairs. One of the important geopolitical results of the First Punic War was that Syracuse, now with a new king, Hiero, was effectively under Roman suzerainty; this would close out any claims by the sons of Agathokles; no doubt this was also one of the purposes of the Roman embassy in 241 BC.

Ptolemy had to watch the condition of the Seleukid kingdom, with which peace had been made with Seleukos II, though not with Antiochos, his brother. If Antiochos won his Fraternal War, he could well turn to reverse the verdict of the Syrian War. True peace, as in a lengthy period without any sort of conflict, was not possible while Ptolemy held Seleukeia, and a

Seleukid king might easily find grounds to denounce the peace treaty and recommence fighting again once the kingdom was reunited; it behoved Ptolemy therefore to ensure that that condition did not come about. He certainly had garrisons in what might be thought to be Seleukid territory, as at Ras Ibn Hani, north of Laodikeia, where the soldiers had time to record their presence in a detailed inscription.[16]

The condition of Greece, as ever, caused concern. The removal of Antigonos II in 239 BC was helpful, but the political condition of the Greek states was in constant flux. The new king of Macedon, Demetrios III, was preoccupied with problems on his northern frontier, where his barbarian neighbours had been provoked into hostilities by the royal accession, as usual. Ptolemy was able to simply take note of Greek events for some time. The main Greek powers – the Aitolian League, Athens (which was under Macedonian occupation), the Achaian League, and Sparta – were involved in the usual diplomatic dance, switching alliances and enmities as the situation changed. There were plenty of opportunities for outsiders, notably Macedon and Ptolemy, to interfere and meddle. Aratos of Sikyon dominated the Achaian League, helped along by a regular subsidy from Ptolemy, and was also liable to conduct an official, or perhaps guerrilla, war to gain his ends.[17] Aitolia for a time was also a Ptolemaic ally, and set up a statue group at Thermos, honouring Ptolemy and his whole family.[18] Aratos, very conveniently from Ptolemy's point of view, instituted his raids into Athenian territory, where the Macedonian presence had been reduced, apparently expecting, having ravaged the countryside, to be welcomed as an ally; by the 230s, Athens was largely defending itself, and even the commander of the Macedonian forces was an Athenian, Diogenes.[19] But it was from Sparta that the real political disturbances emanated. In the 240s King Agis IV had tentatively attempted to reform the old, much-debased, social 'Lykourgan' system but had failed, since the reform required a reduction of wealth and power by the rich.[20] Ten years later, a new king, Kleomenes III (235–222 BC), made a more determined attempt.

By that time, other changes had happened. Another new king was in office in Macedon, Antigonos III Doson (229–221 BC; he was the son of Demetrios the Fair). At first he was regent for the heir, Philip V, the son of Demetrios II, who was a child, born in 238 BC. The Achaian raids on Athens resulted in the citizens buying off the Macedonian garrisons, rapidly subscribing 150 talents to pay the soldiers' wages, and to set about repairing the city's fortifications.[21] This was another consequence of the Macedonian preoccupation with the northern frontier, and with the accession of a new king; any regency looks unstable, at least at first, and it took a couple of years for Doson to become fully established; he was then recognized as king, which affirmed his political position, though he was also regent for Philip V.

The Athenians were hoping to see the end of the raids when they paid off the garrison, but Aratos still intended that the raids would 'persuade' Athens to join his League. This might have worked if he had actually attempted to drive the Macedonians out of Attika rather than regularly ravaging the Attic countryside. In fact, and hardly surprisingly in the circumstances, the Athenians, having rid themselves of Macedonian military occupation by their own efforts, were in no mood to join with the Achaians, and thankfully relapsed into neutrality, though this condition required the most active diplomacy. In this it was assisted by financial help from Ptolemy III, whose subsidies had clearly helped Aratos in his raiding activities.[22] In the quarrel between Achaia and Athens, therefore, Ptolemy was subsidizing both sides. In the event, however, Athens managed to develop peaceful relations with all the powers. The removal of Macedonian power from Athens had in fact been Aratos' main aim.

Ptolemy therefore was now supporting the Achaian League and Athens with subsidies, though the two were enemies. He had supported Aitolia earlier, during an Aitolian-Macedonian war, but that association had now ended.[23] This had been the purpose of Ptolemy's financial subsidies, but his support went no further than money. In Sparta (where Ptolemy II had subsidized earlier kings) King Kleomenes from 229 BC led a revolution which almost overnight revived the Spartan military strength; then he went to war with the Achaians who felt threatened by his revolution.[24]

Kleomenes was successful in his Achaian War, though he failed to capitalize on the support he might have gathered from other states, such as Argos, where the poor were looking to him to export his Spartan revolution to benefit them. As Kleomenes won his battles, Ptolemy switched to supporting him rather than the Achaians;[25] in other words, Ptolemy was using the subsidies to keep the Greek region in turmoil. In reply to the pressure, Aratos, losing badly, turned to Antigonos III for assistance, Athens having refused him.[26] A coalition of Macedon and the

Achaian League was a threat to others besides Kleomenes, and Athens got financial help and a guarantee of political support from Ptolemy; to this grouping the Aitolians added themselves.

That is, the political condition of Greece was much the same as ever, and the relationships of the Greek states became ragged again. They were wholly unable to combine, outsiders were meddling, and war was resulting. The prime meddlers were, of course, Macedon and Egypt, but these were brought in by the several Greek states, though they were using Greek problems and quarrels as proxies for their own mutual enmities. None of their interference was doing any good for Greece. Athens expressed its gratitude for Ptolemy's support by extravagantly honouring him with statues in the agora, creating a new *phyle* named for him, and a new *deme* to be called Berenikiadai, for his wife. A new Ptolemaia Festival was instituted in 224/223 BC, while a new gymnasium was financed by Ptolemy.[27] All this was to no avail. Yet again, when the crisis came, Ptolemy's promise of support failed to materialize.

It was the same with Sparta. In 224, Kleomenes faced a probable Macedonian invasion and called for more help. He got it, financially at least, but had to send his mother and children to Alexandria as hostages. The purpose of this appears to have been so that Ptolemy had a leash on Kleomenes, but it had no effect since Kleomenes was beaten by Antigonos' forces.[28]

The Macedonian forces proved to be too much for Sparta. By the time the final battle at Sellasia was being fought, in 222 BC, Ptolemy had ceased to give any support to the Spartans; all Kleomenes got out of his Ptolemaic alliance was a refuge in Egypt for a short while after his defeat. Ptolemy declined the opportunity to intervene in Greece in any force, just as his father and his grandfather had done – this is described by one historian as 'against the spirit of Ptolemaic policy in Greece', but it would be better described more accurately as cynical and machiavellian.[29] It was yet another indication of the limits of Ptolemaic armed power – a money contribution, but only a very restricted land force was ever provided, if any at all. It was altogether suitable that neither Aitolia nor Athens came through on their supposed alliance with Ptolemy; though they did both stay out of Antigonos Doson's new Hellenic League, which was intended to be the vehicle for Macedonian control of Greece, just as the old league of Philip II had been.

Ptolemy's policy towards Greece was therefore aimed at continuing to encourage the unsettled nature of the peninsula, mainly as a means of blocking or preoccupying Macedon. Every substantial Greek state had received Ptolemaic financial support at one time or another between 240 and 222 BC, but the result was not gratitude any more than any Ptolemaic advantage from this was followed through. Given the cynical nature of Ptolemy III's policy towards Greece there seems no reason for gratitude to be offered. Instead, Ptolemaic influence was entirely driven from the region, and Macedon achieved its greatest triumph since Alexander's time. Perhaps Ptolemy considered this a success, in that all he had had to provide was money; and Macedon was unable, or unwilling, to project its power very far. It is doubtful if anyone in Greece would have accepted that interpretation if they had reckoned up the events and the consequences of Ptolemaic interferences. Ptolemy might also see it as a success that Macedon, even if it was successful in Greece, was kept fully occupied in those two decades. It was hardly a long-sighted policy.

There had been some major indications that Macedon, under Doson, might become actively hostile to Ptolemy. One of the first military adventures Doson undertook was a naval expedition in 227 BC to Karia, where Ptolemy and his Rhodian ally had powerful interests. There the interior of the region was governed by a former Seleukid satrap, Olympichos, whose centre was at the well-fortified town of Alinda. Exactly what Doson did militarily in Karia is a mystery, but he certainly contacted Olympichos, who had been cut off from his Seleukid contacts by the Seleukid Fraternal War and by Ptolemaic encroachments, and had thus become effectively independent, having developed the basic structure of a state. Olympichos accepted Doson as his suzerain.[30]

The Island League had vanished, and Rhodes, badly damaged by the great earthquake of 227 BC, was in no position to assert itself any more in the islands. There is some evidence of Doson's political presence in several of the islands, and alliances were made with Cretan cities. So the expedition to Karia would seem to have had much wider results than the possible capture of part of Karia itself. Alliances with Cretan powers (Hierapytna and Eleuthera are mentioned) and with Olympichos (in existence until 220 BC) and domination of several of the islands, adds up to a deliberate anti-Ptolemaic policy of expansion in the Aegean.[31] And Doson's expansion had taken place before he defeated the Ptolemaic client

Sparta, in the process of which he took over the patronage of Achaia in Ptolemy's place.

This was the fifth time in little more than a century that a Macedonian king had lunged at Karia. Philip II had made contact with the independent Persian satrap Mausollos in the 340s , and Alexander had conquered the region in 333 BC, in a campaign which included a lengthy and difficult siege of Halikarnassos. Antigonos Monophthalamos had conquered the area in a swift and masterly campaign in 313 BC, and Antigonos Gonatas had briefly campaigned there in 270 BC, in which Kaunos had been held by him for some time.

The purpose of this interest was presumably strategic, and the recovery of Macedonian domination in the islands was part of it. Karia had a number of useful ports, it was positioned close to Rhodes and across the water from Crete. It attracted Antigonid attention just as the same area attracted Ptolemaic interest (as at their naval base at Itanos), and that of the Seleukids, who had an old alliance with Lyttos, close to Itanos. Controlling Karia and its coasts and ports would put the Macedonian king in a very useful position to interrupt Ptolemaic communications between Egypt and the Aegean, though it would clearly require formidable naval power to be effective.

And now Antigonos Doson had made his own Karian attempt, the sixth Macedonian intervention in the area. It was relatively successful, and Macedonian authority was inherited there by Philip V, when he achieved his own sole kingship upon Doson's death in 221 BC, though both the domination of the islands and the Macedonian fleet decayed under his rule. And, of course, Philip himself intervened in Karia twenty years later. Antigonos Doson's apparently eccentric move in 227 BC, when the borders of Macedon were under threat from northern barbarian raids, and the Aitolians were in occupation of southern Thessaly, was not so odd, after all, if it succeeded in blocking and interfering in any Ptolemaic assistance to his closer enemies. This was the year (227 BC) of the great Rhodian earthquake, after which many kings and others, including Olympichos, sent relief supplies to the city; Doson was no doubt capitalizing on the confusion in the area to revive Macedonian interests there, as blatant a move as anything contemplated by Ptolemy.

The independence of Olympichos in Karia was only one of several such principalities which had been able to shift into a similar status during the

Seleukid civil war – these would include Antiochos Hierax also. In such a situation there was no need for Ptolemy to do more than watch as the disintegration of his rival continued. Seleukos II attempted to recover control over Asia Minor in 239–237 BC but failed, leaving Antiochos, now with the epithet 'Hierax' (Hawk) attached to his name, in control of a good part of the centre and northwest of the peninsula, with his putative capital at Alexandria Troas, next door to Ptolemy's territories on the Hellespont.[32] But one of the territorial fragments, the Pergamene kingdom of the Attalids, proved sufficiently robust to overthrow Antiochos' rickety kingdom. He eventually fled, also in 227 BC, into Thrace, and attempted to gain support from the local Ptolemaic governor in Ainos and Maroneia, Hippomedon the Spartan. Instead Antiochos was captured by a group of Thracian mercenaries (or 'brigands'), who then killed him.[33] These were presumably part of Hippomedon's garrison forces. No doubt he could be said to have been acting on his own initiative, but it is much more likely that he was obeying an instruction from Alexandria, from Ptolemy III himself. Eliminating an active but erratic and failing Seleukid king in favour of an Attalid was a preferable policy.

Ptolemy's policy towards the Seleukid Empire was very similar to that he pursued towards Greece, in that it was aimed at promoting a continuation of disruption. The occupation of Seleukeia-in-Pieria was a constant irritant to the Seleukids, but the city declined in importance as a result of the Ptolemaic occupation as those loyal to the Seleukids left and so Seleukid trade flowed through different ports; it was thus a steady drain on Ptolemaic resources, and yet was no generator of revenue. It is not known what Seleukid policy was towards the city and its Ptolemaic occupiers; hostility is guaranteed, and it is probable that all trade with inland Syria ceased, even though this meant a heavy reliance on Laodikeia, and perhaps on Arados, for seaborne trade. Over the period of occupation the population of the city declined considerably.[34] The future would inevitably bring a new Syrian War and Ptolemies and Seleukids and their people will have appreciated this, though it would not happen until the Seleukid kingdom had recovered both strength and unity, nor until one of the contributing kings died.

Ptolemy III was responsible for initiating an extensive programme of fortification designed to protect his province of Syria-and-Phoenicia. In the Bekaa Valley a fortified line between the towns of Gerrha and Brochoi was developed, in such a position that an invading Seleukid force would march a long way along the valley, blocked from any movement to east and west, by the Lebanon and Antilebanon mountain ranges, but would then get stuck at the southern end of the valley, in front of the fortified towns and lines and without any way forward. There was no way out other than retreat, and the northern part of the valley was only thinly populated, so the invading army could not live off the land. Secondly, the towns and cities in Palestine and Phoenicia were extensively fortified. It is not clear exactly when this was done, but few places were fortified sufficiently to resist conquest in the wars of Ptolemy I's time, who at one point razed all their fortifications; when the next war came to Palestine in 218 BC every town was able to, and did, resist, suggesting that the fortifications were fairly new, as well as highly effective. Nevertheless, this was still more expense.

Antiochos I and Seleukos II are both noted as having campaigned as far as Damascus, though this is probably wrong, but whatever was the basis for this report, it certainly means that the Gerrha-Brochoi Lines did not exist in the late 240s BC, since the obvious route to attack Damascus is through the Bekaa Valley and along the valley of the Barada River, which breaks through the Antilebanon, yet the lines did block Antiochos III's advance in 221 BC. So, it would seem that these measures were planned and constructed during Ptolemy III's reign, both the Gerrha-Brochoi Lines (also 'lines of Chalcis') and the fortifications of the Palestinian towns. The assumption must be that the war would be fought on the defensive, which was all of a piece with Ptolemy III's diplomatic aim, which was to hold what he had gained, and to make no attempt, after 241 BC, to conquer more territory.

Just as Ptolemy III was willing to subsidize any Greek state which seemed to be able, even briefly, to occupy the attentions of the Macedonian kings, so in Asia Minor any opponent of the legitimate Seleukid king (Seleukos II) was favoured, whoever he was. Ptolemaic assistance had been given to Antiochos Hierax in suppressing a mutiny of his Galatian mercenaries in Magnesia, though when this was is not known.[35] This might be simply a precautionary move aimed at blunting the mutiny's effects on other (Ptolemaic) cities in the area, and so preventing its spread into the Ptolemaic sphere, but it certainly also suggests a certain degree of support for Hierax. Yet, as the Greeks' experience could have told him, the Ptolemaic level of assistance was extremely limited in scope, and liable to be cancelled without notice, especially in the event of the ally losing. To observers in the early 220s BC it will have come as no surprise to see that Ptolemy's support was switched from Hierax to his more successful enemy, Attalos I of Pergamon.

Hierax's military performance had been erratic. He did defeat his brother in the battle of Ankyra in 237 BC, with the assistance of the Galatians, in whose territory the battle took place, but Seleukos had managed to penetrate deep into his brother's territory first. Hierax had gathered a coalition of allies, including the kings of Pontos and Bithynia, and some at least of the Galatians, though Ziaelas of Bithynia was killed by his Galatian allies in 230 BC; the allies, in other words, were unreliable. When Attalos I entered the fight, promising an alternative to a continuation of Hierax's military antics, or a Seleukid reconquest, Hierax's support, and abilities, withered. The whole period is only partly a Seleukid civil war, for in another aspect it was a contest among the several local powers in Asia Minor – Attalos, Achaios, Bithynia, Olympichos, the Galatians, Pontos. The Achaios family, descended from the brother of Antiochos I, craftily fought on both sides in the Seleukid Fraternal War. Seleukos II in turn had a series of internal crises to cope with, including his sister, divorced from Demetrios of Macedon, who arrived intending to marry her brother. He died in 226 BC, the year after his brother, after a fall from his horse. These dual deaths probably cleared the air somewhat, and the war became one between Attalos and the Seleukid king; but the new Seleukid king, Seleukos III, was as erratic as his uncle Hierax. Attalos had succeeded in gaining control of much of Asia Minor as early as 228 BC.

Ptolemy III could therefore be well satisfied with his defensive diplomacy. It had blocked Macedon in Greece, and now supported the victor in Asia Minor, though to one with a cool head a careful look at affairs since 240 BC it would be clear that Ptolemy was not to be relied on. In the years following the death of Seleukos II, however, the whole unstable situation fell apart. In Macedon the accession of Antigonos Doson in 229 BC was the beginning of the destruction of Ptolemy's system of subsidized confusion. In Asia Minor the accession of Seleukos III, the elder son of Seleukos II, brought a Hierax-type of excitable warrior to the conflict on the legitimate side. He lasted three years and was eventually assassinated by two of his officers in 223 BC. He was succeeded in Asia Minor by another prince of the region, Achaios, an experienced commander, who was dispatched from Syria by the new Seleukid king, Antiochos III. Achaios quickly drove Attalos back into his home territory but then ruled inland Asia Minor afterwards as an independent viceroy, then as king.

This looked at first very like a major Seleukid recovery, and to cope with it, and to support Attalos, Ptolemy sent his eldest son Magas with a military contingent to support Attalos against Achaios' advance. Little is known about Magas' expedition, or what it did, though it was intended to thwart Achaios' advance. It was apparently ineffective and was soon withdrawn, leaving Achaios in control and Attalos confined to his city of Pergamon.[36] It is worth noting that this was the only deployment of a sizeable Ptolemaic force in the Greek or Asia Minor regions during Ptolemy III's reign, except for the presence of garrisons and the expedition into Syria. It was therefore the exception which demonstrates that Ptolemy III generally used methods other than the military to maintain his influence. Since Athens defected from his alliance, Kleomenes was beaten, the Aitolians broke away, the Akhaian League teamed up with Macedon, and Attalos was beaten, one may say that the policy of intervening in a non-intervention way was a comprehensive failure – but it lasted until Ptolemy III's death, and kept everyone else busy, so perhaps he would not have agreed.

The death of Seleukos II in 226 BC opened up the possibility – indeed, the likelihood – of a Seleukid attempt to reverse the verdict of the Third Syrian War, and given the overwhelming power of the Ptolemaic navy, the attack would come in Syria. (Ptolemy could have launched a pre-emptive attack but seems not to have considered it.) There are some indications that such an invasion was the new king's preference, but it is probable that his council was divided between those favouring an attack on Ptolemy III and those wishing to attend to Asia Minor first. When Seleukos III died, in 223 or 222 BC, Achaios was sent to perform the latter task, and Antiochos III was persuaded, or insisted, that an attack on Ptolemy's territories was the best policy. It was exactly for this contingency that the fortifications in Syria-and-Phoenicia had been prepared, but Ptolemy III did not see the result; he died late in 222 BC.

Chapter 3

Ptolemy III and Egypt

Ptolemy III had succeeded in two major enterprises in the first year of his reign, though in neither case was he the main instigator. He was operating in the wake of two women, both princesses, both called Berenike. He had succeeded in marrying Berenike ('II') of Cyrene, to whom he had been betrothed for some years, but it is likely that the main impulse for the marriage was Berenike's, who was anxious to get out of Cyrenaica after participating in the murder of Demetrios the Fair. For Ptolemy, apart from the acquisition of a fairly spectacular wife, the marriage also brought the addition to his territories of a major province in Cyrenaica.[1]

The second unexpected success was in his war against the Seleukid king, Seleukos II, though again he was hardly responsible for that success, and was only in Syria for a short time. The way into northern Syria was opened for him by the actions of his sister in Antioch, after her husband's death, when she was able to seize power for a short time. His 'conquest', which was celebrated and greatly exaggerated in the next years, was a brief episode in which he only took a single sitting. But it illustrates his (and his father's) methods, using small forces, leading to defeat.[2] His only prize which was in Syria, after five years of warfare, was one city, Seleukeia-in-Pieria, a poisonous acquisition which guaranteed that a future war would take place. And the peace which ended the war was due to the rebellion of Seleukos II's brother, Antiochos Hierax, with whom Ptolemy had nothing to do. The peace treaty was made in 241 BC, but Ptolemy could claim no more credit for the peace than for the war – though he did claim it.

The result of the war was a certain extension of Ptolemaic territory, but in major respects it was a defeat, and the cause was Ptolemy's impulsiveness. The extension of Ptolemaic power along the southern and western coasts of Asia Minor, and into the Hellespont and Thrace, was as unconvincing as the proclaimed Syrian victory. All conquests by anyone in these areas were subject to the constituent cities, who swayed easily with the way the political winds blew. They could not be counted as loyal cities in a crisis.

Nevertheless, Ptolemy III's successes, ill-grounded and precarious though they were, seemed spectacular enough, and the Ptolemaic kingdom had thereby grown to its greatest extent. Ptolemy III's predecessors might have used this extra territory, its resources, and their new and enhanced geographical position to work for further expansions. Some of Ptolemy I's campaigns suggest that he had been as ambitious to gain control of the greater part of Alexander's conquest as any of his competitors, notably Seleukos I and Antigonos, but he did not have the strength to attempt it; Ptolemy III now rested on his laurels and the evidence for the rest of his reign suggests that he had decided he had won enough, and that in foreign affairs he could relax and watch, as the Seleukid brothers fought each other and their empire shed provinces. Then there was the rebellion, relatively easily suppressed though it was, which brought him home from Syria in 245 BC. This indicated that the problems of Egypt required his attention.

How involved in affairs of state Ptolemy had been during his father's reign is not known, but Ptolemy II does not seem the sort of king who was likely to have given anyone very much authority – except for a time in the campaigns in the Aegean where admirals commanded, and where his forces were eventually defeated, and where his son, who had been given governing authority in Ionia, was killed. Ptolemy II had remained in Egypt most of his reign, apart from a visit to Cyprus at the beginning; similarly, Ptolemy III's expedition to Syria had actually begun as a similar voyage to Cyprus, presumably going for some sort of coronation, or a rearrangement of the government, or both. He only shifted into a campaign in Syria later, as the opportunity opened up. The Syrian campaign does not seem to have cost him very much exertion personally – he seems to have spent his time in Syria in Antioch or Seleukeia, but it developed into a military campaign of considerable expense, involving major armed forces on both sides. This was not Ptolemy's forte, and the Egyptian rebellion provided a useful means of pulling out relatively gracefully.

Like his father, Ptolemy III after his initial brief foray to Cyprus in Syria, stayed in Egypt. By the time of his accession in January 246 BC, the system of government in Egypt had been running for seven or eight decades under his grandfather and father. It had been revised, at least in financial/taxation matters, by Ptolemy II in the Revenue Laws of circa 259 BC, and he had adjusted some laws by decree, for example by restricting the practice of enslavement for debt.[3] In these circumstances, the new king did not need to do more than appoint, or reappoint, the senior bureaucrats, such as a successor for Apollonios the *dioiketes*, who disappeared from the record in 246 or 245 BC. There was always, of course, plenty for any king to do, but no great effort was needed other than to keep the machine operating, unless the king chose to exert himself.

We know almost nothing about the life of the Ptolemaic court during Ptolemy III's reign. Berenike produced six children in the first nine years of her marriage, which would preoccupy plenty of the servants, not to mention the lady herself.[4] She is recorded in some dubiously acceptable items as being assertive in the mode of Arsinoe II in declaring her opinions and interfering in royal decisions.[5] She was allocated the task of dealing with certain legal decisions affecting women and women's rights – which could be incipient feminism, or more likely, Ptolemy handing on a difficult issue to his wife to avoid the hard work.[6] It is likely that she was involved in the decision-making in Egypt when Ptolemy was away from Egypt in 246 BC, and when the revolt of 245 BC began, and appears to have been involved in relief efforts after the low Nile. There is, however, little information about the activity of the king in such affairs, still less his wife, though the implication of these items in which Berenike appears to be assertive is that Ptolemy was inattentive and lazy, playing dice, for example, rather than attending to his royal duties. The anecdotes, however, are not enough to bring forward any satisfactory conclusions.

The general situation of the Ptolemaic kingdom helps explain a development which emerged at the end of Ptolemy's reign, and which was trailed in the last chapter. The king had inherited a working and efficient administration, so all he needed to do was to attend to some of the more difficult internal issues, and to foreign policy. The way was thus open for the emergence of a set of powerful administrators who could take the weight of the detailed governmental activity off his shoulders; this, after all, is the purpose of a bureaucracy, leaving the king or government to make the major decisions and give direction to the machine. These men appear at the end of the reign, but rarely during the reign, in command of the court under his young son and successor, and to be able to do so they will have been prominent and powerful in the last decade or so of Ptolemy III's time. The most prominent of these men was Sosibios, son of Dioskorides, and there were certainly others. However, we do not see them in action, which is partly due to their bureaucratic anonymity, but also to the authority of the king, in whose name they were acting and whose name and authority therefore shielded them.

Berenike, at least in the exiguous sources for Ptolemy's reign, tends to loom rather larger than her husband, but as a king in her own right (of Cyrenaica), and a murderess, this is hardly surprising. She arrived from Cyrene and at the same time as the geographer Eratosthenes, originally also from Cyrene, came from Athens; their arrival at much the same time is unlikely to be a coincidence.[7] Eratosthenes settled into a productive life of research in the Museum/Library for the next half-century. He was appointed tutor to the royal children, and became the head of the library after Apollonios.

Eratosthenes overlapped in Alexandria for a few years with a fellow Cyrenian, the poet Kallimachos, who may have been influential in putting forward Eratosthenes' name for the library post; most of Kallimachos' Egyptian life had been during the reign of Ptolemy II, but his most notable poem (at least today) – *Berenike's Lock* (*Coma Berenices*) – was composed at the time of Ptolemy's absence in Syria, an unusual case of a first-hand reaction to contemporary events. He described Berenike's reaction to the news that her husband, recently married, had ventured into war in Syria, dedicating a lock of her hair to the goddess, only to discover that it had been taken away the next day – the immediate theory, in obsequious reaction, was that it had been taken by the goddess herself. The goddess in fact was Arsinoe II, and it was in her temple at Zephyrion just outside Alexandria, founded by Admiral Kallikrates thirty years or so before, that Berenike was praying. The fact that Berenike was appealing to that particular goddess, and was herself as assertive in affairs as Arsinoe had been, looks very significant.[8]

Kallimachos fell into dispute with Apollonios over poetry, but that was in the 280s BC. Apollonios had attempted to write an epic during his early years in Alexandria, when epics were out of fashion; he had been jeered at, and had removed himself to Rhodes. There he revised and lengthened his epic poem, the *Argonautika*, and returned to Alexandria in the 260s BC to a sort of triumph. He became tutor to the future Ptolemy III. His *Argonautika*, with its curious prefiguring of the extension of Ptolemaic power during the Third Syrian War, may be considered in some way as an encouragement for that war, even a type of claim for the territory it describes; but the return of the voyagers through the west was an empire too far for any Ptolemy, despite a friendship which had developed with Rome, and despite the heritage of Magas' active diplomacy. Apollonios, however, did include Cyrenaica in some detail in the voyage, possibly as an indication of the continuing Ptolemaic claim to that land. Apollonios lived on through Ptolemy III's reign, and may possibly have added to his poem when Cyrenaica became Ptolemaic again in 246 BC – or it may have been a clever prediction of the political union of the province with Egypt. All in all, the poem looks very much like a sort of tribute to Ptolemaic royalty and political achievements, and an earnest of their later achievements as well.[9]

Kallimachos was both a poet and a librarian – though never the head of the Alexandrian library. His poetry is various, and to a degree experimental (hence his dispute with Apollonios), but his library work was in creating a catalogue of the place's contents. The library was half a century in existence by the time he began this work, and clearly the accumulation of books, enthusiastically gathered by Ptolemies I and II had begun to overwhelm the users, and without a cataloguing system individual works were difficult or impossible to find. Necessity therefore forced the catalogue, since it became obvious that in its initial haphazard state the collection was all but useless.

The coincidence of Apollonios' argonauts' adventure and Kallimachos' tribute poem to Berenike with these men's close association with the royal court (and Eratosthenes' work on, especially, the geography and geographical possibilities of the Ptolemaic Empire), demonstrates the clear dependence of the Museum/Library on the Ptolemaic state. The king provided the buildings, paid the salaries of the librarians and scholars, bought the books, and chose the scholars to head the organization – this also indicated the dependence, to a degree, of the Ptolemaic government on the library. The institution served the Ptolemaic state, partly in the renown the Museum accumulated, but also as a research organization on which the government could draw. This is an issue worth pointing out, since the library is too often regarded as in some way independent of political affairs; it was not.

Ptolemy III also continued the exploration and exploitation of the lands of the Red Sea, capturing and transporting elephants and other wild animals, the first for the army, the second for his palace zoo at Alexandria. Regular expeditions went from Egypt, composed of military personnel under the command of a series of aristocratic officers. Some new ports were established, especially in the furthest south, at the Bab el-Mandeb,[10] where a monument commemorating Ptolemy's successes (supposed successes) in the recent Syrian war was erected; it was still there eight centuries later.[11]

These places had to be supplied from Egypt. Some of the ships used for this service appear, from a couple of references, to have been built and appointed specifically as elephant-carriers; they carried cargoes of grain south to feed the troops, and elephants back.[12] This was an arduous service, and more than one of the ships was sunk, and casualties were a constant hazard. At least one expeditionary force on its return put up a thanksgiving monument at Philae, grateful to have survived the experience.[13] More than one of the commanding officers became priests of Alexander and the Deified Ptolemies in Alexandria, the pre-eminent priesthood of the city later – Pythangelos in 213 BC, possibly Andronikos the year before; Pythangelos' daughter was also a priestess at Alexandria.[14]

An autocratic government was inevitably deluged with work, for dealing with the bureaucracy was a necessity. It was also necessary that public works of various sorts were undertaken – worship in temples, celebrations of festivals, visits to the parts of the kingdom at a distance from the capital, and so on. The reform of the army and the upkeep of the navy were continuing necessities. In many kingdoms of the Hellenistic age, the construction of public buildings in the name of the king was another necessity. This was especially the case in the Ptolemaic kingdom, heir as it was to the monumental building works of 3,000 years of pharaohs.

In the reigns of the first two Ptolemies a good deal of new building had been done, notably in the new city of Alexandria. As a result, the late third century, the reigns of the next three Ptolemies, shows much less building, partly because resources were being devoted to other projects, such as the army and the Red Sea expeditions – and then from 207 BC onwards such work virtually stopped as the kingdom faced a long series of crises, in the Egyptian South with the great revolt, and in two Syrian Wars.

The information we have on building is virtually confined to the work ordered by the kings. Private building of course continued, almost continuously, but little is known of what it was like. Alexandria certainly contained a large number of large houses, such as the one in which Kleomenes the Spartan was detained in 219 BC, and every rich man in the city that we know of will have had a house of that sort built for him.

As to public buildings many of those deemed essential already existed by the accession of Ptolemy III in 246 BC, so much of the work which took place was a continuation of earlier starts. The temple of Horus at Edfu was started under Ptolemy III, but certainly was unfinished by the time of the great revolt, and work did not resume until peace returned – and then it took another half century and more to complete the building; in style it was emphatically pharaonic, virtually indistinguishable from buildings a thousand years older; this was obviously deliberate, as an appeal to the Egyptian population to recognise that the Ptolemies were legitimate Egyptian kings. Ptolemy III's reign also saw the building of the Birth House at Philae, one a succession of buildings by several Ptolemaic kings on that island. In Alexandria work continued on the temple of Serapis. Perhaps more significant is a temple at Hermopolis Magna where elements of the construction and decoration were dedicated and presumably paid for, by local cleruchs. Others parts were put up in honour of Ptolemy III and his wife Berenike II. A similar dedication to these Theoi Euergetai was at Kanopos.[15]

The next reign somewhat curtailed in its effectiveness by the confusion of the court crisis at the beginning and the Great Revolt at the end, is much less commemorated in buildings. Perhaps Ptolemy IV devoted most of his architectural energies, such as they were, to the building of his great ship, the Forty. The description of the vessel is such that it is best seen as a floating palace, rather than a vessel. It certainly never moved away from the Nile.[16]

The conduct and result of the war had thrown up a number of problems which the king had to attend to in person. One issue, clearly, was the army, which had been comprehensively defeated in the Syrian campaign. It is probable that the condition of his land forces had become clear to Ptolemy III during his adventure into Syria in 246 – 245. He had had to leave the campaign to be conducted by others when the revolt developed in Egypt, and he was called home to take command of the army in Egypt which suppressed the rising. For the first time since 300 BC, a Ptolemaic king had commanded an army on campaign. That the defeats his forces had suffered had taken place after he left Syria for Egypt was a helpful reminder. It could hardly be ignored, however, that his own command of the expedition had been followed by an invasion of Syria-and-Phoenicia by the enemy. This only emphasized that the army was inadequate and the Syrian provinces were open to attack.

It is a tribute to the effectiveness of the Ptolemaic government in the 230s and 220s BC that the condition of the land defences of the empire was attended to, with the result that they were able to defend the kingdom with success. Two major measures were instituted: the renewed fortification of the cities of Syria-and-Phoenicia, and the reorganization of the army. Neither of these is explicitly described, or even alluded to, in our main sources, but items of information, and the net results, dictate that they took place.

The need to fortify Syria-and-Phoenicia had become clear in the Third Syrian War, when Seleukos II's forces had penetrated into the northern area of that province. Orthosia, located south of the Eleutheros River border, was captured, but later recovered, and it seemed that at one time Damascus was in danger.[17] And that was not the first time an army from the north had menaced Damascus and the province; Ptolemy II had had to muster a major force at one point in the First Syrian War, and it was a notorious fact that the province had been lost to Antigonos I more than once.

That Damascus had been menaced, though it does not seem to have been captured, suggests that twice the enemy had been able to march all the way along the Bekaa Valley to reach close to the city. The coast road was dotted with fortified cities from Orthosia to Sidon, and was thus in effect impassable; east of the Antilebanon the land was desert, which was certainly passable by cavalry (as was later proved by Antiochos III), but hardly by infantry. The fortification of the Bekaa Valley was designed therefore to keep the invader out of the Damascus region, for from Damascus Palestine was readily accessible.

The purpose of gaining control of the Palestinian and Phoenician areas had always been to provide a defence in depth for Egypt. (Until it was lost, Syria-and-Phoenicia was not fundamentally valued for itself by the Ptolemaic regime; recruits into the Ptolemaic army from the region were very few, many less than, for example, Cyrenaica, even under Magas.) But possession of the Syrian provinces for a century had demonstrated that it was vulnerable in itself; it was no longer a defensive adjunct for Egypt, but a region requiring defence for itself.

If Seleukos II and Antiochos I could invade Phoenicia, the whole region was vulnerable, and so therefore was Egypt. The aim was to establish extensive fortifications for all the cities, which would delay, at least, a future invader, if they did not actually stop him. The evidence for this was the difficulty Antiochos III had in securing control of the whole region in his campaigns in 218–217 BC; every town was fortified and defended, holding him up a full year, during which the Ptolemaic field army was enlarged and trained.[18] Thus Syria and Phoenicia might suffer, but Egypt would be defended; and since the cities were being cared for by the new fortifications, the Ptolemaic regime could claim to be doing the best for them.

Until the death of Seleukos I in 281 BC the danger of a new attack had been evaded by the existence of a peace treaty concluded in about 300 BC between him and Ptolemy I, but Antiochos I had invaded, and now Seleukos II had done so as well. Ptolemy II had been protected by peace treaties for much of his reign, and the Second Syrian War had been fought mainly elsewhere, but Ptolemy III could look forward with certainty to a new war in the relatively near future, because of his insistence on holding on to Seleukeia. He was protected by his treaty with Seleukos II, made in 241 BC, but by interfering in the Asia Minor civil war he might provoke a new attack. The answer was to work on the fortification of all those cities from the Eleutheros River to Gaza; and as a frontier defence to devise the fortified system for the north which became the Lines of Chalkis.

Seleukid Syria, north of the Eleutheros, was protected by a set of large well-fortified cities founded by Seleukos I, and the Seleukid military base was at Apameia. Any Ptolemaic attack on that area must be either a temporary raid, or, like that of Ptolemy III, one conducted in association with Seleukid internal divisions, a major invasion of the kingdom while it was united would be halted at the first city reached. This would give a considerable advantage to Seleukid forces in a war, since the Ptolemaic base for defence was in Egypt, which would favour the Seleukid forces when able to invade, unless a Ptolemaic attack was more than a raid. The Ptolemaic answer was to develop its own fortification system. This was the 'Lines of Chalkis', a system of two fortified towns – Gerrha and Brochoi – linked by a line of impenetrable ramparts. (Chalkis was a little behind the line, clearly expected to be the headquarters.) This fortification system was planted considerably far south of the Eleutheros River border, blocking the Orontes River valley and compelling an invading force to march a long distance in thinly cultivated country without easy supplies, and then to end up facing a formidable fortification; there the invader was also blocked on either side by the mountain ranges of Lebanon and Antilebanon (and the lake). Passes to the west to the coast, and to the southeast to the Damascus oasis were blocked by these lines, so these targets would be out of reach. It was this system, and the well-fortified cities along the coast from Orthosia to Tyre, which deterred Seleukos III's council in 225 BC, when he wished to inaugurate his reign by a new Syrian War; it had therefore done its job. This defensive system was not apparent in earlier wars, nor in the time of the invasion by Seleucus II in the 240s, so it was evidently the work of engineers deployed for the task by Ptolemy III after 240 BC, based, presumably, on his experience of campaigning in northern Syria – no Ptolemaic king had done this before. The lines and the fortifications of the coastal and Palestinian cities were a single system of defence.

Then, even if the Lines of Chalkis were broken through, or evaded, the invader would now be faced with a long series of cities, large and small, which were also well fortified. In 218 BC, Antiochos III evaded the Palestinian coast, where Ptolemais-Ake, Joppa, Dora, and Gaza were as well fortified as the Phoenician cities to the north; he turned inland, but even there found that even small cities were well defended. All this was also new, and probably due to Ptolemy III's plan, as much as to some local initiatives for defence.

The army was also taken in hand.[19] It had been built up over the previous century by recruiting forces without much system and often in times of emergency, when units might be relieved not paid off. This had produced a wide variety of units of various sizes, often officered by proprietary colonels; the result had been an awkward mixture of units, variously armed, of different sizes and standards of training, and with an expensively large number of officers. In the 230s and 220s BC, probably by a slow and careful bureaucratic process, these individual units were gradually amalgamated into more formal units of a regular size, and officers were now appointed by the king (at least formally so). This involved joining smaller units into larger, and putting them on an official establishment, with clear ranks, and uniform equipment and arms.

In the cavalry, which is the best recorded element (not that that says a great deal) ten 'hipparchies' of 250 men each appeared by the 230s BC, where there had been a mixture earlier; all these apparently replaced earlier and varied units. They were numbered one to ten, whereas the earlier units had been known by the name of the commanding officer, or perhaps by the original recruiter, and some had presumably been disbanded when the commander died or retired, perhaps to be reinstituted later. Equipment and arms could now be standardized and training directed towards responding to a plan and to orders. All of this had been difficult to enforce in the earlier system. This haphazard earlier system may have been the basic reason why the Ptolemaic army did not involve itself in large-scale campaigns after 300 BC; it could best be used by deploying these earlier units, either as garrisons or in reserve. No doubt the problems of the old system had become all too apparent in the five years of campaigning Syria in the 240s BC.

One of the problems must have been that the cleruchs who composed the larger part of the army when it was fully mobilized were also settled as units in their landholdings. These will have possibly been of a fairly uniform size when first settled, but the passage of time had seen land change hands, possibly drastically over the years, families died out, changes by inheritance, all this even though the land officially still belonged to the state. Some of these cleruchies had been settled as far back as the early years of Ptolemy I, others had been planted at various later times, and of varying sizes; it was perhaps due to the continuing pressure of mercenaries opting to be settled.

The great parades, as in the Ptolemaia of 275 BC, or the great battles, provide varied numbers for the whole army, not always wholly reliable, and never for the complete army, since in every case there were others left in garrisons or other duties while the parade or the battle was undertaken. (This vagueness has allowed a wide variety of totals for the whole army to be suggested.) But these are very occasional events – no major battle was fought between 312 (Gaza) and 217 BC (Raphia), and even the totals provided for these events do not indicate individual units, only groups designated by nationality. In between, in other campaigns, relatively small units were deployed – about 1,000 by Patroklos in Greece in the 260s BC, for example. But any army had to be able to do both of these things – fight a great battle as a single force, and send out smaller detachments when necessary; and it also needed a variety of specialized units. It would seem that this was at least part of the rationale – along with bureaucratic convenience and saving of money – in the reforms of Ptolemy III.

The bureaucratic, training, and organizational advantages to the government of these reforms were obvious, and the change permitted a reduction in the number of officers (an expensive resource). A similar process affected the infantry, and this produced an organization of sixteen units of 'Macedonians'; these were men armed in the Macedonian style, that is with sarissas and protected by the standard leather armour; each unit was of 1,000 men, each with 40 officers; when formed, these units made up a phalanx of 16,000 soldiers, plus officers, which was a size advocated by a number of theoretical military writers of the time. This would therefore be the size of army expected to fight a major battle. The individual units were all locally based, so that they could be mustered quickly in an emergency, and called up separately if only a smaller force was needed.

(The whole problem, and its solution, has an uncanny resemblance to the reorganization of the British Army which took place in the eighteenth century, right down to the local basis for the regiments, and their theoretical battalion size of about 1,000 men.)

The evidence for this development is intricate and difficult, consisting mainly of isolated papyri whose contents need to be carefully interpreted and understood to extract their meaning. It does, however, seem to hang together, especially when one realizes that Ptolemy III's war in Syria had been less than successful on land, and that this was the cause also of the failures of Ptolemy II in Syria and Greece. Ptolemy II had always deployed relatively small forces in his numerous campaigns, and these were probably made up of mercenaries recruited for the occasion. Ptolemy III in his Syrian War had to deploy a larger force and over a longer period. It would seem probable that the methods used by Ptolemy III and his father, in deploying seapower, financial power, and intrigue, but using only small military forces, had finally been understood to be inadequate. Too many allies were betrayed, too many minor expeditions had failed – and too often at the expense of the allies (one might instance Athens in the Chremonidean War, and Kleomenes of Sparta) – and a degree of resentment and annoyance had no doubt developed among the states of Greece, so that such essentially political and diplomatic treaties were unlikely to be successful in the future. (It may also be that the inadequacy of the army was the reason Ptolemy III used money so freely in his diplomacy.) Asia Minor was to be subjected to the same treatment in the late 220s, with Magas' expedition, again a small intervention, and with similar results.

This reform programme took place in the interval (241–222 BC) between the Third and Fourth Syrian Wars against the Seleukids. It was certainly a difficult process, which would require careful and persuasive diplomacy in Egypt with both the soldiers and their officers. In terms of government it was certainly something which was initiated by Ptolemy III, even if it had been suggested to him by others – one must assume that there were complaints about the army, and perhaps about Ptolemy's diplomacy – but it was carried out by the bureaucrats. This would be principally by the high command, if such a term may be applied; these were men of high aristocratic status, in particular, who would have easy access to the king on all occasions, men whom he would listen to. No names are recorded as carrying out this delicate work, though it was accomplished without recorded mutinies or, so far as can be seen, massive desertions. One name, however, may be suggested as being quite possibly in charge of the reform of the system. Sosibios was among the highest members of Ptolemaic society, and emerged as the principal minister at the beginning of the next reign. Later, as will be discussed in the next chapter, he was seen to be an accomplished administrator, army commander, and diplomat. All these are exactly the qualities which were needed to bring about the extended changes in the military system, and it seems very likely that it was he who carried the process through.

This reform will have cost much in the way of resources. The expense of the campaigns in the Third Syrian War was presumably one of the triggers of the army reform programme – as was their defeat. There are also other indications that the state was becoming unusually conscious of its straitened finances, a novel situation. Probably Ptolemy's two revenue laws in the early 250s BC were a response to an earlier shortage, and significantly also follow a period of extended and unsuccessful warfare. It is evident, for example, that the navy was neglected during the reign of Ptolemy III. Some of its ships had certainly been used in the Syrian War; Ptolemy was brought to Kilikia and Syria in his own vessels; the campaign along the Anatolian coasts and as far as the Hellespont presupposed a numerous, active, and available fleet, even if a detachment was defeated at Andros in 246 BC. Yet after the war there is no sign of the Ptolemaic navy in use. The war itself, on land in Syria, no doubt consumed resources, as always, but by 218 BC, in the campaign against Antiochos III along the Syrian coast, no more than thirty Ptolemaic warships were mustered. (Some 400 transports were present, but such ships were probably hired or conscripted for the occasion.) In 219 BC it was discussed whether to send Kleomenes back to Greece, presumably with a force from Egypt so as to rekindle the war there, but the expense was deemed to be unacceptable. A fleet is expensive to build, but it requires continuous expenditure to maintain it, and the costs of maintenance are always the easiest to cut. In 201 BC, when Philip V seized the naval base at Samos, the ships there had been put out of use, and there was little maintenance being conducted. Admittedly this was in the time of the great rebellion in Egypt, but it was a sign that the maintenance of the navy was being neglected, even in a time of international war. It would appear that, in the absence of a prominent advocate for the fleet, such as in the past Philokles of Sidon and Kallikrates, the fleet was being allowed to reduce in numbers of ships and the condition of the remainder degraded.

How far this condition was visible either in the Ptolemaic government, or to outside observers, is not known, but some men will have known of it. The deaths of Seleukid and Antigonid kings in 229, 226, 223, and 221 BC, leaving those kingdoms in the hands of teenage boys, and without in the Seleukid case, a war for Syria resulting, evidently reassured the Ptolemaic government that there was nothing to fear from either of them. The death of Ptolemy III certainly caused some confusion in Alexandria, during which it is quite possible that some governmental activities were neglected. The judgment of foreign affairs, however, proved almost at once to be mistaken.

The records of the reigns of Antiochos II, Seleukos II, and Seleukos III, and their wars, dictated that the Seleukid council of Antiochos III should promote the recovery of Seleukid territory in Asia Minor, at least once the strength of the Ptolemaic defences in Syria were understood, if not the condition of the state. A Syrian war had apparently been discussed by Seleukos III's council, and the same decision had been made. The council of the new king, Antiochos III (another teenage king), included his cousin Akhaios, a native of Asia Minor himself and an experienced commander. He was appointed to renew the royal recovery campaign which had failed under Seleukos III, and took command of the Seleukid army in Asia Minor. He quickly drove Attalos' forces from the field, forcing them back to take refuge in Pergamon. Consistent with his overall policy, Ptolemy sent help to Attalos, in the form of some Ptolemaic forces and a commander, his son Magas, who was only a year or two older than Antiochos III.[20]

Magas and Attalos together were no match for Akhaios. Attalos was locked up in Pergamon, Magas was, presumably, driven out in failure – it is possibly significant that little or no information survives of his work there, other than a single reference to his presence. No doubt the defeat was partly due to the smallness of the Ptolemaic force, which was fighting presumably alongside whatever force Attalos could field after his own defeat; they were facing a major Seleukid army, which was no doubt larger than that which Seleukos had led to defeat. This may be the result of the reorganization of the Ptolemaic army, but Magas' adventure came to an end with the death of Ptolemy himself at the end of 222 or early 221 BC. Ptolemy III's last foreign intrigue had thus resulted in yet another defeat. The way was open for Antiochos III to mount an invasion of Ptolemaic Syria.

Chapter 4

Court Crisis and a New War

The death of Ptolemy III late in 222 BC (the date is unclear but between October and December) began a process in which the Ptolemaic state began to collapse. It is a nasty tale of murder and betrayal in which one man, who had been in high authority under Ptolemy III, emerged as a quasi-dictator.

The Ptolemaic state depended on the continuity of the royal family even more than others of the Hellenistic kingdoms. All of them were under the rule of dynasties, and the kings succeeded by hereditary right, possibly interrupted by assassinations and other royal deaths, but the Ptolemaic system was a little different and the succession system was uncertain. Neither Ptolemy II nor Ptolemy III had been the eldest sons of the preceding king; Ptolemy I had rejected his eldest son, Ptolemy Keraunos, in favour of Ptolemy II Philadelphos, the son of a different mother; Philadelphos may have been grooming his eldest son, 'Ptolemy the Son' for the succession by giving him experience of authority as governor in Ephesos in the 260s BC, but 'the Son' did not survive; Ptolemy III was the next in line. This sort of crisis happened in other dynasties, but in all cases it was expected that the eldest son would follow the father, though the practice of designating the son as heir, or appointing him as joint king, confirmed the succession. The eldest son of Antiochos I, having perpetrated some action of which his father disapproved, was punished by execution; this was exceptional, though that dynasty was exceptional also in the number of kings who died by violence. But the example of Ptolemy I showed that direct prerogative-heredity was not necessarily the rule in the Ptolemaic system.[1]

It is worth noting that, although women were excluded under normal conditions from the royal succession, there were two cases in the mid-third century of women taking on the role as successor – Nikaia, widow of Alexander, at Corinth (though she did not last long), and Berenike II in Cyrenaica, in whose name coins were minted for some time after Magas' death and into the reign of Ptolemy III; I would also include her mother, Apama, in the list, for it seems that she exercised power for a time in her own name in succession to Magas, her deceased husband. These precedents were followed in the Ptolemaic family a century later, and in Epeiros and elsewhere in the next two centuries.

Ptolemy III left three living children: Arsinoe, Ptolemy, and Magas; three more – Alexander, a son whose name is not known, and Berenike – all died before their parents.[2] All the children were born within the space of less than eight years – Berenike II, their mother, ceased to produce children after about 239 BC. Having a quiverful of children as potential heirs was dynastically useful; to have four sons so close in age – they were born within the space of only five or six years – risked immediate familial disputes, especially when the succession system was unclear. It did not help that Ptolemy, the eldest of the boys, had been kept in Egypt, while his next brother, Magas, was sent off to war in Asia Minor, giving him a popularity with the forces he had commanded which was not extended to his brother. It will have been clear that the succession was not necessarily determined.

There were therefore two sons of the king available as his successors; Ptolemy III also had a brother, Lysimachos, who had survived throughout the reign in decent obscurity, probably doing odd tasks for his brother. So, given the precedent set by Ptolemy I, all these survivors were in the set from which the next king would be selected. But there were also two precedents set by Ptolemy II. He had maintained and enriched a long list of mistresses, who were able from the riches they had gained to live in expensive houses in Alexandria. His price, apart from sex, was that any children they produced were killed, so as to avoid any of them mounting a challenge to the succession. How effective they were is not known, but some children of his mistresses did evade being murdered: Ptolemy Andromachos, commanding in the Aegean in the 240s BC, may have been one.

There were, therefore, a series of precedents from which to choose in the matter of the succession. The king could be the eldest son, clearly the preferred succession, or an alternative son could easily be chosen; the new king's brother could be expelled (like the children of Ptolemy I's first wife, including Ptolemy Keraunos), or they could, like Ptolemy III's brother Lysimachos stay on amicably and usefully; or the surplus children could be killed off. And then there was Ptolemy II's other precedent; marriage of brother and sister; this had not produced children, but a later sibling marriage might. Then there were the female children of a king. They, in Ptolemaic succession theory, might pass a claim to the throne to a husband, and so princesses may not be permitted to marry, unless to their brother. (This, of course, eventually allowed women to become rulers themselves.) This diffuse 'system' – though it is hardly that – opened the succession very widely: it is possible, for example, that the children of Theoxene, the child of Ptolemy I's first wife by her first marriage, might be able to muster a claim; they were certainly treated as members of the royal family. The succession to a Ptolemaic king was a highly dangerous and complex matter, especially for the successful 'candidates'. Ironically it is possibly because of the dangers of designating an heir in advance, that this diffuse family arrangement developed – for if an heir was publicly identified he might become a target for assassination, or alternatively might himself anticipate his succession and arrange his father's killing.

The immediate events surrounding the succession to Ptolemy III are not very clear. The order of Polybios' words in one of his statements on the issue implies that even before gaining power, before being enthroned, Ptolemy IV had his brother Magas killed. Later, however, he claims that Sosibios was responsible for this and for other killings.[3] But Magas was clearly the most important victim. He was already popular in the army and, having been tested by his father with an independent command, he may well have been in the process of being groomed as the successor of choice for both his father and his mother. By acting first, even as a prince, and before his father's death, Ptolemy IV pre-empted that choice.

Having killed 'Magas and his partisans'[4] (these were never named or counted) the other members of the royal family who were killed are listed, but it was surely more complicated than that. Magas' death did in fact clear the way for Ptolemy as the obvious heir to his father, so why was his uncle Lysimachos killed? He is said, in Polybios' later summary, to have been Sosibios' first victim. The only likely reason is that Lysimachos, quiescent during Ptolemy III's reign, had made some move to displease Ptolemy IV, perhaps to protest at Magas' murder. The family must have been shocked at the death of Magas, and it could be that Lysimachos was regarded as a more suitable candidate to be king than Ptolemy, or perhaps as the eldest male of the family, he was seen as a spokesman. (It would seem that either Magas or Lysimachos might have been a more acceptable ruler.) So if Magas was killed, Ptolemy (and Sosibios) were quickly aware that Lysimachos must go, before his complaints about their conduct stimulated action, or before he took action himself. So one crime was followed by another and then another.

Further, it seems that Berenike II, the mother of Ptolemy and Magas, was as assertive as a widow as she had been as wife. It is theorized that she had favoured Magas as Ptolemy III's successor,[5] though it is unlikely she did anything about it while the old king was alive, and it seems that Ptolemy was quick enough to be proclaimed and enthroned ('Ptolemy IV'), and arrange the death of Magas, to avoid an instant dispute.

Ptolemy IV is depicted by Polybios as hiding away in the palace after his accession, almost invisible to diplomats and courtiers, and devoting himself to drink and sex.[6] This rather suggests a man half scared out of his mind; he was also 'ruling ostentatiously', ignoring, or at least not responding to, any possible criticisms.

In the murder plot against Magas, Sosibios is credited with organizing it, but he did not act alone. He clearly consulted the new king, or perhaps the king consulted him, and met with such a favourable reception that Sosibios was given the task. He is noted as consulting the exiled Spartan King Kleomenes, who was now, with Antigonos Doson dead and the Achaians involved in war, increasingly anxious to return to Greece. He had access, it seems, to Ptolemy, who was not interested in Greek adventures, since the new Macedonian king was even younger than he was, and it was assumed he would not be able to take any initiatives for some time. Giving up on Ptolemy, Kleomenes turned to Sosibios, who was already seen as the king's 'head of affairs' or 'chief adviser'.[7]

They discussed the process of murdering Magas, and Kleomenes pointed out that if Sosibios needed armed help, perhaps as a guard if there was a hostile reaction to the murder, he could call up the Peloponnesian and Cretan mercenaries in the area around Alexandria, 4,000 of them, and Kleomenes assumed he could command them.[8] Sosibios did not, in the event, need them, but he certainly recalled that idea later.

Magas was killed in his bath, either by a dagger thrust or, surely much less likely, by being scalded to death.[9] The actual murderer was named as either Theodotos or Theogos, though the latter is generally regarded as a copying mistake; the only man named Theodotos who is known at the Ptolemaic court was an Aitolian mercenary commander who had held the important command of Ptolemaic forces in Syria-and-Phoenicia – in effect, viceroy of the province. It is clearly relevant that the Aitolian League was a Ptolemaic ally, and was providing a series of important mercenary commanders for the Ptolemaic army; the league was at war at the time with the Akhaian League (this was the war which encouraged Kleomenes' hopes of returning home). At the same time it was expected that a new Syrian war would begin; there were new kings on both sides of the Syrian frontier, and at least one would be expected to attack. Theodotos had perhaps been brought to Alexandria originally to discuss the prospects for the defence of Syria and was persuaded to carry out the murder. Given Magas' popularity, the courtiers on the spot could not be trusted to murder him; a soldier who had for some time been stationed well outside the capital, on the other hand, could gain access to him, given his popularity with the army. Theodotos then apparently returned to his Syrian command at once; he was certainly there later in the year.

Kleomenes' price for supporting Sosibios and the new king remained permission to return to Greece with his family and with a sufficient force to convince the Spartans that they should rise in his favour. But his comment that he was able to call up a large force of mercenaries in the near area around Alexandria was quickly seen by Sosibios, and perhaps by Ptolemy, as a threat; both men, with the death of Magas, were probably on the lookout for threats, and saw them where there were none. An intrigue followed, involving a letter to Kleomenes, delivered to Sosibios, and containing incriminating language, which Sosibios showed to Ptolemy. And Ptolemy, already annoyed at Kleomenes' repeated requests to be allowed to leave, agreed that Kleomenes should be locked up, but in a large house of some luxury which was guarded by soldiers.[10] Kleomenes was a king, after all, and should not be unnecessarily insulted.

Kleomenes realized that this was the end of his hopes of getting to Greece with Ptolemaic support, but was resourceful enough to escape from his comfortable detention. He waited until Ptolemy went out of the city to visit Kanopos along the coast to the east, got the men guarding him drunk in a feast, and broke out with a few followers. But he had not planned any further; perhaps he had not been able to. He was opposed by Ptolemaic officials, failed to raise the population, failed to break into the citadel to release and recruit the prisoners held there, and, in despair, committed suicide. Those with him did the same.[11]

This was exactly the sort of situation which will have enhanced Ptolemy's fears and made him even more suspicious, and still more reliant on Sosibios than before. By this time it is probable that the king's uncle, Lysimachos, had also been killed. The only indication of this is that he is listed by Polybios as one of Sosibios' early victims, though it is probable that this list is not chronological.

And there was one more. The Queen Mother, Berenike II, was a force in herself, probably greater than any of her children, her reputation, her position, all perhaps making her a greater force in the court than Sosibios. But her power lay in her character and in her friends at court, and most of the court inevitably were king's men, since they were in need of his favours, posts, and generosity. Even so, Sosibios, who had been given the task of organizing the killing once more, had to plead with and persuade and consult many of the courtiers to gain sufficient support, or acquiescence, to see to Berenike's murder. This was surely an extraordinary scene. The king's first minister was openly discussing with many members of the court whether or not the king's mother should be murdered, and, since he had to do so openly, there were clearly others who opposed him. It all presumes that Berenike had a considerable reservoir of support amongst the courtiers. The murder decision took some time to be arrived at, and it is surely likely that Berenike knew what was happening: the court was no doubt a gossipy place, and she had supporters who will have heard Sosibios and reported to her. This may have been why she was not openly assassinated by a dagger thrust, like Magas. Instead, the murder was committed by poison, by an unnamed instrument of Sosibios.[12]

Berenike's fate was probably sealed once her husband was dead, and it is a sign of her position of power that she survived for some time. One would suppose that she was angry at the murder of her son Magas and perhaps was on guard as a result. Her reputation as a murderess (of Demetrios the Fair nearly thirty years before) will have made many very wary of her, and Sosibios in particular. If she had managed to kill Sosibios before his plot against her succeeded, she would no doubt have taken his place as the dominant influence in the court; Ptolemy IV would hardly have resisted; as it was, he approved of her murder in advance. When Magas was killed, a number of others, his supporters, were also murdered. There is no record of Berenike's supporters being killed, but one would expect that anyone staying on at the court would be rapidly removed, or remove themselves, one way or another. Those with sense will have left as soon as, or before, the Queen herself was killed. The method of murder, poison, may have been chosen to disguise the murder as illness, in which case a purge of her partisans at the court would not have been appropriate.

All this happened during 221 BC, though the exact sequence of killings is unclear. The situation in the Ptolemaic court could not possibly be kept secret, with the deaths of a sequence of such prominent people, and no doubt many outsiders found the event and the court altogether distasteful. One reaction was perhaps that of the new Seleukid king, Antiochos III. He had been in office for a year before Ptolemy IV's succession. He had been in Babylon when his brother was assassinated, late in 223 or early in 222 BC, and had to move from there to Syria, arriving there sometime in mid-222. Once at Antioch he had to listen to the representations of his council members – inherited from his brother – over what action to take in the face of his various problems. Antiochos was about the same age as Ptolemy, but his accession was much more sudden and traumatic, and his council was even more dominating than was Sosibios.

There were several possibilities for Seleukid action. One of these was instituted at once, when Akhaios, Antiochos' cousin, was sent to take command of the forces in Asia Minor. He succeeded in driving Attalos back to Pergamon, and Magas back to Egypt (and to his death).[13] The second option, which may have appealed to Antiochos as a recent resident at Babylon, was to march east to recover control of the eastern provinces which had been lost to the Parthians and to independence under his father in Parthia and Baktria. The third option was to invade Ptolemaic Syria, which had been possible for several years, since the death of Seleukos II and the expiry of the peace treaty of 241 BC.

As noted already, the precise chronology of these events is subject to discussion. Akhaios campaigned in Asia Minor in 223–222 BC, and Magas returned to Egypt in that year. Akhaios' success probably decided Antiochos on the invasion of Syria. The war therefore began in 221 BC, and will have happened in the campaigning season, between March and the onset of winter. It was triggered partly by the success of Akhaios, and partly by the death, late in 222 BC, of Ptolemy III. The accession of Ptolemy IV, widely seen as an ineffective youth, and the news of murders at the court may have been further inducements. It is necessary to allow some time for the decision to be reached in Antioch, and this in part will have depended on the news of the events in Alexandria. The Ptolemaic commander in Syria, Theodotos the Aitolian, was in Alexandria when Magas was killed, probably early in 221 BC – even if he was not the actual killer – and then he had to get back to Syria. His absence, and the tumult in Alexandria, would be the best time for the Seleukid attack.

The objectives of the Seleukid forces were two, at least in the beginning: the Bekaa Valley defences, and the city of Seleukeia-in-Pieria. In the best tradition of tackling the worst problem first, Antiochos sent his army into the Bekaa. The army had been gathered at Apameia, which was the main Seleukid military base, but it was also the first defensive point at which a Ptolemaic attack would be met; Laodikeia performed the same function on the coast road. This dual purpose of Apameia may have disguised the Seleukid aggressive intention, but in this case it was the base for the attack to the south. Because it was a busy military base it may be that the Ptolemaic defenders were taken by surprise, but the Ptolemaic defences in Phoenicia were designed to minimize the effect of such an attack.

Antiochos had three possible routes for his invasion, but the coast road was well defended with fortified cities, and the route east of the Antilebanon lay through a waterless desert; the Bekaa Valley was thus the best, indeed, in effect the only, approach – but it was enclosed by mountains on both sides, which were no doubt held by detachments of Ptolemaic troops; the valley itself was scarcely inhabited and so had no resources to sustain an army, and at the southern end were the Lines of Chalkis, closing off the routes out of the valley. The whole was a cul-de-sac, and the Ptolemaic forces were on the alert. When he reached the lines, Antiochos was defeated in his attacks, suffered considerable casualties, and had to retreat.[14]

There will have been relief, possibly even celebrations, in Alexandria (and perhaps Antiochos' defeat was the signal for the killing of Berenike). At the time, in the Seleukid kingdom, it was the signal for two men, Akhaios in Asia Minor, and Molon in Iran, to assume royal titles. In Alexandria, relaxation could take place, certainly on Ptolemy's part, since it seems that relaxation and indulgence in pleasure were his personal priorities. No doubt Sosibios was less relaxed, for the condition of the court, after the recent murders and confusion and plots, required him to be alert, even if the king was relaxed.

By contrast, Antiochos was energized. The reaction to the defeat in the Bekaa was such that, paradoxically, he had become much more secure. The defection of Akhaios had prevented him from invading Syria, as he had originally intended; the victory of Theodotos in the Bekaa was apparently regarded as definitive by the Ptolemaic court, which was also preoccupied with the internal campaign of murder, and with the king's marriage, which took place during 220 BC. So Antiochos was able to deal with two other problems without being concerned about a possible Ptolemaic counterattack. There was a rebellion of the Kyrrhestai, in north Syria, and this was suppressed, and the pretensions of Molon were defeated in 220 BC – he and his brother committed suicide after their military defeat. Akhaios made an attempt to invade Syria, but he had kept his aim secret from his troops, and when they discovered it, they refused to continue; they did accept him as king however.

Antiochos' methods were in strong contrast to those of Ptolemy and Sosibios. During the campaign against Molon he had executed a plot against his main minister, the overbearing Hermeias, but he also recruited at least one new minister, the highly capable and loyal Zeuxis, who had been governor of a section of Babylonia, and was very effective in the war against Molon. Even more significant, two generals who had failed against Molon, Xenon and Theodotos Hemiolios, were not dismissed (or executed), but continued to be employed.

The contrast is with the Ptolemaic treatment of Theodotos, the victor in the Bekaa fighting. He fell out of favour at the court in Alexandria. While he was in Syria his enemies had conducted a whisper and rumour campaign against him at the court in Alexandria, no doubt based on his contribution to the murder of Magas, and he discovered when he returned there that he was clearly in danger. He now knew enough about the methods used at the court to remain out of reach of Sosibios and Ptolemy, remaining in Syria. There he contacted Antiochos and was welcomed as another capable recruit to the Seleukid cause. Polybios reports this only after the capture of Seleukeia, but it may have been in train already; he says that Theodotos wrote a letter to Antiochos offering to join him, and had seized control of Ptolemais and Tyre, but one would have expected preliminary negotiations long before this – the letter was Theodotos' decisive move in his defection, just as Antiochos' capture of Seleukeia was his decisive move in the Syrian War, after which Theodotos' treason would open the way for Antiochos' further conquests.[15]

The viciousness of the court at Alexandria, a combination of Ptolemy's fears and Sosibios' ambition and capabilities, had thus removed a respected elder of the royal family, two capable commanders, and an intelligent and forceful queen within a year. In 220 BC, while Antiochos was consolidating his kingdom after defeating Molon far off in the east, Ptolemy married his elder sister Arsinoe, no doubt among extensive celebrations once more.[16] These were now the only members of the royal family still alive. Antiochos was also married about this time (he was the only member of the Seleukid family still alive, apart from the branch in Asia Minor, headed at this point by Akhaios). He married a daughter of the king of Pontos, bride and groom were cousins.[17]

The marriage of a brother and sister was, of course, not unprecedented in the Ptolemaic family, for Ptolemy II had married his sister (also older than he was) over half a century before. There were, however, profound differences between the cases. The earlier sibling marriage had been more a political union than anything else; Ptolemy II continued to take his sexual pleasures outside marriage; insofar as is known, his wife did not object – possibly it was part of the agreement between them, not that she could have prevented him. But the marriage of Ptolemy IV and Arsinoe III was explicitly intended to produce children who would be successors to the kingship. Ptolemy had indulged himself sexually before his marriage, as he did afterwards. His main mistress, though not the only one, was Agathokleia, the granddaughter of the Syracusan king, Agathokles. Her mother Oenanthe was also said to have been one of the king's mistresses.[18] The sibling marriage also removed Arsinoe early from the possibility of marrying outside the family, and so kept the succession close; this was no doubt a prime consideration.

The earlier case of the marriage of Ptolemy II and Arsinoe II had created shock amongst the Greeks, and so this later case was less controversial. The marriage of Ptolemy IV and Arsinoe III certainly solved the problem of the succession for the moment, and the newly married couple soon produced children; it also solved the problem of Arsinoe, who otherwise would not have been allowed to marry at all, since that would have provided her husband with a strong interest in removing Ptolemy. The marriage therefore would seem to be in part a product of Ptolemy's fears and paranoia. A further advantage is that Arsinoe appears to have been personally popular, which can probably not be said of her husband.

Chapter 5

The Fourth Syrian War

The court crisis and the murders in 221–219 BC overlapped, not surprisingly, with the beginning of the new Syrian War, the Fourth. This began with Antiochos III's invasion of Ptolemaic Syria in 221 BC, was suspended after his defeat at the Gerrha-Brochoi Lines, and while he dealt with the rebellions of Molon and the Kyrrhestai. The war resumed in 219 BC at a time when the Ptolemaic court was preoccupied with the problem of Kleomenes. It solved that problem in its usual way, by another killing. But in the process, the Ptolemaic commander-in-chief in Syria and Phoenicia, Theodotos, the murderer of Magas, defected, probably in fear of his life. He and Antiochos could then collaborate on the new invasion of his erstwhile province. Antiochos still had not recovered his Asia Minor province, but since Akhaios' army had refused to march into Syria to face the king – and more particularly, the king's army – he could ignore the matter for the moment.

The invasion of the Bekaa Valley took place in 221 BC and resulted in Antiochos' defeat and retreat. There was no Ptolemaic riposte, which one might have expected. Nor did Antiochos apparently fear one, since he at once marched east to attack Molon, and then climbed into Iran to loot a temple. He spent at least a year on this expedition, and yet Ptolemy did nothing. Did he imagine that one victory would end this new war? To be sure, he was busy in 220 BC, when he was married to his sister, and in 219 BC with the crisis over Kleomenes, but that cannot have lasted very long. One must put the absence of Ptolemaic reaction to the opening of the new war down to negligence and a complete lack of imagination.

It was in that period, 221–219 BC, that Theodotos the Aitolian was left in command in Syria, and came to the conclusion that his survival in the Ptolemaic system was so unlikely that he determined to defect. On the other hand, Theodotos had to be sure that he was not abandoning a corrupt court for an incompetent king; he waited to see if Antiochos could justify his claims and prove his abilities. That is, he had to be sure that Antiochos had learned from his defeat at the Gerrha-Brochoi Lines.

He in fact showed his quality, both in his defeat of Molon, and in his first successful Syrian War move. His first target was now Seleukeia-in-Pieria, the former centre of his kingdom, whose capture would resonate widely throughout the realm.

There was, of course, a garrison in Seleukeia, but the city was somewhat isolated as a result of the development of the Ptolemaic defensive system.[1] It was in fact 160 kilometres away from the main Ptolemaic concentration of power in Syria; the defence of Seleukeia was clearly expected to be undertaken by the garrison, holding out long enough to be relieved by the navy – but the navy was in decay. The main Ptolemaic forces were in the southern end of the Bekaa Valley, at the Gerrha-Brochoi Lines; there were others in garrisons in the cities along the Phoenician coast, but they, unlike the forces in the southern Bekaa, were not mobile, and their orders were to defend their cities, not sally out to defend another city. When Seleukeia was under attack, the city's garrison could not be reinforced except from Cyprus, but this would take some time to organize. Reinforcements could only come by sea, from Cyprus or the Phoenician cities, and eventually from Ptolemais-Ake or Egypt. The forces in the Bekaa could not intervene, unless the attack degenerated into a static siege.

The attack therefore had to succeed quickly. Antiochos had to be persuaded to undertake it, and credit is given for this to the royal doctor, Apollophanes, an exiled native of Seleukeia, for persuading him and the council to make the attack. There is clearly more to it than the doctor's advocacy, for the plan was so quickly implemented that it had obviously been under consideration before the decision was made, presumably during the winter of 220/219 BC. This would be the first indication to Ptolemy that the war had not been finished by the victory in the Bekaa. The danger of an invasion from the Bekaa as a distraction was countered by a detachment under a general called Theodotos Hemiolios, which was sent into the valley to block the passage. The small Seleukid fleet was mobilized under the admiral Diognetos and instituted a sea blockade; even if this force was not strong enough to fight the Ptolemaic fleet, it could certainly prevent supplies getting in. Thus the political isolation of the city was further emphasized by new military isolation. The whole enterprise was a gamble, and if it stretched out, defeat was very likely.[2]

Direct attacks against the city walls were difficult, since the city climbed the hills whose steep sides were exaggerated by the walls, and it would be difficult to muster a large enough attacking force at any point. The obvious point of attack was in the lowland by the sea and in the harbour area. No doubt the walls here had been kept in good repair, but this was the most vulnerable point. The land was flat or low-lying, and there was an area called by Polybios 'the suburb', presumably an area outside the wall on the lowland, which was less well defended. Two attacks were mounted in this area, one commanded by Diognetos by 'the men from the fleet', the other commanded by Ardys, against the suburb. Other areas of the wall were menaced, but these were subsidiary to the main assaults by the harbour, and were designed to stretch the defenders' manpower thinly.

There was yet another aspect to the plan. As soon as the Seleukid army reached Seleukeia, messages went into the city, apparently quite openly, offering rewards to 'the officers in command' if they would betray the place. Presumably this occurred under the cover of a summons directed at the main commander in the city, a man called Leontios. All the officers so addressed, including Leontios, apparently refused. But the offer had been so open and publicized that the next-lower layer of officers reacted favourably, though they set the condition that a successful attack on, say, the suburb, was necessary to give them the excuse to advocate surrender. When the initial attack was therefore made, and Ardys captured the suburb, the corrupted officers set up a howl that the city was lost, and persuaded Leontios to negotiate. Antiochos speedily agreed to spare the population (including presumably the Ptolemaic soldiers and any Ptolemaic immigrants); Leontios surrendered and Antiochos took possession. The population was left alone, and those who, like Antiochos' doctor, had gone into exile to avoid Ptolemaic rule were able to return. No doubt the Ptolemaic officers joined Antiochos; they could hardly go back to Ptolemy.

Polybios now claims that, as Antiochos was occupying the city of Seleukeia, he received the message from Theodotos that he had seized control of the city of Ptolemais-Ake in Palestine, the governing centre of the Ptolemaic province, and that one of his officers, Panaitolos, had seized Tyre.[3] Polybios makes it seem that this came as a surprise to Antiochos, and that the offer came immediately following the capture of Seleukeia, but there were several months between the two events: the city was taken in spring, Theodotos defected in August. But Theodotos would scarcely have taken such a step without knowing it would be welcomed by Antiochos, so three months were probably taken up with the negotiations and Theodotos' preparations. He would need to prove his defection by such a deed before Antiochos could publicly accept him, and that is what happened when Theodotos seized Ptolemais and Tyre.

This was certainly a serious blow to the Ptolemaic war effort. Seizing these cities would disorganize the Ptolemaic forces in Syria-and-Phoenicia, especially since it was their commander-in-chief who was defecting. The Ptolemaic defence system had thus been cracked, but it had not been broken. Another commander, Nikolaos – another Aitolian – brought troops under his control in Palestine to besiege Theodotos in Ptolemais-Ake. The loss of Tyre opened the coast road, if Antiochos could pass the Gerrha-Brochoi Lines and cross the Lebanon range. The towns of Gerrha and Brochoi, which anchored the lines, were besieged by Antiochos' forces as soon as he could get them there (a force had been in the valley under Theodotos Hemiolios for some time). This gave Nikolaos time to send a mercenary contingent, commanded by the Cretan Lagoras and yet another Aitolian, Dorymenes, to block the only accessible pass across the mountain, the route to Berytos. Antiochos, however, was quick enough to foil this operation. He left his heavily armed troops – the sarissa-armed hoplites – to besiege the two towns, and took the light-armed troops – which would have been called peltasts in an earlier century – to bypass the defences by climbing the flanks of the hills, and then contest the pass. Perhaps the Ptolemaic force there was taken by surprise, or perhaps it was outnumbered, but the king's assault drove them back down the mountain towards the sea.

He was then joined by 'the rest of his forces', though we do not know if Gerrha and Brochoi were taken or merely masked – probably the latter – and the army marched down to the coast road, past captured Tyre, and met Panaitolos and Theodotos near Ptolemais.[4] The Phoenician cities north of Tyre remained to their Ptolemaic garrisons, as did Sidon to the south. Nikolaos had withdrawn his besieging forces as the main enemy approached. The Ptolemaic defence had thus far failed, though Antiochos' advance had been delayed by the need to mask Gerrha and Brochoi and Sidon, and by the fight at the pass. His next target, assuming that the capture of Ptolemais gave him control of Palestine, was intended to be Pelusion, the guard of Egypt, which would have involved a long march along the coast road, the capture of Gaza, and the crossing of the Sinai Desert, again by the regular coast road.[5] This would clearly take a considerable time. The distance from Ptolemais to Pelusion was at a minimum 700 kilometres, a marching distance of at least a month and more realistically two months or more; and this was without reckoning in any resistance to overcome – one would expect Gaza at least to be defended against him.

In Egypt the shock of the breaking of the defence line was considerable, compounded by the treason of the Aitolian commanders, following on the capture of Seleukeia. Almost before they had heard of the attack on Seleukeia, the news of the arrival of Antiochos' forces in Palestine will have come. Plans for the defence of Egypt were hurriedly made, and they bear the hallmarks of the cunning mind of Sosibios. He dominated the response with Agathokles, the brother of the king's mistress, another competent conspirator.

There is no record of any orders going to Palestine, but it would seem likely that Nikolaos was given instructions to delay Antiochos as much as possible, which he did by putting garrisons into all the defensible cities with orders to fight, not surrender. Small cities and open towns had to be allowed to surrender, but there were plenty of places which could form a strong defence. It was assumed that Antiochos' forces would nevertheless get through to the Egyptian border.

Pelusion was re-fortified, and the approaches flooded. No doubt the old forts were reoccupied – they had stopped the Persians and Antigonos, so this was yet another defensive system to block an attack on Egypt. The wells along the route across Sinai were blocked up. Forces were collected, mercenaries hired and imported, and the mercenaries employed in the overseas territories were ordered to Egypt. Plans for a fighting defence to delay Antiochos' advance were thus made, and measures taken to recruit reinforcements and make military preparations. Diplomatic delaying tactics were also devised, again with the aim of gaining time in Egypt to construct the army of defence. Elaborate measures were organized to prevent the full extent of military preparations in Egypt becoming known.

Alexandria was to be the centre of these preparations. This was where the mercenaries from overseas would arrive, but it would not be there that the main army would gather. The army changes which had been carried through in the previous two decades seem to have largely escaped notice outside Egypt, so the new system would come as the first surprise to Antiochos. With the new mercenary forces the Ptolemaic army would eventually equal Antiochos' force in size when the two came to battle. Both also recruited 'native' forces as reinforcements, but Antiochos seems to have relied on Arabs and others, who were less than fully disciplined and must be classified as light forces; the Ptolemaic measure was to recruit Egyptians, presumably from the Egyptian militia called the *machimoi*, plus new recruits as reinforcements. These trained as hoplites in order to form a second phalanx. To do this, time was clearly needed, hence the elaborate delaying tactics.

The process of recruiting, transporting and organizing the mercenaries from Greece and the Aegean world was supposedly kept secret at Alexandria, but such work could hardly be hidden, and it served to hide the other preparations being made within Egypt. One Seleukid agent loitering in the Athenian docks area would be able to see what was happening, and another in Alexandria could give a fair idea of numbers – and Alexandria was a large port in constant contact with the outside world; secret activities on the scale suggested would be impossible. But that would not matter, and having divined this Ptolemaic secret, Antiochos' people would not be inclined to look any further. By insisting on visiting diplomats being taken to Memphis without stopping in Alexandria, the suggestion was reinforced.[6] The eventual appearance of an extra phalanx, trained somewhere in Egypt, and really and successfully kept out of sight, was the second surprise Antiochos received.

Antiochos gave up the plan of a swift attack on Pelusion, perhaps when he realized the extent of the preparations for defence which were being made at and around the city, perhaps when news came of the preparations at Alexandria, or perhaps when, in his march along the coast, he found that the first town south of Ptolemais-Ake, Dora, was stubbornly and successfully defended. Ptolemy brought forward a force to Pelusion as well. Nikolaos was still active with an army in the Palestinian interior where the Seleukid forces were harassed while he supported and supplied Dora. The envoys from Ptolemy arrived with suggestions for a diplomatic negotiation. When the winter season approached, Antiochos, who was still besieging Dora, agreed to a four-month truce.[7]

This truce was not much of a concession, since the winter was usually a time when campaigning was suspended, a suspension which normally lasted for four months. The Ptolemaic envoys suggested a negotiation to end the war. Antiochos fixed the place for the discussions at Seleukeia, where he would be the host of the meeting, thereby making it clear that one of the terms of any peace would be that the city would become his.[8] He evidently knew that other Ptolemaic envoys had reached Akhaios, and they were attempting to concert actions between him and the Ptolemaic forces. Polybios claimed that the Seleukid troops were dismissed for the winter and that Antiochos 'neglected' to exercise them, but this would have happened anyway in the winter season – the soldiers were to go home, and therefore not draw on government supplies. And it is not to be believed that all the army swiftly and simply dispersed. A substantial proportion remained in occupation of the conquered lands, and a field army remained on guard in case the truce collapsed (or if Akhaios made a move).[9]

Negotiations at Seleukeia during the truce predictably got nowhere. Antiochos made it clear that Seleukeia itself was not for returning, so the issue was control of Syria-and-Phoenicia. He had occupied a large part of this Ptolemaic province, but not all of it. Nevertheless, he claimed it all, citing the fact (as he would have put it) that his ancestor Seleukos I had been unlawfully deprived of it in 301 BC by Ptolemy I. Needless to say Ptolemaic envoys did not agree, and spun out the talks with all sorts of irrelevant diversions. It will have been obvious that they were doing so, which may have been taken as attempting to delay the inevitable resumption of the war (though the truce had a time limit). The treason of Theodotos was raised, and Ptolemy wanted Akhaios included in the peace, which was impossible for Antiochos. Both sides talked about the justice of their causes, when in fact they were really discussing power. Both sides were quite happy to go on talking, having stated terms knowingly unacceptable to the other, and knowing that no result was ever likely until a decision was reached in the fighting.[10] As the period of truce came to an end, and the winter quarters ended with the arrival of spring, both sides mustered their armies and prepared to renew the fighting.

Both sides had also spent the time of truce in preparations for this moment. Antiochos' army re-mustered, and was accompanied, for the first time, by a substantial naval force. This was partly made up of his own ships, those Diognetos had commanded at the attack on Seleukeia, and of formerly Ptolemaic ships which had been captured at Tyre and Ptolemais.

He now had a fleet of about forty warships.[11] The Ptolemaic forces, still under Nikolaos, had established a base of supplies at Gaza, from which the resistance in Palestine could be reinforced. The Ptolemaic navy, on the other hand, was greatly reduced from its earlier glory, and Perigenes the commander now had only thirty warships in his command.[12] It must be assumed that there were no other Ptolemaic ships available, that some had decayed to uselessness, but others were held at bases in the empire.

The rival plans for this part of the campaign brought the armies to a fight north of Tyre. Antiochos marched south, this time along the coast road, meeting only minimal resistance. He captured and burnt the towns of Trieres and Kalamos and captured Botrys and Berytos. He then paused and sent out a force under Theodotos to clear the passes towards the Bekaa, so that he would not be attacked in flank and rear when he moved on. This was a different campaign than the year before, deliberate and more massive, as he was employing his full army.

The Ptolemaic forces facing him were, as in the diplomatic fencing earlier in the year, intended to slow Antiochos down, and perhaps wear his army out in advance of the final meeting. A detachment occupied a narrow part of the coast road at Porphyrion, and Perigenes brought up the fleet to provide support on the seaward flank. He was accompanied by 400 transport ships.[13] This is far too many to be simply carrying supplies, and it was no doubt carrying a landing force, intended to cut the road behind the Seleukid army. (Four hundred ships could easily be carrying several thousands of soldiers.) The battle which resulted was fought on both sea and land. The two fleets fought to a draw, which might be considered a victory for Perigenes' fleet, it being the smaller. On land the tactical skill of Theodotos was displayed by seizing the high ground inland of the pass, and so defeating Nikolaos' force on the shore. As it was seen that the Ptolemaic land force was beaten, Perigenes withdrew the fleet as well. Nikolaos' army had been at first successful, fighting well. The war was not going to be easy.[14]

Nikolaos' force suffered considerable casualties, and just as serious, his army had fled the battlefield, so providing Antiochos with a further boost to his own confidence and that of his army. He had evidently worked out in advance his further method of campaign for the conquest of Palestine. Sidon was blockaded, so as not to be delayed as he had been the year before at Dora, and with Tyre and Ptolemais in his hands, he was able to concentrate on the inland areas of Palestine. Having by-passed Sidon he turned east and campaigned along the route of the Jordan River, from Philoteria just south of the Sea of Galilee (a Ptolemaic foundation – surely this was as much a psychological blow as a military) to Skythopolis and onwards to Atabyrion. Whatever instructions to resist had been issued were disregarded by some of the Ptolemaic garrisons. Both Philoteria and Skythopolis surrendered tamely; the garrison at Atabyrion rashly ventured on a sortie and was defeated and the town captured.[15]

Antiochos crossed the Jordan River to the east bank and captured a line of cities and towns along the King's Highway moving south – Pella, Kamos, Gethros, Abila, Gadara, and Rabbatamana. The purpose of this campaign was probably to prevent Ptolemaic forces in these places being organized into a field force to make an attack on him as he aimed for Gaza. In the process the first wider signs of the effects of these Seleukid victories (and perhaps of the defection of the senior officers) on the Ptolemaic army came with the defection of several officers and units to him. Some places resisted well – Rabbatamana, for example – but Antiochos and his commanders displayed an unusual skill in siege warfare, while his army was clearly buoyed up by his successes.[16]

This successful campaign put Antiochos in control of much of Palestine, and the land across the Jordan, but it had taken time, so that after Rabbatamana was captured it was time to go into winter quarters again. The army would certainly need a rest, time to heal wounds, burnish and repair equipment, and recover. Antiochos, as a signal of his successes so far, took up his own winter quarters in Ptolemais-Ake, the Ptolemaic provincial capital.[17] And yet, the Ptolemaic strategy was also working. The Seleukid conquest, incomplete still, had so far taken two full campaigning seasons, and there was a good part of Palestine still in Ptolemaic control, together with Sidon, Gaza, and possibly the forts of the Gerrha-Brochoi Lines. The Ptolemaic resistance was meanwhile allowing the new Ptolemaic army to be built up and trained.

According to Polybios 'at the beginning of spring' – that is, March (217 BC) – the two sides 'completed their preparations'.[18] He implies that the armies forthwith marched to fight each other, but as elsewhere, he has compressed events, and the battle which resulted did not take place until mid-June. He covers these three months with the comment about 'preparations'. On the Seleukid side this must have included a preliminary campaign in southern Palestine, since Gaza was in Antiochos' control at the time of the battle. On the Ptolemaic side the commanders had no intention of meeting Antiochos' army in comfortable fertile territory. The Ptolemaic preparations therefore included gathering the full force of the army in one place for the first time – Pelusion is mentioned – and making careful supply preparations for a desert march, then waiting until the Seleukid army was committed to its own desert march. No doubt Antiochos hoped the Ptolemaic army would itself be committed first, and compelled to march through the desert, but he was outwaited.

Much discussion has taken place over the composition of the two forces, which Polybios described in some detail, but the essence is that the Ptolemaic force was larger, and, having come straight from training, was possibly better disciplined than the Seleukid, which may have become over-confident after its string of successes.[19] The main difference lay in the presence of the supplementary phalanx of Egyptians, armed in the Macedonian style, in the Ptolemaic army. Antiochos' force had the advantage in cavalry and elephants, but as the battle was fought it was the eventual clash of the phalanxes which was the decisive action. A battle with these forces was hardly an exercise in subtle generalship. Antiochos' cavalry, led by Antiochos himself, defeated the Ptolemaic horse on the left wing, and his elephants defeated the Ptolemaic elephants, but neither of these forces turned to attack the phalanxes, which were always vulnerable to well-handled cavalry or elephants attacking from the flank. The push of the larger Ptolemaic phalanx against the Seleukid was therefore decisive. There were just two elements of subtlety involved in the clash. Theodotos attempted to assassinate Ptolemy in the night before the battle by infiltrating himself into the enemy camp, but only succeeded in killing the king's doctor. Ptolemy himself, and his sister-wife Arsinoe, showed themselves to the army before the battle began to inspire the soldiers, as did Antiochos on his side. More significantly, during the fighting Ptolemy had to take refuge from the cavalry fight inside the infantry phalanx and in a decisive move showed himself to the soldiers and inspired them to the decisive push of pike (or push of sarissa). Once driven into retreat, of course, any phalanx gradually disintegrated; the Seleukid force collapsed and shredded; the men fled for safety.

The defeat of Antiochos' army was the end of the war – except for making peace. The sequence here is confused. Polybios ignores an episode in which Ptolemy undertook a short campaign into Seleukid Syria, north of the Eleutheros River boundary. He did claim that the population of the Ptolemaic province welcomed Ptolemy as he travelled north, but since he was escorted by the Ptolemaic army, and was a vicious character known to have been responsible for several murders, the enthusiastic welcome was probably purely self-defence; there is no other indication at any point that the Ptolemaic regime in Syria and Phoenicia had any popularity.

Ptolemy was in no hurry after the battle. The Seleukid forces rested at Raphia during the night, but moved on next day, followed by the Ptolemaic forces at some distance. Antiochos moved steadily north, collecting his garrisons on the way. Ptolemy followed fairly steadily. When Antiochos sent envoys to suggest negotiations for peace, it was Sosibios who went to Antioch to discuss the terms. Ptolemy's progress included visits to Joppa and Tyre,[20] and presumably to Ptolemais and Sidon; he made a dedication to Serapis and Isis – archetypal Egyptian deities – at Laboue near the Eleutheros border;[21] it seemed for a time that he aimed to invade Seleukid Syria, but then pulled back.[22]

The evidence of the Raphia Decree, that Ptolemy actually did invade Seleukid Syria and plundered 'a few cities', is not convincing; nor is the interpretation that he was really putting down a rising in his recovered province.[23] The authors of the Raphia Decree, which is dated November 217 BC, did not know at first hand what had happened on the Seleukid-Ptolemaic border; the evidence they used was probably an official account from the Ptolemaic government, recording a token crossing of the border (as at Laboue); the Ptolemaic authorities would be as anxious as ever to exaggerate their achievements. It is notable that Ptolemy made no attempt to resume the fighting at any point in his progress northwards. There would be no disputed terms that would delay the peace.

The peace treaty which resulted was, despite the victory at Raphia, by no means a diplomatic victory for Ptolemy. The negotiations might well have reverted to the sterile talks of the previous year, but they were this time conducted between Antiochos and Sosibios, both of whom will have been businesslike and keen to reach an agreement. So Antiochos kept Seleukeia-in-Pieria; Akhaios was omitted from consideration; no tribute was paid.[24] And the conclusion of peace, as usual, meant that the two kings could now rest easy until one of them died. This agreement was a sentence of destruction for Akhaios, who had been abandoned by Ptolemy, and it gave the green light for Antiochos' great expedition to the east. This was not, as has been claimed, a display of Ptolemaic 'consummate statecraft'.[25] Instead it simply put off, until Ptolemy IV died, the reckoning over Syria.

Ptolemaic Egypt had been forced to exert itself very greatly in resisting Antiochos' invasion. The cost was probably much greater for the Ptolemaic government than it was for the Seleukid kingdom. The failure to mount a serious naval campaign may be an indication that all resources were being devoted to the new army. The Ptolemaic army had only by dint of desperate measures – recruiting several thousands of mercenaries, arming 20,000 Egyptians – succeeded in one single battle. Until the Battle of Raphia, admittedly a neat and successful campaign, every military encounter in the war had been a Ptolemaic defeat, and the Raphia battle was very close to a defeat also for a time, and the failure of the Ptolemaic army to exploit the victory is telling. The dilemma of Ptolemaic power remained. Egypt's military resources were inadequate when faced by a major military power, in part because the government relied mainly on 'Greeks and Macedonians' as manpower in the army, that is, cleruchs and mercenaries. When the policy was to keep the enemy in play and at a distance by small raids and betrayable alliances, the kingdom could survive profitably; in a larger war it had to expend massive resources to raise a sufficient force to be able to resist. The end result could only be an eventual defeat, and the loss of power and of its overseas provinces.

Chapter 6

An Accumulation of Problems

Ptolemy IV had been unexpectedly energetic and effective in the battle at Raphia, though he left the diplomatic aftermath to Sosibios. Indeed, between December 219 and November 217 BC he travelled on at least six occasions from Alexandria to locations in northern Egypt: to Phakoussa, twice to Pelusion, twice to Memphis, and once to Bubastis.[1] To these may be added the Raphia battle in June 217 BC, in which he took an active part, the trip to Kanopos which persuaded Kleomenes to make his prison breakout, and on top of all this there was his long journey through Palestine and Phoenicia to the border with the Seleukid kingdom. Some of these destinations are hardly unexpected: Memphis was his alternative capital and the site of his ceremonial coronation, and at least one of these visits was to attend a meeting with a group of Egyptian priests – a state occasion therefore, and in a time of war in Syria, Pelusion was an obvious place for the king to visit.

However, this is the total of 'visits to the *chora*' – that part of Egypt which was not Alexandria, that is to say, the vast majority of it – we have a record of for Ptolemy IV's reign. After November 217 BC there is, for the remainder of his reign, no indication that the king ever left Alexandria. After the frequent visits and journeys in 219–217 BC this seems somewhat surprising, and one wonders if the apparent energy of the first five years or the apparent lethargy of the latter twelve years was the real style of the man. There is also no record of any visits between his accession to the kingdom at the end of 222 and the visits to Phakoussa and Kanopos in 219 BC, but he may be excused in that period since he was so busy killing his relatives, surviving plots, marrying, and preparing for war. And after 207 BC the rebellion which developed in the south of the country might well have compelled him to stay in the palace, or at least in the city, though one would have thought that the king's visible presence in the *chora* would have been a sensible political move, in view of the multiple crises which by then were facing the kingdom.

The records we have of other kings visiting the *chora* are a clear contrast. Ptolemy II, in a reign of thirty-six years, travelled in the *chora* at least thirteen times, again mainly in the north, but his visits were chronologically well distributed, the only lengthy gap being in the last years of his life, when he was perhaps less mobile – he reportedly suffered from gout; Ptolemy III travelled out of Alexandria five times in twenty-five years, though only once to the south, to Edfu, and this includes his voyage to Cyprus and Syria in 246–245 BC, to which might be added his coronation at Memphis, which is not actually recorded but which presumably took place. Ptolemy V inherited the kingship as a child, but between 197 and 180 BC, as an adult, he travelled to Memphis four times, to Raphia, and to Naukratis and other places in the Delta, and attended the siege of Lykopolis in 186 BC – seven journeys in eighteen years. Ptolemy IV's failure to leave Alexandria after 217 BC is therefore clearly anomalous, especially after his busy earlier years. Of course, it is possible, indeed very likely, that the record is deficient, as suggested by the additions which can be made to other kings' itineraries and which are noted above, but this will apply to all these reigns, and there are reasonably good records for the others, so one might expect it of Ptolemy IV.

Given the probable personal laziness of Ptolemy IV noted by Polybios, the attractions of life in the royal palace, and the willingness, or perhaps eagerness, of Sosibios (and Agathokles) to assume the burden of administration, there was no need for the king to venture out.[2] All that he needed for a luxurious life of pleasure and play and self-indulgence – 'shameful amours and senseless and constant drunkenness', according to Polybios[3] – existed in the palace and the city (though this appears to be based on hostile sources).[4] But it also seems that conditions in the *chora* meant that it was no longer safe to journey there, or at least that the land was disturbed.

There is a vague and chronologically displaced reference in Polybios which seems to indicate that Ptolemy had to fight against members of the army while in Syria. The soldiers were Egyptians rather than Greeks. Polybios seems to be referring to the aftermath of the Raphia campaign, and various dates, including 217 and 213 BC, have been suggested. This would suggest early disaffection of the Egyptian soldiers, to be connected with the great revolt which began in 207 BC. But that revolt in the south seems too distant from Raphia to be the reference here. Furthermore, that chronological distance hardly persuades that the great revolt was a direct result of the employment of Egyptians at Raphia, ten years before.[5]

A rebellion put down in 217 BC or thereabouts seems therefore very likely, and since Polybios is unclear and confused about it, and disdainful of such events, it is perhaps best classified as a mutiny, or as mob riots.[6] A short passage in the Raphia Decree of November 217 BC confirms that there was trouble, but since this was largely a propaganda document, praising the king and developed by temple priests, it would not be specific on such negative events. A full-scale rebellion developed from 207 BC in the south, in the Thebaid, but this was a much more serious affair than mutinies and riots, which were normally brief, as were those in c.217 BC. But such events do not spring from nothing, even if in our sources they appear without warning and seem to be deliberately obscured. The fact is that the sources available for the decade 217–207 BC are exceedingly poor. Some events can be dated in that period, however, and clearly contributed to the rebellion.

The fact that Ptolemy stayed in the palace, or at least in Alexandria, is one of those 'events', or rather conditions. He was clearly all too ready to leave the active administration of the kingdom to his ministers, notably Sosibios, without adequately checking what they were doing, and part of their activities was no doubt to divert some of the public resources and revenues to their own possession, and helping their fellows to do the same. The country was run by a bureaucracy, a system which, once organized with rules and practices, can operate quite automatically, leaving the men supposedly in charge to make only the crucial decisions, but it is always liable to expand both in numbers of clerks and officials and in its range of action. So we may assume a degree of increased expenditure, and of corruption in the government system, this on top of the great cost of the Fourth Syrian War. Yet, as will be seen, Ptolemy had enough resources to spend lavishly.

Ptolemy had seized on the idea of possessing a great ship. This was to be bigger than any other. It was technically a warship, a 'forty' (the largest earlier ships had been 'thirties', though nothing bigger than a 'thirteen' was used in battle). Actually, it was a vast floating palace, richly furnished and decorated. The description (in Athenaios) makes it clear that it was a typically Ptolemaically extravagance, notably in the cost of construction, but also in its rich and elaborate fittings and furnishings.[7] Not only that, but Ptolemy had a monster state barge built as well.⁸ Neither of these vessels ever really sailed anywhere, except perhaps for short distances along the Nile. These vessels in themselves, though ludicrously extravagant as well as useless, could be excused as state enterprises built to impress foreigners, which was a function of royalty, especially Ptolemaic royalty. They were certainly costly, but the country was rich, at least from the point of view of a man living in Alexandria and in the royal palace. And yet if in themselves they were unlikely to beggar the state, these ships were typical of the extravagance of the whole palace system, devoted as it was to display, luxury, and pleasure; this was a vast consumer of resources rather than a contributor to them.⁹

It seems likely that Ptolemy was challenged – or felt he was challenged – by the existence of the great Syracusan merchant ship *Syracusia*, built for King Hiero II of that city in about 240 BC. This was a vessel specifically designed as a cargo carrier. It was about half the size of Ptolemy's forty, about 61 metres in length and 15 metres on the beam, whereas the forty was 103 metres long and 17 metres in the beam. *Syracusia* has been estimated as having a carrying capacity of between 1,700 and 3,600 tons, depending on the cargo, whereas the forty, constructed as a warship, could carry 7,250 men. All these figures are, of course, estimates. But the point is that *Syracusia* was built about 240 BC, designed by Archimedes; the forty was built between twenty and thirty years later. Since *Syracusia* voyaged to Egypt, it seems probable that it was the ship which piqued Ptolemy IV's curiosity and stimulated him to order a ship of his own – twice the size.

Hieron II of Syracuse, having had the ship built, intended to send it around the Mediterranean distributing gifts to needy cities. But it was found that most ports could not accommodate it, so when it visited Alexandria, he made a present of it to Ptolemy III, who renamed it *Alexandris*. Only one ship in the ancient world was bigger than the forty, and that was a ship built specifically at the order of the Emperor Caligula to transport an obelisk from Egypt to Rome. In other words, none of these three great ships really had any use other than as display pieces to impress the subjects of those rulers who had them built.¹⁰

All this was government expense coming on top of the costs of the Fourth Syrian War, which was undoubtedly far more expensive than earlier Syrian wars – the entire phalanx and the extra phalanx were only two enormous items; the hired mercenaries were even more expensive.

The army which fought at Raphia was larger than any earlier Ptolemaic army, and the cost of embodying so many extra soldiers – and training and maintaining them for a year or more and recruiting a large number of extra mercenaries – will have drained the royal treasury. The cost is estimated at 1,000 talents every three months,[11] and since the army was mobilized for at least two years, this alone amounted to at least 8,000 talents, to which costs of the garrisons in Egypt and the empire must be added. At the end of the war Ptolemy distributed 300,000 gold pieces among the soldiers (another 1,000 talents).[12] Given the division of ranks, the private soldiers received a small payment, the officers a large one. More expense, more discontent.

And when the soldiers were demobilized and paid off and went home (at least those who lived in Egypt) they found that their taxes were as rigorous as ever, perhaps even more so, for the war, from which they had returned victorious and rewarded, had now to be paid for. Mercenaries who were paid off will have taken their accumulated pay to their homelands or to the next employment, thus removing from the state a considerable quantity of hard cash. It seems probable that the palace, the administration, the great ship, the barge, and corruption quickly soaked up much of the current revenue from taxation and the accumulated treasure, and the peasantry found itself under greater pressure than ever. This is not easy to quantify, of course, since the record keepers of Ptolemaic Egypt were not normally concerned about the welfare of the peasantry, and the king was wallowing in idle luxury, scarcely leaving his palace for ten years, and so without any direct means of investigating peasant conditions, if he had ever wanted to.

There was some manipulation of the currency involved in this period (the end of Ptolemy III's reign and through until perhaps 200 BC) in which a new tariff of silver to bronze was gradually instituted. This in itself may not have had much effect in a country where most of the population used coinage only rarely, mainly when paying their taxes, but it also seems that there was a general shortage of coin as well, which would certainly feed inflation. (It would be easy to point to the mercenaries' export of coin as an obvious cause of the shortage.) Parts of Egypt had always been coin-short, particularly the south, and the distribution of coin usage was erratic, geographically and over time, and partial, but in Ptolemy IV's reign the shortage appears to have spread to the north, which had the benefit of proximity to coin-rich Alexandria, avid for supplies, paid for in cash.

Again, the effects of this are difficult to quantify, but it is one more item to be added to the list of economic effects of the Fourth Syrian War.[13] it is generally assumed that these currency manipulations are no more than technical adjustments, but it is difficult to accept that they had little or no effect on the population at large; it is also worth noting that these currency changes took place (more or less between 225 and 200 BC) at a time of both great expense and unrest in Egypt.

Many of these alterations are, if not conjectural, then difficult to pin down in their effects on the whole population. The growth of peasant resentment clearly took place between the demobilization of the army in 217, and the beginning of the great revolt in 207 BC; this is not to say that this did not exist earlier, but it clearly reached the stage of an anger which grew into the rebellion by 207 BC. This included the release of the 20,000 Egyptians who had been recruited and trained to fight in the Macedonian style in the phalanx at Raphia, and while this, at ten years' distance, cannot be a direct cause of the revolt, it would be surprising if some of the leaders were not trained soldiers from that time. The subsequent financial stringency certainly reduced the employment of mercenary soldiers, but it also seems to have led to a reduction of the fleet, and a reduction in maintenance and in the employment of sailors, most of whom were Egyptians, some volunteers, but most were conscripted. As a result in 219 BC only thirty ships would be mobilized to campaign in Syria.[14] This period of ten years is about right for the growth of anger among the peasantry of southern Egypt, and the realization that neither adequate rewards for gaining the victory at Raphia, nor relief from taxation pressure could be expected, and an appreciation that the court in the great city was absorbing great quantities of taxation revenue in financing palatial events and activities.

It also seems that the links between the king and the Egyptian priesthood hardly existed any more. The king, a devotee of Dionysos, did not pay much heed to the Egyptian religious pretensions, though the usual subsidies went to the temples, where the priests were kept in comfort as a means of keeping them as supporters of the government. But for the peasantry in pharaonic times the Pharaoh himself had been a necessary part of their worship and of their view of existence, and when the kings worshipped only Greek gods, the link was broken. The religious centre of pharaonic Egypt had always been in the south, at Thebes and nearby cities, and this had been downgraded by the kings' continual residence in the north – only two royal visits to the south are recorded between 282 and 182 BC – five reigns.[15] The Egyptians in the south did not know their king, saw their religious beliefs, in effect, scorned, and yet they paid an increasingly large share of their produce in taxes.

The absence of Ptolemy IV from the *chora* is conspicuous because it is such a contrast to his activity there, and in Syria, in the first five years of his reign. It is easy to take Polybios at his word and ascribe the king's immobility in the palace to his decadent style of life – 'amours and drunkenness', as the historian summarizes it.[16] There seems no doubt that this was encouraged by Sosibios and Agathokles and the court generally, but that does not necessarily mean he did nothing else. He was, for example, clearly involved in the building of his great ships, the forty and the monster barge, and probably only he could have insisted on (and paid for) their construction. Both Sosibios and Agathokles were rewarded with large gift estates in the *chora*, the former at Tebtunis, and Agathokles in the far south near Thebes.[17]

But by separating the king's personal life from the political events which occurred during his reign, it is possible to emphasize, and indeed to exaggerate, the former, and to push to one side the latter, and so to conclude that he was extravagant and neglectful. But those political events did take place, and since this was an absolute monarchy, they did so in the king's name. It is easy to ascribe Ptolemy's policies to his ministers, notably Sosibios, as Polybios repeatedly does, and to point out that his mistress, Agathokleia, was the sister of one of these powerful men, and so to imply that Ptolemy paid only nominal attention to affairs of state, leaving crucial decisions to the ministers. However, just because it was an absolute monarchy, the subordinate statesmen, for their own welfare, had to consult and inform the king.

So we may assume that the absence of the king from any travels after 217 BC was due to a whole set of reasons, of which personal laziness was only one. Others included: the troubles in the *chora* and in Syria after the end of the Fourth Syrian War, which lasted an indefinite time; the king's disinclination (possibly) to travel; and his chosen lifestyle. But it was also due to the primary fact that it was in Alexandria, and specifically in the royal palace, that political discussions took place and decisions were made. The reputation for an enjoyment of pleasure and leisure which the king acquired, does not exclude his willingness to engage in decision-making, nor indeed to work. We cannot blame everything on Sosibios, though it is evident, notably in view of the disaster which befell Agathokles and his family after Sosibios died, that Sosibios was the real driving force among the ministers. He was a master courtier, intriguer, and politician, who was capable of securing decisions in council, or persuading the king, whichever was necessary, and carrying them through into effect. He was evidently trusted by the king and with good reason. One may not like Sosibios, but he was evidently an effective minister, and this was one of the main reasons he held power.

The eventual victory in the Fourth Syrian War no doubt enhanced the prestige of the Ptolemaic kingdom internationally. It did not expand the empire which Ptolemy IV ruled, but it did give him the international authority to participate further in foreign affairs, and there are traces of his actions throughout the eastern and central Mediterranean in the ten years after the peace of 217 BC. In these regions there were three geographical areas in which Ptolemaic policies were active, although, as in earlier reigns, they were directed at particular ends which were favourable to the Ptolemaic regime. These were inevitably the same regions in which earlier kings from Ptolemy I onwards had been involved, but in Ptolemy IV's reign they began to become linked together, thus complicating matters even more than usual. The balance of Ptolemaic interest in each region shifted with the local events. Ptolemaic policy, therefore, as it always had, tracked these local developments, partly to keep up with them, partly to influence them, and partly to avoid becoming too involved. For Ptolemaic policy, exemplified above all by the policies of Ptolemy II towards Greece, was still aimed at keeping trouble at a distance from Egypt, to which end relations with local powers were continually adjusted, which is a polite way to summarize the constant shifts of alliances and subsidies directed at the Greek states. The overall aim, as in the possession of the empire, was defensive; just as Syria-and-Phoenicia was possessed to keep Seleukid power away from Egypt, and Cyrenaica to keep the Antigonid kings at a distance, so foreign policy was aimed at keeping potential enemies fully occupied, so that they did not approach Egypt. It was all connected, but it was bound in the end to fail. Ptolemy IV's policy was thus very largely a continuation of that pursued by his three predecessors.

DISCOVER MORE ABOUT PEN & SWORD BOOKS

Pen & Sword Books have over 4000 books currently available, our imprints include; Aviation, Naval, Military, Archaeology, Transport, Frontline, Seaforth and the Battleground series, and we cover all periods of history on land, sea and air.

Can we stay in touch? From time to time we'd like to send you our latest catalogues, promotions and special offers by post. If you would prefer not to receive these, please tick this box. ☐

We also think you'd enjoy some of the latest products and offers by post from our trusted partners: companies operating in the clothing, collectables, food & wine, gardening, gadgets & entertainment, health & beauty, household goods, and home interiors categories. If you would like to receive these by post, please tick this box. ☐

We respect your privacy. We use personal information you provide us with to send you information about our products, maintain records and for marketing purposes. For more information explaining how we use your information please see our privacy policy at www.pen-and-sword.co.uk/privacy. You can opt out of our mailing list at any time via our website or by calling 01226 734222.

Mr/Mrs/Ms ....

Address...

Postcode........................... Email address..

Website: www.pen-and-sword.co.uk Email: enquiries@pen-and-sword.co.uk
Telephone: 01226 734555   Fax: 01226 734438
Stay in touch: facebook.com/penandswordbooks or follow us on Twitter @penswordbooks

Freepost Plus RTKE-RGRJ-KTTX
Pen & Sword Books Ltd
47 Church Street
BARNSLEY
S70 2AS

The three regions Ptolemy IV was interested in influencing were, from west to east, Sicily and the surrounding powers, Greece, and Asia Minor. In these last two the aim was to thwart any action by Philip V or Antiochos III which might enhance their power, since these were the only powers, at least at the beginning of his reign, which could seriously threaten the Ptolemaic kingdom. These were Ptolemy's traditional Great Power enemies, to be watched with extra care. With Antiochos this was necessary above all because it was essential that the peace of 217 BC not be jeopardized. This ruled out any direct or overt hostile action, though covert activity was quite possible. With Macedon no peace had ever been made with Philip V's ancestors, and certainly not since Philip and Ptolemy had become kings in 221 and 222 BC respectively. Open war was to be avoided if possible, though intrigues and the encouragement of other enemies of Philip was quite possible.

In the western Mediterranean, Ptolemy's father had been a friend of King Hiero of Syracuse, who had sent him the great ship *Syracusia* (renamed for the occasion *Alexandris*) with a cargo of grain.[18] Magas of Cyrene had also developed useful political contacts in the West, but the scope for diplomatic action in Sicily was much reduced when Syracuse became involved in the Second Punic War. King Hiero died in 215 BC and his grandson and successor Hieronymos then attempted to bring Ptolemy into an anti-Roman alliance with himself and Carthage.[19] He also sent his two younger brothers to Alexandria, probably to keep them safe in the event of trouble in Syracuse, repeating King Agathokles' action in 290 BC, sending his wife Theoxene and their children to Ptolemy I, her stepfather, to keep them safe. Ptolemy IV's minister Agathokles was a grandson of that King Agathokles; possibly Hieronymos hoped that the arrival of more royal sons of Sicily might act as an inducement to the alliance he was hoping for.[20] Ptolemy IV avoided involvement (just as Ptolemy I had done) but perhaps only because Hieronymos was assassinated in 214 BC, and Syracuse was taken over by a republican regime; then Syracuse was locked into a Roman siege for the next two years; Ptolemy now kept well clear of any Western entanglements. The arrival of Rome so directly onto the Ptolemaic horizon was a new factor in foreign affairs, though it had been present less obviously since the 270s BC.

In Asia Minor, in the same period (216–212 BC), Antiochos III campaigned to suppress Akhaios, whom he regarded as a rebel. He invaded Akhaios' territory the year after his defeat at Raphia once he had concluded the peace treaty with Ptolemy, in the full knowledge that this peace protected his Syrian frontier, but also that Ptolemy would very likely give clandestine help to Akhaios. This consisted of funding some Aitolian soldiers to go to reinforce Akhaios, and when the latter was locked up in the siege of Sardis, by sending a group of Cretans to attempt to bring him out – they failed.[21] The intervention must have been either to enable Akhaios to continue fighting, or to hold him available as a threat to Antiochos. This meddling might have been enough to cause Antiochos to charge Ptolemy with breaching the peace – it was certainly a flagrant and fairly public Ptolemaic interference in Antiochos' internal affairs by soldiers paid by Ptolemy and whose mission was apparently organized by Sosibios – but it was more in Antiochos' interest to allow the peace to continue – he went off on his great campaign as far as India, knowing that the peace was secure, and so therefore also was his Syrian frontier. And, of course, the publicity blew back on Ptolemy, whose defeat in the clandestine efforts was just as public. The capture and execution of Akhaios was a public humiliation for Ptolemy.

In Greece Ptolemy's main concern was the rise of Philip V. The Ptolemies were always apprehensive of any increase in Antigonid strength. From being a disregarded teenager at his accession in 221 BC Philip emerged during the War of the Allies (220–217 BC) as a decisive commander, if a somewhat erratic politician, and a king with a ruthless streak, prone to vent his annoyance by sacking a captured city. Ptolemy sent an envoy in 217 BC to join with three of the Greek states, Rhodes, Chios, and Byzantion – to attempt mediation to end the war in Greece. Philip met them, then sent them on to the Aitolians, his principal enemy, but neither side paid any attention to the neutrals' efforts.[22] The group was in fact not so much neutral as anti-Philip, and Philip would see that. An earlier attempt by Rhodes and Chios had also failed, so it appears that both Byzantion and Ptolemy had then been enlisted to increase the authority of the intervention;[23] probably Rhodes was the main instigator, concerned that the war was interfering with its commerce, which would be an argument which both Ptolemy and Byzantion could respect. The fact that peace was made soon after the neutrals' second appeal had little to do with their attempts, and more with the news of Roman defeats in

Italy at Hannibal's hands, and with Philip's apprehension of the possible advantages to Macedon of a Carthaginian victory.[24]

Ptolemy had good relations with Aitolia, which had sent mercenaries to Egypt in large numbers for years, and especially in the Fourth Syrian War (despite Theodotos' and Panaitolos' defections), and other Aitolians had gone at Ptolemy's behest and expense into Asia Minor to help Akhaios. So the neutrals' intervention was in fact an attempt to prevent Philip from defeating Aitolia, which Philip would fully understand. The friendship with Aitolia continued, and Ptolemy IV made attempts to extend his good relations in other areas of Greece: into Boiotia, where statues to him were put up at Oropos,[25] Orchomenos,[26] and Tanagra,[27] no doubt in return for some Ptolemaic favour or subvention, and he and Arsinoe sponsored (*in absentia*) the festival at Thespiai,[28] which was revived in 215 BC after a break during the fighting. Rhodes continued to maintain its friendship with Ptolemaic Egypt, for good commercial reasons, and dedicated a statue to Ptolemy IV also.[29] Philip was elected president (*prostatos*) of the Cretan Federation, though this was only an honorary position, and there remained a Ptolemaic presence at Itanos. One of the island's main cities, Gortyn, dedicated a statue to Ptolemy, so this rather implies that the Federation was less than the whole of Crete;[30] Ptolemy was also able to recruit Cretans as mercenaries as freely as he did Aitolians in all his wars, and to employ Cretans in the attempt to extract Akhaios from the siege at Sardis; Crete was a diplomatic contest zone between the kings.

The intervention of Philip in wider affairs eventually brought a Roman declaration of war against him in 211 BC, which in Greece became a recrudescence of the previous War of the Allies, as Aitolia joined in on the Roman side, and so against Philip. In fact, the Aitolians succumbed to Roman persuasion, but Rome was using Aitolia just as the Ptolemies used other Greek cities, to keep the Antigonid kingdom fully occupied as cheaply as possible. In 209 BC Ptolemy and his former associates, Rhodes and Chios, joined this time by Athens, met Philip at Phalara in Thessaly on his march south. They succeeded in organizing a thirty-day truce, but it had no larger effect,[31] and in fact the war extended to Asia at about the same time with the involvement of King Attalos of Pergamon (though this did not last long). Attalos had in fact succeeded Akhaios as Ptolemy's chosen friend in Asia Minor. Neutrals, always including Ptolemy and Rhodes, made further efforts in 208[32] and 207 BC, as Rome showed declining interest in the fighting in Greece and the Aitolians came under greater pressure from Philip and his allies. This again indicated quite clearly that it was to save Aitolia as much as to secure peace that the neutrals were attempting to intervene. By 207 BC a larger neutral delegation – Ptolemy, Rhodes, Byzantion, Chios and Mytilene, and perhaps Athens – made a larger attempt, again without success, since Philip seemed to be advancing.[33] It became clear to the Aitolians that Rome would offer no more help, and that alliance with that city offered no profit, and in the winter of 207/206 BC the neutrals made another attempt.[34] How far their efforts were influential is unclear but the Aitolians did agree to a peace during 206 BC, despite Roman objections and disapproval.

In all this the leading power, albeit rather in the background in the Greek section of the overall war, was Rome, and the Ptolemaic regime's diplomatic interventions became steadily more involved with the Italian city. The precise cause of this involvement was the Second Punic War, whose effects, unlike in the First Punic War, spilled over into Greece and ignited the Second Macedonian War. At the time Ptolemaic Egypt was clearly the major military and naval power in the East, or so it seemed, and so necessarily became involved, at least diplomatically, in all the political developments, for this is how Great Powers always act. Yet it was quite possible for all those in Greece who were involved in the Second Macedonian War between 211 and 205 BC to ignore Ptolemaic attempts to bring peace; Philip certainly repeatedly brushed off Ptolemaic attempts to set up peace negotiations; and there is no sign that the Aitolians tried to use Ptolemy's influence to do so either. This would suggest that Ptolemy was only marginally serious in his political interferences, and that there was little military or naval power behind his diplomacy. Rhodes and Byzantion, and perhaps Athens, were commercial powers, far more concerned than Ptolemy about peace. But all the neutrals were too-obviously hostile to Philip to be considered credible neutrals in a peace negotiation. Their individual interests were too closely involved.

Ptolemy IV was also very careful to avoid any hostilities with Rome. He was clearly willing to contribute clandestinely against Antiochos in Asia Minor, or in Greece by developing diplomatic relations in Boeotia and Crete and in assisting Aitolia diplomatically, but Rome was obviously a different matter. Any prospect of reviving the Syracusan monarchy by using the refugee princes was extinguished by the Roman capture of the city and Roman friendship with Aitolia was severely damaged by the latter's 'desertion', in the Roman view, of Rome. Rome, like any other state, interpreted events in its own interest, and Rome's loyalty towards its allies was as equivocal as that of the Ptolemaic kingdom to its allies, while expecting any ally to be unequivocally loyal to it.

The initial lesson about Rome was perhaps when Hieronymos of Syracuse attempted to enlist Ptolemy on the side of Carthage and Syracuse against Rome. Suddenly it was clear that such old friendships as those with Syracuse, largely informal as they were, could be dangerous. Ptolemy was rescued by the assassination of Hieronymos, and from then on he was a determined neutral with regard to Rome, so that his interventions in Greece, which can best be interpreted as in the Aitolian interest if for anybody, were weak, since it was rapidly clear that Rome's annoyance at the Aitolian unwillingness to go on fighting had been evident from early on. Ptolemy's response to the Roman embassy in 210 BC, supposedly of congratulations to the king and queen (an unlikely pretext since they had been married for ten years and in that year Arsinoe largely severed relations with her husband) or to request a supply of grain, is not known, though he may have agreed to supply the grain – it was a bad time for Rome.[35] Ptolemy helped Decius Magius, a Capuan leader captured by Hannibal when he took his city; he had been sent to Carthage, but had ended up in Egypt by the vagaries of the weather.[36] These were timid gestures of support for Rome, but indicated friendship rather than the reverse. There was no such gesture towards Carthage, except for the participation of the priest king of the Siwah oasis, which was technically part of Ptolemy's territories, who was a commander in the Carthaginian forces.[37]

The feeble diplomatic interferences in the war in Greece happened on four occasions between 209 and 206 BC, with no apparent result. Ptolemy IV was certainly anti-Philip and pro-Aitolia, as were his ancestors, and Rome was allied with Aitolia, but Ptolemy evidently exercised no real influence either way. Rome was determined to keep the war in Greece going so as to keep Philip occupied in Greece, and no doubt the Ptolemaic envoys fully understood that – after all, this had long been a part of Ptolemy's Greek diplomacy. When Aitolia eventually made peace despite Roman disapproval, the neutrals might congratulate themselves on their failure, so that they escaped Rome's enmity, for the moment.

The arrival of Rome as a member of the coterie of powers in the eastern Mediterranean complicated diplomacy for all involved. Ptolemaic purposes in foreign affairs were still, however, the same as in the reigns of the first four kings: to block off any advances in power by the Seleukid and Antigonid kingdoms, generally by means of developing friendly relations with the enemies of these kingdoms, and even provoking them to war to preoccupy a greater enemy. But in the long run this could not work, and this was only partly because of Roman intervention. In effect the Ptolemaic diplomatic effort was used, as before, to see that wars continued, not that they were resolved. That policy was unpopular with its victims (enemies and allies) and it was ultimately a failure. Ptolemy IV was following in his predecessor's tradition of betraying allies and attempting from the comfort of the Alexandrian palace to manipulate the lesser powers. But Philip and Antiochos, and now Rome, could not be manipulated in that way; instead, they were equally skilled manipulators. The situation was thus changing.

The period following the end of the Fourth Syrian War therefore contained those developments which had led to the collapse of the Ptolemaic state in the following decade. The kingdom was heading for trouble with its Egyptian peasantry, who were feeling betrayed after rescuing the regime at Raphia, and it had built a tradition of betraying allies which left no reliable allies available anywhere. The army and navy had hardly been used after 217 BC, and had decayed, while Antiochos III had been achieving spectacular successes in the east and in Asia Minor, and Philip building a major reputation in Greece, just as Rome had in the west. In the next decade all these developments and changes, in a true reckoning of the cost, would coalesce to ruin the state.

Chapter 7

Rebellion and Court Coups

Explaining a major rebellion has always been a difficult task – the English Revolution and the American Civil War may be enlisted as prime examples to illustrate the difficulties and the controversies which arise – but it becomes effectively impossible in the case of the great rebellion in Egypt in the late third century BC. The absence of any contemporary record attempting to explain the causes is a basic part of the difficulty in even attempting a modern explanation of what happened. The one historian who might have attempted an explanation is Polybios, but he dismisses the rebellion as 'a war ... which contained nothing worthy of note', no fixed battles, no sea fights, no sieges.[1] It is possible that he attempted an explanation of the war elsewhere in a part of his text which has disappeared, but his basic disdain is evident, and it is unlikely he was convincing.[2]

The sources for the war itself are just as difficult as those for its cause. There are a number of details, but any overall account can only be stitched together out of discontinuous items, in the knowledge that even more detail is missing.[3] These consist of indirect notices, generally dated by a king's reign, which gives the political authority in power at a particular place on a particular date – but that may change the next day, and could have changed the day before. It does not help that the spelling of the names of the Egyptians who made themselves pharaohs changes almost with the historian. So we are compelled to make estimates of the extent of the authority of the various kings, and to speculate about motives.

There can be no doubt, however, about the importance of this war – in which a considerable part of Egypt seceded from Ptolemaic rule, and reverted to pharaonic rule. This condition of affairs lasted for twenty years, and undermined the strength of the Ptolemaic kingdom at a crucial period. It is in fact crucial to the future of the Ptolemaic state. It is the equivalent of the collapse of the Seleukid state in the previous generation, which permitted Ptolemy III to walk into north Syria attended only by his personal guard, and was followed by a prolonged civil war and the loss of territory.

The Seleukid kingdom revived, and recovered most of those places taken from it during its period of collapse, and more, thanks to the ability of Antiochos III. The Ptolemaic kingdom did not revive in the same way after this civil war, probably because its collapse was much more serious, and it lacked a king as capable as Antiochos – though Ptolemy VI had the makings of a capable king – or one ruling as long as he did without interruption. It certainly continued in existence as a political entity, and lasted in the end a generation longer than the Seleukid kingdom, but the rebellion of 207–185 BC was the first of a series of such civil wars throughout the rest of its existence, and it was accompanied by repeated court disputes, *coups d'etat*, court scandals and the murders of kings, resulting in a serious reduction in the prestige of the monarchy, and a reduction in the effectiveness of the regime; it also attracted the repeated attention of outside kingdoms seeking to steal parts of its empire.[4]

The period covered in this chapter is a depressing record of such problems, and in retrospect it can be seen that the court crisis at the beginning of Ptolemy IV's reign (Chapter 5) was the first of a series of these which lasted through to the end of the dynasty. The following ten years (Chapter 6) seem like a taking of breath in preparation for an even greater crisis, which included the same ingredients – murders, rebellion, *coups d'etat*, invasions. But this crisis in the Ptolemaic kingdom was even longer than the preliminary in the 220s BC, or that of the Seleukid kingdom. And, of course, the Ptolemaic kings had only themselves to blame.

The rebellion which initiated the twenty-year crisis began in or about September 207 BC. The earliest signs of rebel activity are at Thebes, where the deposit of taxes into the bank in the city ceased in September, presumably meaning either that the tax receipts had been appropriated by rebels, or had not been collected at all;[5] at Edfu, building work on the temple in the city – a temple founded and funded by the Ptolemaic kings – ceased at about the same time.[6] Whether these interruptions meant that these places had come under the control of the rebels, or had simply been raided, and so their operations were disrupted, is not certain, but in neither case did the interrupted operations resume for the next decade and a half.[7] Another source, awkward and late, is the record of a legal case in 117 BC, in which reference is made back to events more than eighty years earlier in the reign of Ptolemy IV; the former owner of a building was attempting to recover it from the family which had held it since the rebellion; calculating the date (and assuming the lawyers and the plaintiff could count, and were accurate) takes the event back to the same time as the episodes at Edfu and Thebes. Together, these several events imply the existence of serious fighting in the south by the autumn of 207 BC.[8]

It is worth noting that Agathokles, the minister of the king, had been given a large estate between Thebes and Harmouthis. This had been awarded him by Ptolemy IV, and so after 220 BC. It lay between the two cities which were early implicated in the rebellion, and it is therefore certain that he lost control of it. He had no doubt distributed plots to cleruchs. One wonders how much the fact of Agathokles' involvement in the planting of cleruchs close to the Theban temple had on the origins of the rebellion. Cleruchs for one were fairly rare in the south, and the revolt is widely credited to the resentments of soldiers who had fought at Raphia.

There does not seem to have been any reaction by the government in Alexandria to these rebel successes, and a year or so later the rebels certainly held both Thebes and Edfu, and the garrison of Greek troops which had been at Thebes had been driven away upriver to Elephantine and the first cataract.[9] By 206 BC the rebel commander, Haronnophris (Har-wennefer, in Egyptian), had been proclaimed pharaoh at Thebes; the earliest dated document attesting this is an ostrakon from Karnak dated 11 November 206 BC. And this gives the generally accepted date of 206 BC for the start of the revolt, though the evidence from Thebes and Edfu puts the first events in the year before, therefore Haronnophris' reign began between September 207 and November 206 BC.[10]

These early hostilities were significantly directed at the bank at Thebes where the tax receipts were collected, and at the temple at Edfu whose role was no longer simply religious but had become part of the government taxation system; the temple controlled large estates, and the priests had privileges and pay from the Ptolemaic regime. To the peasantry, rightly, these priests were therefore part of the general oppression, and so they were a target. This emphasizes both the anti-government activity of the revolt, but also that the religious system was perceived as an oppressor by the peasantry.

This had been prefigured in the separation of people and religion which had been developing in the previous generation. No doubt the peasants still worshipped their old Egyptian gods, but this was now separated from the temples as an institution. And by accepting a pharaoh as king – that is, an Egyptian – the rebels had thus developed into an organized political movement, whatever the preliminary events had been. The rebellion was developing into a revolution.

No doubt these events were not taken seriously at first in distant Alexandria (though other places must have been aware), where the government was perhaps dismissive of peasant enmity. The problem was probably left to the southern garrisons to deal with. But the garrison of Thebes, the old Egyptian capital, had been driven out, and so probably had any troops at Edfu, and at any towns between them, and as far south as Elephantine, the southern border of the kingdom; taxes were no longer being collected, and a rival king had appeared. By 205 BC the matter had surely been seen as serious even at Alexandria. But then, during 205/204 BC, another court crisis developed. Ptolemy IV died some time before July 204 BC, which is the date of the last known document of his reign.[11] His death, however, which was probably sudden (he was less than forty years old) is said to have been concealed for some time (not necessarily for very long) by the ministers Sosibios and Agathokles, who were determined to keep power in their own hands.[12] Ptolemy left a son, his only child, who had been born in October 210 BC. He had been associated as joint king since 209 BC, and now became sole king as Ptolemy V. The obvious regent for him would have been his mother, Arsinoe III, but she detested what her husband had become in his devotion to pleasure, and was hostile to the two ministers, who had encouraged his dissipation. They therefore had her murdered, probably not long after her husband's death.[13] They then read out a document which they claimed was the dead king's will (judged by Polybios to have been a forgery, a claim widely accepted, though that does not matter). They had gathered an assembly of bodyguards and officers – a travesty of a Macedonian army quasi-legislative assembly – for the occasion, and then assumed the position of joint royal guardians, though Sosibios died soon after. Agathokles' sister, Agathokleia (Ptolemy IV's former mistress), and their mother, Oenanthe, were put to care for the six-year-old king.[14]

This series of events clearly preoccupied the court, perhaps for some time before the king's death if he was ill, just as had the crisis at the death of Ptolemy III. But it was not merely a court problem. The death of Ptolemy IV may have been concealed (for an uncertain period of time) so that the ministers could seat themselves firmly in power before announcing it, and so that Arsinoe could be murdered, but they knew they also faced another probable crisis. The king's death voided the peace treaty of 217 BC and left Antiochos III free to attack once more in Syria. He had, in the time since that peace, retaken Asia Minor from Akhaios, and had conducted a great campaign to the borders of India, establishing his superiority over a series of now-independent kingdoms from Parthia to the Kabul Valley and the Hindu Kush, and incidentally training his army to high efficiency and with a wide variety of military skills. In 204 BC he was once more in Asia Minor, and the news of the death of Ptolemy IV allowed him to move against the cities in the Asia Minor coastal region which were in effect in the borderland between the two kingdoms.[15] These encroachments were mainly directed against areas and cities which were not actually under Ptolemaic control, but which were clearly threatened by any further Ptolemaic advances. So the advances Antiochos had made were not quite enough to bring on a war, but it was a clear sign to the new regime in Alexandria that Antiochos would not remain content to stay within his former boundaries, or encroaching onto no man's land, for long. Large areas of Asia Minor were vulnerable, but it was obvious that Syria-and-Phoenicia would be his prime target.

The Seleukid army had therefore been in active operations continuously, in Asia Minor, in the East, and again in Asia Minor, ever since its defeat at Raphia, and had succeeded in all its campaigns; it was a flexible and skilled instrument, and Antiochos had developed his command skills in parallel. In that time the Ptolemaic army had been, so far as can be seen, inactive, and was probably reduced to small garrison forces scattered throughout the empire and in Egypt (such as the garrison which was driven out of Thebes by a peasant force). This would be the typical reaction into relaxation by an army and government following a decisive victory, when further challenges cannot be easily discerned. In addition, it is evident from events in the next Syrian war that the Ptolemaic navy was wasting away, both in numbers of ships and in sailors. Sosibios and Agathokles – or at least the first of these – must have been fully aware of the contrast between the forces of the two kingdoms, and the danger which the new situation posed to them and to the Ptolemaic kingdom.

The ministers who were so eager to take power, therefore inherited a whole series of major problems – they had to establish themselves in control of the court and of Alexandria, they had to prepare their armed forces for a new Syrian war, and the rebellion in the south of Egypt had to be combatted, or at least contained. Of these issues the least important was the third. The pretensions of Haronnophris as king or pharaoh was a clear step up in the rebellion from the usual problems of strikes and raids and withdrawals – 'a process common enough to earn its own name of *anachoresis*' - in which the aggrieved peasantry indulged.[16]

It seems likely that the peasants in the south had been acting in this way for some years, and that the raids on Thebes and Edfu were their first advance from strikes and withdrawals; the proclamation of a pharaoh would be the next move. If this gradual evolution was what had happened, there is some excuse for ignorance by the Alexandrian authorities of what was going on. This is, of course, all of a piece with the decay of the navy, the failure to exercise the army, and the general defensiveness of the conduct of foreign affairs, a process of increasing wealth among the Alexandrian aristocracy, based on office holding and land grants, and overseen by Sosibios, who used his authority to reward supporters, or buy off opponents; but this also turned the aristocrats' attention inwards, concerned above all with their own affairs, and much less concerned with the good of the kingdom, on which they relied for maintaining their wealth.

And yet the emergence of a pharaoh in the south, with its anti-Ptolemaic and anti-Greek connotations, was clear evidence that the situation was a good deal more serious than usual. The new pharaoh was by no means powerful enough to constitute a serious threat to the northern part of Egypt, with its combination of plenty of soldiers and a higher population of Greek inhabitants who were capable of being mobilized quickly. In estimating the degree of threat of the problem Sosibios and Agathokles had simply decided that Haronnophris could be left alone for the moment; the greater threats were those which came from the north. And yet the example of the pharaoh acting independently in ruling over a substantial part of Egypt could only inspire other Egyptians; it was clearly a mistake to avoid dealing with the southern rebellion until Haronnophris had both emerged and settled himself.

Haronnophris managed to take Abydos by 201 BC (his Year 5), which was not a very threatening progress.[17] The garrison at Elephantine held out apparently without difficulty throughout the revolt. It has been suggested that the rebel regime never managed to block the river traffic,[18] which, if so (though one must have some doubt about this conclusion), would allow supply to reach Elephantine regularly, though the only example on record comes at the very end of the war, in 187 BC.[19] It has also been suggested that the pharaonic regime did not include any sort of administration for such tasks as taxation and customs supervision,[20] though it is clear from the documents which survive that some sort of administration did exist; since taxation and general oppression were the main grievances of the rebels, the pharaonic regime could not impose itself in the same way. It would, though, take over royal land and that of absent Greek owners, and collect dues and rents.

For a brief space of a year or so the Alexandrian court considered the many forms of the crisis, while acting to ensure its own survival. But plans, once made, quickly go wrong. Sosibios died soon after the proclamation of the regency, leaving Agathokles in a control which was precarious.[21] He continued to deal with the rebels in the south by ignoring them, though he must have personally suffered a loss of income from the lost lands near Thebes. The threat of a new Syrian war was clear, and he attempted to evade it by sending envoys to Antiochos, to King Philip of Macedon, and to Rome. Some, or even all, of the men he dispatched were his competitors or enemies, sent off as much to get them away from Alexandria, out of conspiring distance, as to conduct their diplomatic negotiations. Philammon, identified as the actual murderer of Arsinoe, was no doubt very glad to leave, given the undisguised public grief and anger at her death; the rumours of her death by murder, and by whom, had come out quite quickly; Philammon was appointed *libarch* in Cyrenaica, a post similar to that held years before by Agathokles' father. Pelops son of Pelops, who had been governor of Cyprus for a decade, was now sent to negotiate with Antiochos; his earlier post will have made him familiar with the Seleukid threat. Ptolemy son of Sosibios (probably the eldest of his two sons) went to King Philip with a proposal that the new king should marry Philip's daughter, something which had been discussed earlier.

Philip son of Agemarchos was to go to Rome, at least in theory, but he was actually expected to stay in Greece, his homeland, visiting friends and relatives – he came from Megalopolis – and in fact he did not bother to go all the way to Italy. Apart from greeting his Greek friends, and perhaps being relieved to be out of Alexandria, he must have realized that with the Second Punic War still on, Roman intervention in the East was not possible.[22] This was presumably others' pleased decision also. (Scipio Africanus was even then campaigning in Africa, and Hannibal was being shipped from Bruttium to Africa to contest his presence.) Indeed, the Roman embassy which had come to Alexandria in 210 BC, possibly asked for assistance against Carthage, but had been either refused or ignored. There is a difference between the accounts of this mission; Livy claims it was to present gifts to the king and queen, though why then is never explained; Polybios thought it was to ask for the supply of grain, which is more likely, given the damage which had been done to Italian agriculture during the war.[23] It was to be expected that Rome would behave in the same way in the face of the Ptolemaic requests for help; the help was thus never requested.

The result of sending these envoys to Antiochos and Philip and Greece was likely to draw attention to Egyptian weakness; at some point both kings offered assistance to the Ptolemaic regime in dealing with an Egyptian rebellion in the Delta region but this was refused. The offer was made at some time early in Ptolemy IV's reign, though exactly when is not known.[24] It is the only direct reference to troubles in the Delta at this time. The kings were unlikely to have referred to the rebellion in the south, since its continuation was so much in the interests of both kings. Continuing disturbances in the Delta area after the Fourth Syrian War – what Polybios calls Ptolemy IV's war against the Egyptians – and the discontent which followed the demobilization of the Egyptian phalanx, would explain Ptolemy IV's failure to travel after 217 BC, and could have provoked the royal offers. Of course, both Philip and Antiochos had ulterior motives in making their offers, and would clearly expect concessions in return for their help. That help was refused: Ptolemy would hardly wish to be a king who had to get help from his enemies. Quite likely Antiochos and Philip expected that rejection (how would they have reacted in similar circumstances?), so the offer was probably not serious; indeed, it is more likely to have been, and to have been seen as, a not-so-subtle insult.

The dispatch of Agathokles' envoys to the two kings had an effect which Agathokles can have hardly expected. Philip and Antiochos, from dynasties which were traditionally friendly to each other, and who had several times inter-married, had clearly been in contact over the question of Egypt earlier. Far from responding to Agathokles' diplomatic overtures, they were stimulated to contact each other once more and then to negotiate a treaty in which they agreed to attack and partition the Egyptian empire, detailing those parts they would each take. This is the 'Syro-Macedonian Pact'. Precise details of the agreement have not survived, if indeed they were ever committed to writing, but there is no reason to reject its existence.[25] The news of this partition treaty, when it was relayed by Rhodes – a Ptolemaic client – to Rome, certainly interested the Romans, but it was also clearly yet another appeal for Roman help from the regency regime in Egypt. There was no reply from Rome. There is some doubt that Rhodes knew the precise details, which, if not written down, would not be surprising, and the Rhodians may have exaggerated what was known or suspected in order to get Roman attention. If Rhodes told the Romans about it, Egypt was also no doubt informed; Rome at least paid no attention.

By then Agathokles had succeeded in arousing the opposition of the Alexandrian mob. The Alexandrians had liked Arsinoe, whose murder could not be kept secret.[26] Agathokles had become the object of plots to remove him, something which was very likely to happen once Sosibios died. Polybios described him as indulging in 'drinking and debauchery' and ascribes to this the growing dislike of him which he apprehended. Yet having removed a whole set of prominent men who were his enemies, notably the envoys, and surrounded himself with cronies, he had left himself vulnerable.[27] The most prominent opposition authority was now Tlepolemos, sent to Pelusion as military governor of that important post. He put himself at the head of the discontented and, behind the screen of a loyal garrison, he gathered allies among army commanders and provincial governors.[28]

The opinion of Tlepolemos, who developed a habit of sharing offensive jokes about Agathokles with his dinner guests, led the latter to move against him. Tlepolemos, however, had gathered the support of governors and units of the army, and Agathokles' move failed.[29] The authority of Agathokles' government also suffered by the arrival from the south of refugees driven out by the early successes of the Egyptian revolt, which may have been the first time those in Alexandria outside the government understood the scale of the revolt.[30] Agathokles' failure to attend to it while attacking his internal enemies could only increase his unpopularity. Evidence which emerged later shows that the houses these people had left were taken over by squatters, who in several cases were able to retain possession after the revolt was over.[31] The discontent fanned by the arrival of these refugees added to Agathokles' troubles.

Agathokles struck out at those he considered his enemies, including imprisoning Danae, Tlepolemos' mother-in-law, which further angered the city mob.[32] But when his own mother took refuge in the Thesmophoreion (the temple of Demeter) and one prominent victim of Agathokles' vengeance, Moeragenes, escaped from arrest just before he was to be executed, and took refuge with the soldiers, it was evident that Agathokles' regime was heading for a collapse.[33] The city boiled with riots and rumours; some of the latter were no doubt exaggerated, or even invented. Agathokles secured the person of the king and held him in a part of the palace. There they were located by a group of now-mutinous soldiers. He sent out one of his associates, Aristomenes son of Menneas, who had been priest of Alexander and the Deified Ptolemies for 204/203 BC, as his negotiator; Aristomenes' father had held the same priesthood in 231/230 BC, so he was of the highest layer of the Alexandrian aristocracy. Agathokles, grandson of a king, and Aristomenes, were the sort of men who commanded instant respect, but Agathokles' reputation, though not that of his messenger, was suffering badly by now.

The demands of the soldiers were for the king to be sent out. After some delay Agathokles, presumably persuaded by Aristomenes, who had his own agenda in all this, surrendered his hostage. Part of the crowd rejoiced and went off with the king, but the rest were determined to deal with Agathokles. Interestingly, they asked the king for permission to punish those who were guilty of offences against him, and when he nodded assent – he was only six – Sosibios son of Sosibios, who was in the crowd, reported this to the crowd and then took the king to his own home for safety.[34] This was not a mob out of control, fuelled by fury, but a rational crowd with a clear purpose. Aristomenes had gone out into the crowd to negotiate, Sosobios son of Sosibios was amongst them; the whole affair was clearly well organized.

The crowd, having thus been given royal permission, murdered Agathokles, Agathokleia, and Oenanthe in a public torture-and-execution session in the city stadium.[35] Philammon, the murderer of Arsinoe, had meanwhile returned to the city from Cyrenaica, and was pursued by a group of ladies who had been in Queen Arsinoe's household; they broke into his house and killed him, his son, and his wife 'with clubs and stones'.[36]

Polybios' description of Oenanthe's behaviour in the temple of Demeter, when she reviled those of her ladies who offered her assistance and consolation, and that of Agathokles, who evidently had taken to drink, and when he had the king as hostage, released him without any attempt at bargaining, is a description of a family in fear and trembling and dissolution. They were both clearly at the end of their tether, quite unable to cope with the situation they faced, and equally unable to see any way out – paralyzed with tribulation and indecision. Polybios makes no mention of the reaction of Agathokleia, though she was evidently as much blamed as the others, and suffered the same punishment.

The respect everyone had for the person of the king is clear. He was held but early released by Agathokles, and went out into the baying crowd, but was treated with respect there. Sosibios was able to conduct him home – his own home, not the palace – without difficulty. There was evidently no danger that the Alexandrian rioting would develop in a republican direction, even though Ptolemy V was the last of his dynasty; to eliminate him would bring on a real revolution, yet this was rejected. This sequence had happened at Cyrene less than half a century before, with one king assassinated, and the heir, Berenike, spirited off to Egypt as the king's wife; there was also a confused republican coup; it is clear that Alexandria was populated by loyal royalists.

Tlepolemos, together with Sosibios son of Sosibios, who had secured the person of the king, jointly emerged as regents in Agathokles' place. Despite the descriptions of the mob violence which Polybios rather revels in, the actual seizure of power by Tlepolemos had been accomplished by his command of the Macedonian royal forces in the city (who had been roused by Moeragenes' plight). That is, behind the crowd's murders and riots, Tlepolemos was conducting a military coup, and had enlisted Sosibios as his partner, no doubt because Sosibios was the son of the dead Sosibios, and held the person of the king. Of course, such a coup was conducted in the king's name, and was theoretically aimed to 'restore' the king's authority.[37] One must suspect that it was Tlepolomos who was behind the intervention by the troops, and even the crowd actions; he and Sosibios were evidently allies all along.

Tlepolemos was an experienced administrator (his father had been governor in Karia in 246 BC) and soldier. He therefore had the aristocratic ancestry, and the conventional abilities of a Ptolemaic official, but Sosibios owed his position to his father's name, and to his association with the king, and he did not last long. Tlepolemos himself soon became unpopular once the situation in the city calmed down; his was the characteristic failure of a soldier in politics, unable to master the governmental administrative system or the politics of his position. He lasted for a year or so but proved incapable of dealing with the diplomatic problems which smothered him. By 202 BC he had been ousted by Aristomenes son of Menneas;[38] the Alexandrian revolution, if such it was, overthrew Agathokles only to see his successor then replaced by Agathokles' own follower.

In the south Haronnophris had succeeded in expanding his kingdom north along the Nile as far as Abydos and possibly to Ptolemais, and south towards Elephantine, though a Greek garrison continued to hold that place all through the wars.[39] It seems that any advance north of Abydos was only temporary, if it took place at all; at Tenis-Akoris, just north of Abydos, the family of a wealthy Egyptian called Hakoris later boasted that he had been loyal to Ptolemy all along, making it clear that the town had never been occupied by the rebels.[40] If so, this meant Ptolemais was not taken – though Hakoris could be exaggerating, or lying. This revolt, or 'disturbance' had already contributed to the overthrow of Agathokles by forcing refugees to flee to the north, and highlighting his negligence. It had clearly been a mistake by Agathokles (and perhaps by the elder Sosibios) to ignore the events in the south; the result of the crisis in Alexandria was clearly connected with the revolt's effects.

Pharaoh Haronnophris controlled the traditional Theban kingdom, but more relevantly, it gave him control over the trade routes to the Red Sea. Edfu, Thebes, and Koptos, all in his territory, were all termini of routes between the Nile and the ports on the Red Sea, developed at great cost by Ptolemy II, and the connection had been continued by his successor. The capture of elephants, however, had proved less than profitable. At Raphia the smaller Ptolemaic animals – seventy-five of them – had failed against the larger and better-trained Indian elephants of Antiochos. The interruption of the elephant hunts may therefore have been a financial advantage to the Ptolemaic regime in reducing its costs; other trades could continue, based on more northern Red Sea ports, and not needing such a specialized infrastructure. The trade in incenses from South Arabia continued along the old road through Arabia, which could also be used by the Indian spice and cotton trade; the customs duties at Gaza no doubt expanded.[41] This had been a major source of customs revenue for the Ptolemaic regime under previous kings and was now partly lost and partly redirected either to the rebel regime or through Gaza. And, of course, the Ptolemaic trade and the agricultural production of the Thebaid region was lost to the Alexandrian government as well. No doubt the disturbances in Alexandria interrupted the regular collection of taxes in other parts of the kingdom.

The precise reasons for the outbreak of violence in Alexandria are difficult to isolate, but the cession of power to ministers, the revolt in the south, the tension brought on by the expectation of a new war, the negligence of Agathokles, the waste and extravagance of Ptolemy IV, all contributed in various ways. The result was a decisive weakening of the Ptolemaic regime, and an unexpectedly long life for an essentially weak southern rebellion. Most important, an obvious opportunity was presented to the kingdom's outside enemies. It was, obviously, a case of attempted political suicide.

Chapter 8

Egypt Beset: the Fifth Syrian War

The diplomatic agreement between Philip and Antiochos to partition the Ptolemaic Empire was agreed in the winter of 203/202 BC; Antiochos would take Syria and Phoenicia, and Philip the cities in the Aegean and the Straits, Karia, and Cyrenaica. All these were areas which these kings and their dynastic predecessors had predatory and long-lasting interests in acquiring.[1] This is, of course, only an assumption, partly from previous ambitions, and partly from the unreliable sources which comment.

Philip was a little slow off the mark, and never did declare war on Ptolemy, but in 202 BC Antiochos began his invasion of Syria – the Fifth Syrian War – and Philip moved in 201 BC. Antiochos' invasion of Syria this time came by a different route than in the previous war, suggesting that some investigation and careful planning had been made. Instead of the city-blocked coastal route and the fortified Bekaa Valley, Antiochos took a cavalry force and rode along the desert route east of the Antilebanon. This brought him to Damascus unexpectedly. It also outflanked all of the Ptolemaic defensive positions and the fortified cities. It was necessary to use only a cavalry force for the attack, for the desert route is too long and dry for an infantry march, which would be detected well in advance also.[2] In fact he is said to have arrived at a time of festival in Damascus, an additional surprise. This is unlikely to have been a coincidence; more likely it was a well-planned move.[3]

Having secured Damascus and the surrounding oasis, the Ghuta, which provided a rich source of supplies, Antiochos brought his infantry forces through the Bekaa Valley; indeed it is very likely that he began the campaign by starting his infantry and elephant forces through the Bekaa to fix Ptolemaic attention while he led his surprise attack east of Antilebanon. From the Damascus side he could take control of the eastern part of the Barada Gorge, which gave him control of the Barada route into the Bekaa, and so threatened the Ptolemaic Brochoi–Gerrha lines from front and rear simultaneously. He therefore got his infantry forces through to join the cavalry at Damascus, probably without a fight.

From the Ghuta, Antiochos could reach Palestine with relative ease, by the road southwest from Damascus, which ran across south of Mount Hermon. The conquest by this route ignored the whole Ptolemaic position in Phoenicia, which had held him up so badly in 218 BC. As a result, the Ptolemaic position in Palestine, thus attacked unexpectedly, largely collapsed, though the fortified cities in Phoenicia continued to be held by Ptolemaic garrisons, but these were not strong enough to interfere in his campaigns. By the end of 201 BC Antiochos had occupied the Bekaa, Damascus, much of inland Palestine, and held Gaza under siege, but had not yet tackled any of the coastal cities. The Gaza siege lasted a long time, perhaps throughout the campaigning season of 201 BC. Polybios lays emphasis on the steadfastness and heroism of the garrison and the citizens.[4] Gaza, of course, had been recently enriched by becoming a major centre for the collection and redistribution of Arabian and Indian products.[5] It was in the citizens' interests to be loyal to the Ptolemaic regime, just as it was in the regime's interest to hold the city as a forward defence for Egypt. It was once again functioning as the strategic gateway to Egypt. For Tlepolemos, as a former governor of Pelusion, Gaza was the equivalent fortress at the entrance to Egypt, the twin of Pelusion situated at the other end of the road along the Sinai coast, and he would understand this (as indeed would any Egyptian who had fought at Raphia). It is not at all certain when the city was taken, if it was, though the Ptolemaic army was later able to get past Gaza to invade Palestine from the south, which rather suggests that Gaza held out against the siege.[6] Polybios comments on the determined defence of the city, but omits to say what the result was.

In Alexandria, perhaps as a result of the defeats in Syria and Palestine, Tlepolemos was overthrown. He owed his reputation to his military abilities and his membership of the Ptolemaic aristocracy, but he had failed to hold Palestine, despite Gaza's garrison fighting hard. As a result he was overthrown (his personal fate is unknown), and his place was taken by Aristomenes, who was an experienced official/courtier, a former associate of Agathokles and presumably before him of Sosibios, but probably not an experienced military commander; it is probable that Aristomenes had been merely waiting on an opportunity to oust Tlepolemos.[7]

In a sense the coup returned power to the party of Sosibios. Aristomenes had thus probably been involved in all the earlier intrigues and had experience of government under Ptolemy IV; he will certainly have witnessed, perhaps at a distance, Sosibios' seizure of power and Agathokles' loss of it. His experience and his history had put him in opposition to Tlepolemos, but his participation in releasing the king from Agathokles' grip suggested that he was more level-headed than most of those involved; he certainly lasted longer in power than Agathokles and Tlepolemos put together, and he even survived the intrigues of Polykrates. Tlepolemos' failure to effectively defend Syria-and-Phoenicia amid all the tumult in Alexandria obviously gave his enemies an excuse, and the scope, to get rid of him. He had not, to be sure, had an easy task, made worse by a personal preference, so we are told, for expensive dinners.

The war until then had been a contest between the Seleukid and Ptolemaic kingdoms. The oral agreement to partition the Ptolemaic Empire between Antiochos and Philip was little more than a sketch of the future, whose details were to be filled in by victory. But Philip had proceeded cautiously, unusually for him. While Antiochos campaigned in Syria as far as Gaza, he had campaigned in Thrace, the Straits, and Ionia and Karia. In the course of this he took over the Ptolemaic posts of Maroneia and Ainos, at the latter the Ptolemaic governor Kallimedes surrendered the city, as well as some of the independent cities in the region, without a fight.[8] At Samos Philip captured the Ptolemaic dockyard and the fleet stationed there, discovering that some of the ships were useless, maintenance having been neglected, no doubt as an economy measure, and others he had not time to fit up for use.[9] Whether he intended to seize the ships, or the dockyard supplies, or make use of the island as a base, is not known, but it was certainly in a very useful strategic position if he chose to keep it. When a Ptolemaic force came to drive him out, he simply withdrew his forces. (Samos was soon afterwards set up as an independent state by Rhodes.) These events were not part of Philip's war, and he could claim that he and Ptolemy were at peace, though he was stretching the meaning of peace very thin.

It was clearly therefore impossible, amid the series of attacks in Syria and the Aegean, to block Philip's advance against these essentially peripheral areas, and he had to be left to get on with whatever he intended, though it looks as though Aristomenes' government made a less-than-serious effort to defend their Aegean territories; the ships and dockyard at Samos were seized without resistance, for example, and Kallimedes deserted. But Philip mismanaged his logistics. Twice he had to appeal for supplies to Antiochos' governor in Sardis, Zeuxis, and later, at the end of 200 BC, he was camped in Bargylia in Karia for the winter. He had nonetheless severely damaged the Ptolemaic position in the Aegean and in western Asia Minor even without declaring war – his favourite way of proceeding. The cost, however, lay in the progressive alienation of many states by his rough campaigning.

Agathokles and then Tlepolemos in Alexandria between them had, despite their problems, nevertheless made a good start on organizing the defence of the kingdom against Antiochos' attack, when it came, even if the Aegean posts had to be left to defend themselves. They were faced with the usual Ptolemaic problem in a major war – the inadequacy of its military manpower – and this time it was clearly impossible to recruit Egyptians; resort had to be had to the mercenary market.

Skopas, an Aitolian soldier-politician who was in exile in Egypt, was commissioned to recruit a new army of mercenaries in Greece.[10] Part of their purpose had been to take the place in Alexandria of the soldiers with whose loyalties Tlepolemos had been tampering, but Agathokles fell from power before this could be implemented, and Tlepolemos moved in, and continued recruiting. When Skopas returned to Egypt he was put in command of the mercenary army he had recruited and was sent to recover Palestine after Antiochos' successes in 202–201 BC. Tlepolemos was thus adopting Agathokles' ploy of employing his enemy (Skopas, who had been originally sent out by Agathokles) and then sending him on a mission, out of the city.[11] These soldiers had been arriving since 204 BC, with an increased tempo once the war had begun, and while Antiochos was capturing Damascus and campaigning to Palestine. This, of course, was essentially the same method as that used by Sosibios in 218 BC, but this time the recruiting could not be kept secret, especially since, as the numbers of men Skopas collected grew, the Aitolians objected to their losses of manpower and restricted his work. Service with Ptolemy was sufficiently popular among Aitolian soldiers that Skopas had to be prevented by the Aitolian strategos from recruiting more than 6,500 men.[12] These men, joined to the main Ptolemaic field army which was reinforced by cleruchs called to the colours, were available in Egypt by the winter of 200 BC to campaign to retake the lost territory. Tlepolemos had been responsible for organizing this force, but it was Aristomenes who launched Skopas and his men in their counter-attack.

Then the Ptolemaic government suffered another blow. The constant disturbance, confusion, and killings in the court had had a similar result as in 219 BC; the Ptolemaic governor of Syria-and-Phoenicia, Ptolemaios son of Thraseas, deserted to Antiochos. He was repeating the actions of Theodotos in that earlier court crisis, and for the same reason, the corruption and mess in the court in Alexandria. His original appointment is not dated but he probably held the post under Sosibios, Agathokles, Tlepolemos, and Aristomenes, so there was plenty of opportunity to end up on the wrong side of any of these men. He may have been content that the soldier governor Tlepolemos was in power at the start of the war, but when he was replaced by Aristomenes, who was more a politician-administrator; perhaps he lost heart, not wishing to be on the losing side. It may also be that he found he was being lined up as scapegoat for the defeat – he was, after all, in command when Syria was lost. Like Theodotos, he was welcomed by Antiochos, and was swiftly reappointed as governor of Syria-and-Palestine, which had been his former post in the Ptolemaic system. He was the fourth generation of a family originally from Aspendos in Pamphylia, all of whom had served in high positions as Ptolemaic governors and commanders; that such a man should desert the Ptolemaic cause was most ominous.[13]

Skopas was sent with his army into Palestine in a counter-attack in the winter of 201/200 BC (while Philip was camping at Bargylia), and was quickly successful. This was perhaps due as much to the fact that it was a winter campaign and so as much the result of that surprise as of the quality of Skopas' generalship; the use of Gaza as a starting point was also probably a surprise. He recovered much of the territory which had been taken by Antiochos earlier, as far as northern Palestine, but, like that of Antiochos in 218 BC, his progress seems to have been slowed by the need to besiege some of the places where Antiochos had left garrisons, in this case including Jerusalem. Antiochos meanwhile held on firmly to Damascus, and so retained his entrance into Palestine. Skopas marched his forces north, either to take up a defensive position or to attack Antiochos' forces in Damascus. The Ptolemaic control of the Phoenician coast had not yet been disturbed. It was clearly possible for the Seleukid forces which gathered during early 200 BC to march to Damascus by way of the Bekaa Valley without being hindered. Jerusalem now appears as a place of some importance for the first time, and it seems that the population there had come out decisively on the Seleukid side, and the city had to be physically captured by Skopas.[14]

In Egypt, Skopas' success in recovering control of Palestine from Gaza to Mount Hermon, must have looked good in propaganda statements. But without Damascus and the Bekaa, the reconquest was clearly incomplete and insecure. Nevertheless, this appears to have encouraged Aristomenes to use some of the army still stationed in Egypt, which he had retained under his hand, no doubt for 'security purposes', to campaign south to recover control of the rebel-held territory from Haronnophris. Skopas was then attacked by Antiochos with his full field army, elephants, and militia. Skopas was hindered by not having the full Ptolemaic levy available – there were substantial forces in the Phoenician cities and in Egypt (both in garrisons and in the south), and in the Aegean posts, none of which were available to him; on the other hand, there were similar forces held back in Seleukid territories, but Antiochos had much greater resources.

Skopas' reconquest of Palestine took all of 200 BC. Antiochos retired from much of the region for the winter of 200/199 BC, leaving garrisons in various places. He had probably been fully aware that, having collected a major force of mercenaries as reinforcements and called up much of the militia forces, the Ptolemaic government, whoever was in charge, would make an attempt to reconquer the lost lands in the next campaigning season of 199 BC. At the same time, he himself called up his full army, bringing into the line those men, colonists and citizens, from the many cities of his kingdom. This was only the second time in his reign that he did this (the first was for the Battle of Raphia). Normally he campaigned with a professional force of about 35,000 men: calling up his reserves more than doubled the size of his army (and still left substantial garrisons scattered from Asia Minor to eastern Iran). Meanwhile, the Ptolemaic army had decayed somewhat in the years of idleness, a considerable contingent had to be sent to face the southern rebels, and other forces had to garrison restless Egypt, while still more forces were preoccupied in facing Philip's campaign in western Asia Minor. The pressure on the Ptolemaic regime was thus developing relentlessly, with war within Egypt, war in Syria, war of a sort in the Aegean, and these last two were in process of intensifying.

Aristomenes turned to Rome, asking for help. As it happened the Senate in Rome was in process of manoeuvring to be able to mount an attack on Philip, revenge for his alliance with Hannibal. The Ptolemaic appeal allowed that kingdom to be added to those whom Rome claimed to be protecting against the Macedonian king.

Rome was not wholly unknown to the Ptolemaic kings. Ptolemy II had made contact with the city in 273 BC when it was clear that his ally Pyrrhos of Epeiros was about to have his adventure in southern Italy and Sicily snuffed out.[15] Ptolemy II and III had thereafter carefully refrained from involving themselves in either of the Punic wars, and had not interfered when Syracuse, another Ptolemaic friend, had been conquered, sacked and annexed by Rome – and this even though one of Ptolemy IV's counsellors, Agathokles, and his nurse Agathokleia, were descended from a Syracusan king, and had come to Egypt as refugees. None of these early diplomatic contacts were really any more than fleeting, or perhaps they were simply investigative, to see what was going on in the western Mediterranean region. The initial contact by Ptolemy II in 273 BC might have been an attempt at initiating a diplomatic friendship, but later the kings had pulled back to a careful non-intervention policy in Western affairs, no doubt in part because the Ptolemaic kings tended to be preoccupied elsewhere.

When Rome eventually intervened in Greece with its First Macedonian War (215–205 BC) this brought a more concerned Ptolemaic attention. By this time the power of the two great Western states, Rome and Carthage, was all too obvious. Rome, with a major enemy army campaigning in southern Italy under Hannibal, the most accomplished general of the Hellenistic world, was still able to send armies into Spain and to Greece, able to conquer the first and fight another Great Power, Macedon, to a standstill. It behoved any Hellenistic king and state to watch events in the West more carefully, as the Aitolian statesman Agelaos precipitately pointed out as early as 217 BC.[16] (Antiochos III went off on a long campaign into Iran and India, but when he returned he was fully aware of Rome's new presence in the eastern Mediterranean.) Ptolemy IV received a Roman diplomatic delegation in 210 BC, but this had no result; nor did his attempt to mediate peace in Greece between Rome and Macedon. He found that no one was interested; victory was their only aim. The attempt did demonstrate that the Ptolemaic kings were interested in what was going on, though it revealed their inability, even at the height of their power, to influence events.[17]

Philip V had in fact been careful to avoid any real hostilities against any Ptolemaic possessions in the Aegean in 201–200 BC. He had, it is true, made free use of the Ptolemaic island of Samos and its dockyard, and the governor of the city of Ainos on the Thracian coast had deserted to him, but he had not used violence against any of Ptolemy's possessions – Maroneia may be an exception, but it was surely covered by Kallimedes' treason.[18] He left Samos when Ptolemaic forces arrived to expel him. (The island then shifted into independence under Rhodes' patronage. Rhodes had similarly extended its 'protection' over the Island League of the Kyklades.) There was no time limit to the implementation of the division of Egypt's empire between Philip and Antiochos, and Philip was no doubt perfectly content to see Antiochos fighting his way south through Syria, thereby, if he won, destroying much of the Ptolemaic military strength. Philip could then help himself to his own share of the spoils with much less trouble.

In the event he didn't get the chance. The Ptolemaic regime turned to Rome for protection in part because of Philip's behaviour in Greece, which came as close to war as he could go without actually declaring it. At the same time, Rome turned to Egypt in search of some excuse to attack Philip in revenge for what the Romans saw as Philip's treacherous success in the First Romano-Macedonian War. Rome's diplomacy was quite unscrupulous. A Roman embassy of three men, a most high-powered one, consisting of C. Claudius Nero, the victor of the battle in which Hannibal's brother Hasdrubal was killed and his reinforcing army destroyed, P. Sempronius Tuditanus, who had commanded the Roman army in Epeiros in the former Macedonian war, and M. Aemilius Lepidus, a young man from one of Rome's most eminent families, was to tour the eastern states, first in Greece, and then going to Ptolemy V and Antiochos III, investigating conditions, making contact with rulers.[19]

The embassy went to Greece to offer assurances to Rome's 'friends', which included Athens, Rhodes, and the Aitolian League, at least. The appeal for help and protection which came from Ptolemy reached them and they added him and his empire to the list. The appeal put Ptolemy and his kingdom into a vague status of Roman client. Since the war in Syria had already begun, this scarcely affected Antiochos III, which might have been the most useful power to be protected from, but the

Romans were not about to take on both Philip and Antiochos at the same time. It did apply, however, to Philip, who had not started fighting Ptolemy yet, at least not officially, but who was in Rome's aggressive sights. When M. Aemilius Lepidus confronted Philip at Abydos in the autumn of 200 BC he was speaking on behalf of all Rome's 'friends' as well as Rome itself.[20] He demanded, in effect, that Philip leave Greece, including the Ptolemaic possessions. It was, though Philip did not at once grasp this, an ultimatum.

The appeal for help had gone directly from Alexandria to Rome, probably by way of Greece, so the two delegations may have met on their journey. No answer arrived directly, though it was used in Lepidus' ultimatum, and he must therefore have known of the Ptolemaic appeal.[21]

The Roman delegation travelled on to visit Ptolemy and Antiochos, ostensibly seeking to mediate a peace treaty between them. At Alexandria, they will have met Aristomenes, and at Antioch, Antiochos. By the time of these visits, after Lepidus confronted Philip at Abydos, Rome was at war with Philip.[22] No doubt sending the youngest and most junior member to deliver the declaration was a Roman insult, and possibly intended to mislead him. The Egyptian and Syrian visits took place while Skopas was in occupation of Palestine and Antiochos was collecting his army to campaign in the spring. With both sides fully geared up to a new campaign the Roman delegation had no chance of mediating, if they even tried to, and the fact that they had now embarked on a war in Greece blunted any display of power they might have made. The proposal to mediate was probably no more than a means of visiting the two kingdoms to assess their power and resources. The Roman army which had been sent against Philip landed in Epeiros as they were still travelling.

Philip was compelled to turn away from his campaign in the Aegean. He returned to Macedon but then, provoked by an Athenian declaration of war and an attack on his subordinates, he spent much of 200 BC campaigning destructively in Attika. The Roman forces made only minor movements. Once war between Rome and Macedon had begun, the Egyptian government could relax, or at least concentrate on its other troubles. It was clearly in little danger from Philip if he had to concentrate on heading off the Roman forces. In Syria, however, Antiochos returned with his full army in a new invasion of Palestine in 199 BC, and at once faced Skopas' army in battle.

The precise numbers and make-up of the opposing armies are not recorded on this occasion, but both had strong hoplite phalanxes, cavalry, and elephants, and Antiochos had the full levy of his kingdom, and so probably a similar-sized army, or greater, as that which had fought Raphia, 70,000 men. The balance in all parts was in favour of Antiochos. He had a larger phalanx, a larger number of elephants, and as before, he had Indians, whereas Skopas had the smaller African animals. Amongst the cavalry, moreover, in addition to his greater numbers, Antiochos had a contingent of cataphracts, mailed horsemen on especially strong horses.

The battle was fought near the small city of Panion, south of Mount Hermon, and as close to Damascus as Skopas had been able to reach. It was clearly a complicated encounter, mainly in a relatively restricted area of flattish ground, dominated by surrounding hills and mountains, and divided by the Banyas River, which at one point was difficult to cross. To determine what actually happened in the fighting is especially difficult since the only ancient source for the battle consists of Polybios' criticisms of parts of an account by Zeno of Rhodes, and Zeno's own account does not survive. It seems, however, that the decisive moves were made by Antiochos' elephants, which drove off the Aitolian cavalry, and by the cataphracts which seriously damaged the Ptolemaic cavalry. The Ptolemaic phalanx was then assailed by Antiochos' cavalry and elephants on both flanks and pinned down by the Seleukid phalanx in front. (This had been the manoeuvre Antiochos had failed to make at Raphia, so he had apparently learned the lesson of that fight.) The Ptolemaic phalanx disintegrated, suffered heavy casualties, and the survivors fled in disorder.[23] This, of course, was the classic battle pattern such as fought by Alexander and Hannibal with the difference that it was elephants which were decisive.

Skopas commanded the largest organized contingent of survivors, 10,000 or so, mainly, it seems, his fellow Aitolian mercenaries, a preference, or coincidence, which cannot have pleased his employer. He withdrew them from the battlefield in good order and marched to take refuge in Sidon, one of the fortified cities Antiochos had so far ignored. Skopas no doubt hoped to be evacuated by sea, or even reinforced for a new attempt, but Antiochos laid siege to the city and the army, and it was his ships which arrived to form a blockade, and the Ptolemaic government could not gather enough ships to relieve the blockade, or men to break the siege.[24]

The Seleukid army besieged Skopas in Sidon throughout the winter of 200/199 BC and then, simultaneously, campaigned in Palestine and Phoenicia to remove all Ptolemaic forces, a campaign which went on into 198 BC. Meanwhile, Philip came under increasing pressure from the Roman forces, which, after a good deal of dithering, finally got into Thessaly during 198 BC. Therefore, both major enemies of the Ptolemaic regime were fully preoccupied throughout 200 and 199 BC. It was at this time that Aristomenes sent the second Greek expeditionary force against the rebel pharaonic regime in the south.[25]

This may have seemed a foolhardy venture, when the main Ptolemaic army was fully occupied in Palestine and then besieged in Sidon, but it made some strategic sense. Aristomenes and his colleagues must have feared that Antiochos and the rebel regime in Upper Egypt might make an alliance, and make a joint attack on the main Ptolemaic geographic base from Lower Egypt and Palestine. This combination would be made even worse if Philip drove out the Romans and joined in the Syrian War aiming to secure those parts which the Syro-Macedonian Pact allocated to him. The rebel regime was presumably the weakest of Ptolemy's many enemies, and if it could be removed, the forces involved would be available for fighting against Antiochos when, or if, he invaded Egypt from Palestine. It was therefore quite rational to deal with the rebel regime while it was possible, and at the same time to encourage Rome to keep Philip preoccupied, while Skopas was no doubt instructed to hold out in Sidon as long as possible.

The army that was sent to the south was not necessarily large. It had to march, or possibly sail, along the Nile as far as Ptolemais before it met any serious opposition. Then a series of river towns had to be captured, Abydos, Dendera, Koptos. During the operation, Pharaoh Haronnophris died, whether in the fighting or from natural causes is not known. The latest known document in Haronnophris' name is dated July/August 199 BC; the first in his successor Chaonnophris' name (Ankh-wennefer) is in October/November 199 BC,[26] which puts his death in the late summer; by that time Skopas had been removed from Sidon, but Antiochos had still to mop up the last Ptolemaic posts in Palestine and Phoenicia. The Ptolemaic offensive also reached and captured Thebes, which, along with the pharaoh's death, might have brought hopes to the Ptolemaic government that the rebel regime was destroyed.

This successful campaign might have energized the Ptolemaic army, but the Pharaoh Chaonnophris was perhaps more inventive and effective than his predecessor. (His relationship to Haronnophris is not known, though he is sometimes assumed to be his son.) It took some time for him to recapture Thebes, which probably finally took place in 198 BC, suggesting that the rebel recovery was strong, vigorous, and effective, and next year (197 BC) Chaonnophris sprang a surprise. A detachment of his army marched past the Greek forces north of Thebes and seized control of the town of Lykopolis, called Zawty by the Egyptians (now Asyut), 250 kilometres north of Thebes. This was a clever strategic move, for Lykopolis lay at a narrow point of the Nile valley, so control of the town gave Chaonnophris some control over the traffic along the river, as well as cutting the land route close to the river. This appears to have blocked any more activity by the Greek forces, perhaps by reducing their food supplies. Their communication and supply routes were cut so long as the rebel force held Lykopolis and perhaps other places along the river. Lykopolis and its area were very badly damaged in this operation, and are reported to have been rendered a desert by the end of the war.[27]

There were two cities called Lykopolis in Egypt – that in Middle Egypt, which Chaonnophris' forces had captured and held, and another in the Delta which is vaguely located in Greek sources either in the Busirite or the Sebennytic nome,[28] or possibly just south of Mendes;[29] but it is located in the Busirite nome according to the Rosetta Stone, which, since it is almost contemporary with the events there, and was composed by Egyptian priests who lived in the area, may be taken as accurate. It is usually assumed that this is the object of a campaign by Ptolemy V in 186/185 BC to suppress the last remnants of the rebellion, but it is just as probable that this refers to the former, the city in Middle Egypt which Chaonnophris captured, and which experienced so much destruction and extensive damage to the surrounding countryside, according to a set of papyri from that city.[30] That is, both of the cities called Lykopolis were subjected to a siege, but a decade apart. This implies a long and difficult campaign, which is what is described by the sources for Ptolemy's siege.[31] The fighting in the Delta, at the other, northern, Lykopolis, was perhaps instigated by the news of the Ptolemaic defeat at Panion. The subsequent weakening of the regime, and Chaonnophris' successful offensive in the south, perhaps revived the earlier dissent in the Delta. The Delta had been disturbed for twenty years, on and off, and these events could well have encouraged a revival of that Delta discontent. The siege of the Delta Lykopolis was clearly an elaborate affair, though it did not necessarily take very long. Yet it was no doubt a major distraction from what Ptolemy was doing at the same time, and clearly aided Chaonnophris.

The Ptolemaic government made several attempts to relieve the siege of Sidon (while still fighting at both Lykopoleis), but these are only known by the name of the commanders of the relieving forces – Aeropos, Menekles, and Demoxenos – all of whom failed, defeated by the vigilance of Antiochos' intercepting forces.[32] It is probable that Antiochos could use some of the forces he had assembled for the siege to defeat the relief attempts, and meanwhile also to capture several of the places in Phoenicia which he had bypassed so far, and to retake places such as Jerusalem which Skopas had collected earlier.[33] Each place that was captured reduced the possibility of a successful relief of the forces in Sidon, but when Sidon finally capitulated, probably in the summer of 199 BC, Antiochos still had to campaign to take Tyre, Ptolemais-Ake, and Joppa. When these were taken, by mid-198 BC, he had secured all of Syria-and-Phoenicia. There is no mention of Gaza, which had perhaps surrendered quickly to avoid yet another siege. His new governor of the region was Ptolemaios son of Thraseas, who had done the same job for Ptolemy IV and V.[34]

At about the same time the Roman army in Epeiros, now commanded by the inventive and flamboyant T. Quinctius Flamininus, at last broke through the Macedonian defences; the Greek War was thus transferred to Thessaly. For the next year fighting in Greece continued, interrupted by truces and peace conferences which had no results. It was thus a very different war than that which was being fought in Syria, where only the informal truce of armies going into winter quarters happened – and not even then sometimes. Both sides in the Greek War were too busy to have time, resources, or attention left for the Syrian War.

The Syrian War was not yet finished, however, even when the last Ptolemaic resistance was overcome in that country. Skopas, having evacuated his men from Sidon and returned to Alexandria, was at once sent back to Greece to recruit a new mercenary force, so that the defence of Egypt would be possible if Antiochos decided to invade, and perhaps the rebel regime could be crushed.[35] Given that the Aitolian League was now participating in the war against Philip, it is unlikely that Skopas would be able to recruit many men, at least while the war continued. All the surviving Ptolemaic forces would no doubt now need to be concentrated in the north to defend Egypt proper (which may have assisted Chaonnophris in the recovery of Thebes and his advance northwards during 199 and 198 BC). Skopas recruited more men, but by the time he had done so it was clear that the Syrian provinces had been decisively lost. Antiochos now turned to invade the Ptolemaic lands in Asia Minor; he was not satisfied with Syria only, but it looked as though he did not wish to seize Egypt.

Antiochos spent the rest of next year, 198 BC, organizing his conquests, which would need to be well-garrisoned, at least until peace was made. He must have at least considered the possibility of invading Egypt itself, so that threat existed at least until the end of 198 BC, and no doubt this would pin down most of the Ptolemaic forces to places in the Delta. If the 'Syro-Macedonian pact' had the status of a sworn treaty (which is highly doubtful), and if it included a specific division of Ptolemaic territories to be conquered and shared between Antiochos and Philip (which is probable), there could be a good reason for Antiochos refusing to invade Egypt proper. Also, the difficulty of the invasion would be clear, and the memory of the defeat at Raphia was no doubt present. And Antiochos knew there were valuable spoils available elsewhere.

So Antiochos' next targets were the remaining Ptolemaic territories in Asia Minor, which he attacked in 197–196 BC. He marched his army from Syria by land through the centre of the peninsula as far as Sardis, and sent a fleet of 100 ships by sea along the south Anatolian coast. He had built a navy of these warships, the first time the Seleukids had made such a serious effort at sea.[36] This force included some ships of a considerable size, and some of them could have been constructed in the seafaring ports of Phoenicia in 198 BC, where the Ptolemies had built their ships earlier. The success of the siege of Sidon suggests that Antiochos had been able to blockade the city by sea, a manoeuvre he had used in 219 BC at Seleukeia-in-Pieria, and in the campaign in Phoenicia in 218 BC. Building up his navy had therefore evidently been a project over a number of years. But a true Great Power had to be strong both on land and sea; Antiochos was imitating Ptolemy and Rome, and further back Carthage, Syracuse, and Athens.

This navy was sent along the south Asia Minor coast to mop up all the Ptolemaic posts there.[37] Only one place, Korakesion, on the border of Kilikia and Pamphylia, resisted seriously, but was taken by siege after only a month.[38] This was, and is, a formidable fortress which should have been able to hold out much longer, so its resistance of only a month might suggest it had been left with a shortage of supplies, or a collapse of morale, or a minimal garrison, or all three of them. Earlier the fleet had removed the Ptolemaic forces from the posts maintained along the Kilikian coast, and then bypassed the Pamphylian cities to reach Lykia. The Seleukid fleet bluffed its way past a Rhodian squadron attempting to block its passage by its own bluff, and collected more conquests in Lykia and Karia and Ionia as far as Ephesos, leaving some to Rhodes in Karia.[39] The Ptolemaic Empire now consisted only of Egypt, Cyprus, and Cyrenaica together with the island naval bases in the Aegean, all the rest of its overseas empire having been captured.

While this campaign had been proceeding, the war in Greece had ended with the defeat of the Macedonian army by the Romans and their allies at Kynoskephalai in Thessaly. A peace conference produced a treaty; the Ptolemaic kingdom was not represented at the discussions, so the Roman 'protection' which had been a part of the Roman justification for the war, did not involve returning lost Ptolemaic lands. At the Isthmia at Corinth in summer 196 BC, Flamininus announced the Roman decision to withdraw from Greece, and to leave the cities of that country 'free'. Philip was shorn of some territories and partly disarmed. Meanwhile, Antiochos had secured the Ptolemaic territories in Asia Minor simultaneously with the defeat of Macedon and the triumph of Rome. He went on to take over more cities in the Straits which had been abandoned by both Philip and Ptolemy, and moved into Thrace – all territories he could lay claim to by possession at some point in the past, as with Syria-and-Phoenicia.

The steady losses of Ptolemaic forces and imperial lands to Antiochos' forces in 197 and 196 BC clearly exerted heavy pressure on the government of Aristomenes. An opposition figure had arisen, Polykrates of Argos, who had been governor of Cyprus between 203 and 197 BC. He had been an appointee of Agathokles – of whom Aristomenes was also an associate. Rivalry for power developed between the two men, fuelled by Polykrates' deliberate cultivation of the king – he had brought with him from Cyprus the accumulated treasure collected during his governorship, and handed it over to the king.[40] In 197 BC he organized the *anakleteria*, the coming-of-age ceremony for the king, who was almost fourteen by then. This

A bust of Arsinoe II photographed in the Louvre Museum, Paris. (*Gary Todd via Wikimedia Commons*)

A bust of Ptolemy II from the Naples National Archaeological Museum. (*Marie-Lan Nguyen via Wikimedia Commons*)

A bust of Ptolemy III from the Naples National Archaeological Museum. (*Miguel Hermoso Cuesta via Wikimedia Commons*)

Berenike, princess of Cyrene and wife of Ptolemy III. (*CNG Coins via Wikimedia Commons*)

Gold coin of Ptolemy IV Philopator.

Arsinoe III, daughter of Ptolemy III and sister and wife of Ptolemy IV, murdered in 205/204. (*CNG Coins*)

Ptolemy V. (*Cgb.fr via Wikimedia Commons*)

The Rosetta Stone in the British Museum; a record of a series of concessions to the Egyptian priesthood by Ptolemy V – recorded, of course, by the priests. (© *Hans Hillewaert via Wikimedia Commons*)

A Ptolemaic king wearing the double crown of pharaonic Egypt – symbolizing the union of Upper and Lower Egypt; probably a later Ptolemy when it was necessary to conciliate the Egyptians – possibly Ptolemy VI.

Kleopatra Thea and Alexander I Balas, minted at Seleukeia-in-Pieria on the occasion of their wedding, 150 BC, arranged by Ptolemy VI. (*CNG Coins*)

Ptolemy's Enemies

Antiochos III. (*Auguste Giraudon via Wikimedia Commons*)

A bust of Antiochus IV from the Altes Museum, Berlin. (© *José Luiz Bernardes Ribeiro / CC BY-SA 4.0*)

Coin of Antiochus IV depicting a victorious galley. (*CNG Coins*)

The Temple of Horus at Edfu. Begun under Ptolemy III and built in a very pharaonic style with the addition of the classical elements, such as the columns. Work ceased during the Great Revolt and the building was not finished until the reign of Ptolemy VIII. (*Adobe Stock*)

Asyut, ancient Lycopolis, a town at a narrow point of the Nile Valley, hemmed in by hills. This is the place Chaonnophris chose to seize in his offensive against the Ptolemaic government of Ptolemy. The result was extensive devastation of the surrounding area, and fighting for several years.

made Ptolemy V, in theory at least, capable of ruling without a regent. A coronation ceremony followed a year later, in May 196 BC, at Memphis in the temple of Ptah.[41] These ceremonies were perhaps aimed at reinforcing the ministers' political authority, rather than passing direct power to the king, but it will also have done the same for the teenage king.

Between them, despite their rivalry – which the newly engaged king perhaps helped to moderate – Aristomenes and Polykrates dealt with an apparent threat from Skopas, who lived on in Alexandrian exile after being driven out of Sidon. He had accumulated a major fortune by his entrepreneurial activities as a recruiter of mercenary forces and from loot collected as commander in Syria. Exactly what threat he posed to Aristomenes is hardly clear, other than having collected a considerable band of followers, many of them fellow Aitolians, who were no doubt helping him to spend his wealth. Perhaps there were memories of the crisis over Kleomenes, which Aristomenes at least would remember.

There may have been some feeling against Aristomenes. He was the first regent-minister for forty years to be a native Alexandrian. Sosibios had been the son of a man from Taras in Italy, Agathokles was descended from a Syracusan king, Tlepolemos was of Iranian origin and was probably from Asia Minor; the tradition of appointing high officials from elsewhere than Egypt was strong, and, of course, their origins rendered them vulnerable. Aristomenes, by contrast, probably had local supporters (and no doubt opponents in the city); Polykrates, his rival, was from Argos. And now here was Scopas, an Aitolian. On top of his defeat in Syria and Asia Minor, and of the sudden revival of the rebel regime, the arrival of Skopas in Alexandria brought a new political crisis in the city.

Scopas had been driven into exile from Aitolia because of his political activities, which had included such populist suggestions as a cancellation of debts, one of several elements in the extreme democratic programme of revolutionaries at this time. None of these qualities will have commended him to the Alexandrian court, and this was emphasized by his military defeat, and his apparent guard of fellow Aitolians. He was attracting both local Egyptian and home support. Perhaps as a replacement, he appeared to be building a political programme and a military force at the same time. It may have been in pursuit of his populist agenda, or due to his 'notorious' greed and 'rapacity' that he and a Ptolemaic commander called Charimortos 'stripped the Palace' of valuables.

This was presumably the royal palace in Alexandria, though possibly not the place which the young king inhabited – there were plenty of buildings in the city which could be called palaces. The king's youth would not require a large staff, so perhaps part of the Palace was unused. It is certainly odd that these two men were able to steal from the palace. (Charimortos had been a commander of elephant hunts in the Red Sea country; Polybios says that when he raided the Palace, his 'savagery and drunken violence' was remarkable.)[42] Those were hardly a programme and activities that would appeal to men rich enough to become priests of Alexander and the Deified Ptolemies, but they might please the poor, and possibly the defeated, disgruntled soldiers. Alternatively, the story of the theft from the palace might well be disinformation put out by Apollomedes and his group after the event, distracting from the sudden elimination of the victims, and hoping to provoke the sort of indignation which would justify their actions.

Aristomenes moved against Skopas, first by summoning him to the royal council, which was clearly a threat, and which Skopas ignored. When he did not respond, Aristomenes sent another messenger to summon him, but this time accompanied by a considerable force of 'soldiers and elephants', quite sufficiently intimidating, one would have thought, to secure compliance – but how strange to use elephants as a police force. This succeeded in prising Skopas out of his house, and away from his followers/bodyguard. At the council he was accused and condemned; he died in prison, from poison apparently administered personally by Aristomenes, that very night.[43] (This extravagant arrest and hasty dispatch does rather imply that Aristomenes had a real fear of Skopas' potentialities as a political opponent.)

The situation in Alexandria was thus by no means stable. A second Greek of a dubious reputation in the city was Dikaiarchos, who had been employed by Philip V of Macedon on various clandestine missions, some directed against the Ptolemaic lands, or Ptolemaic friends such as Rhodes; he was condemned and killed at the same time as Skopas.[44] The presence of such capable, adventurous and difficult men in the city at the same time was evidently a disturbing one – or perhaps the power and fear of Aristomenes was causing the disturbances. The regency government was obviously extremely sensitive to such men – and ruthless in removing them. It is notable that Polykrates was a member of the council which condemned the men, and that he cooperated with Aristomenes in their condemnation while clearly angling to replace him.[45]

So the political atmosphere in Alexandria, though perhaps less toxic by 196 BC than earlier, was hardly calm and serene. The end of Antiochos' campaign in Asia Minor during that year coincided with King Ptolemy's coronation and with the condemnation of Skopas and Dikaiarchos, which thus seems to be a deliberate preparation for concluding a difficult and humiliating peace treaty; popular annoyance at the defeat and territorial losses certainly anticipated would be a fine foundation for a coup by such as Skopas. Earlier, the beginning of Antiochos' Asian campaign had coincided with both the *anakleteria* and Chaonnophris' advance. Polykrates had used the ceremony to distract from the disasters overseas, and even those at home – a typical politician's trick. All these events together signalled that change was imminent, and it was marked by the partial displacement of Aristomenes as the king's main minister in favour of Polykrates, apparently a decision of the king, possibly ensuring and exercising his new post-*anakleteria*, post-coronation authority.[46] It was, however, under both men's ministerial authority that the Syrian War was brought to an end, a situation which meant that both were responsible for the peace treaty's terms.[47]

In 195 BC, after negotiations of which nothing is recorded, peace was made between Antiochos III and Ptolemy V, on the basis of the cession to Antiochos of his conquests in Syria and Asia Minor. (Antiochos had also made an attempt to attack Cyprus, but was foiled by a storm.)[48] A Roman delegation had attempted to interfere in the peace negotiations, meeting Antiochos in a conference at Lysimacheia in Thrace; the attempt failed; the Romans were comprehensively out-manoeuvred by the king, and the peace was made exclusively between the two antagonists.[49] The actual terms agreed can only be determined from the later territorial distribution of the lands, but briefly the Ptolemaic kingdom lost all its Syrian and Asia Minor territories but kept Cyprus and Cyrenaica and several posts in the Aegean.

In addition a marriage treaty was agreed, whereby Ptolemy V, by that time fifteen years old, was to marry Antiochos' daughter Kleopatra, who was a few years younger than that.[50] She was the first non-Ptolemaic woman to marry into the Ptolemaic family since the time of Ptolemy I, apart from the murdered Berenike II, who was in fact a collateral member of the royal family. Kleopatra, nicknamed 'the Syrian' ('Syra') by the Egyptians, brought into the family her own Macedonian name, which became a fixture in the dynasty, largely replacing, or perhaps supplementing, Berenike and Arsinoe; she also brought in a refreshing set of genes, which assisted in ensuring that the future kings were genetically much more healthy. The use of her name in future generations may be a sign of the strong impression Kleopatra made, despite the near-insult of her nickname; the marriage took place in the winter of 194/193 BC at, of all places, Raphia (possibly a compromise choice of venue which salved just a little of the Ptolemaic hurt at the result of the war).[51]

Chapter 9

Ptolemy V

The child Ptolemy V, born in 210 BC, grew up in a kingdom at war, civil and international, and in a court which was murderous and treacherous. It is, on the face of it, surprising that he survived, but since he was the only member of the royal family left alive, after his father died and his mother was murdered, he was useful to those in the court. It was only by acting in the king's name that they could pretend to any authority, and, of course, award themselves rewards from the royal treasury.

Ptolemy watched, as he grew up, as minister after minister – Sosibios, Agathokles, Tlepolemos and others – fell away, died, was dismissed, or was murdered. He witnessed a huge rebellion in the south of Egypt which detached a major part of the kingdom into independence for much of his reign, and saw the defeat of his empire and his fleets, so that the empire which he inherited, stretching from the Dardanelles and the borders of Macedon to the southern Red Sea, and from Cyrenaica to northern Syria – the most powerful kingdom in the world so far as he knew – was reduced to Egypt alone, plus Cyprus and Cyrenaica, and a substantial section of Egypt was in rebellion.

The cost of all this was not simply in territories lost, or in manpower destroyed, but also in resources forfeited – Syria-and-Phoenicia, for example, was a particularly wealthy region in trading and manufacturing terms, and is estimated to have produced between 2,000 and 4,000 talents in tax revenue annually out of a possible annual revenue for the whole empire of around 14,000 talents.[1] This was now unavailable. The rebel areas subtracted still more, while the rebellion reduced the Red Sea trade. Further, there was the cost of mounting repeated expeditionary forces, both in Syria and in Egypt, which were repeatedly defeated. The richest kingdom in the Hellenistic world had lost its primacy in all aspects.

Reviving from this parlous state was slow and painful. It was, by 185 BC, only after he had been king for over a quarter of century that Ptolemy V could consider all Egypt as under his rule. Large parts of the land had been severely damaged in the fighting which spread over the southern half of the country, and in the Delta and the Red Sea trade was much reduced because the rebel state controlled the land termini of the routes to the Red Sea ports. It was no longer possible in the state of the finances of the kingdom, to hunt for elephants, muster a large fleet, or gather a sufficient army to mount attacks to recover the lost lands. Whereas in 217 BC the Ptolemaic army had been larger than the Seleukid at the Battle of Raphia, in 199 BC, at the Battle of Panion, the reverse was the case – and the casualties at Panion had been heavy and appear to have especially fallen on the cleruchs.

Furthermore, during Ptolemy's reign the configuration of the political world he faced changed fundamentally. A cold-eyed consideration of the wars his kingdom had fought against Macedon under Philip V and against the Seleukid kingdom under Antiochos III showed that his kingdom had survived by the skin of its teeth. It was only Antiochos' decision to turn north and campaign in Asia Minor and the Straits which diverted him from invading Egypt. The kingdom's survival was not therefore down to its strength or to the conduct of its diplomacy or its army, but to Antiochos' obsession with Asia Minor, and then to the intrusion into the cosy Hellenistic political system of a brutal outsider, Rome, which had not been considered part of the political system until it blundered in, bringing with it a much more unpleasant method of warfare and an unscrupulous set of diplomatic assumptions and methods.

King Philip had been making good progress in gaining control of the Straits and the Aegean, and it was clear by 200 BC that he could sweep Ptolemaic power out of the whole region whenever he chose. He no doubt looked forward to using his fleet to secure Cyrenaica, especially in view of the dismal condition of the Ptolemaic fleet, as revealed in the condition of the ships at Samos, and the failure to employ a fleet of any size to hinder Antiochos in Syria. But then he suddenly found himself at war with the Roman Republic. This stopped his undeclared war with Ptolemy in its tracks, and his defeat in that war so reduced his political strength and armed power, and the range at which he could operate, that Macedon was no longer any threat to its Greek neighbours, still less to the other Hellenistic kingdoms or to Rome. And then, as Ptolemy V was marrying his Seleukid bride Kleopatra 'Syra', the daughter of Antiochos III, in was by that time beginning to take his full part in affairs. Aristomenes remained as a valued minister until 192 BC, when he committed suicide, apparently under royal compulsion,[7] but to say that he was out of favour between 196 and 192 BC need not mean he wielded no influence in those years, and the exact reason for his suicide is unknown. If he was out of power there would be little point in compelling his suicide, unless his wealth was such as to stimulate royal greed. Polykrates does not seem to have succeeded him as senior minister even then, nor at any point, but since both exercised power until Aristomenes' last year, it would seem best to assume that they worked in tandem, possibly under the king's increasing influence. Indeed, Aristonikos son of Aristonikos, who was priest of Alexander in 187/186 BC (not a position Polykrates ever reached), seems to have become chief minister in succession to Aristomenes, and he also worked alongside Polykrates. By then Ptolemy was evidently more or less in command of his court, though in the result this seems to have been somewhat precarious.

Aristonikos was an Alexandrian, possibly the first chief minister to come from Egypt for three or four reigns, apart perhaps from Aristomenes. He was a eunuch, also unusual, an inhabitant of the court, and a friend of Ptolemy V from childhood. He played an active political part in Ptolemaic affairs from the 190s BC, and after. He was a diplomat, but was also employed in the 180s BC to command military expeditions, not such an unusual combination of roles. In 196 BC he was recorded as a cavalry commander in the war in the south, and in 185 BC he was in Greece exercising his diplomacy and recruiting mercenaries.[8] The date is significant, for Ptolemy V in that year had finally ended the last Egyptian resistance. He had employed Polykrates to force the surrender of its last leaders, at Lykopolis in 185 BC. Polykrates had done this by giving his word that these leaders would survive. Ptolemy instead insisted on their execution.[9] It seems to have been a clear display of anger by him, annoyed at the length of the time they had resisted, or possibly he meant it as a deliberate lesson for any later rebels; it did, however, also humiliate Polykrates, who had been unable to make good his word of honour; this may have been also the king's purpose – a typical combination of political results desired from a single project. It thus appears clear that Polykrates did not reach the high position he had aimed at due to the king's resistance, though he continued to be employed by Ptolemy; he had the reputation of great wealth, he had gathered a considerable estate, and he and his wife and daughters won the chariot race at Olympia several times. He had fought at Raphia back in 217 BC, and had governed Cyprus with success (he returned to Egypt with a considerable cash surplus extracted from the Cypriots) in 203–197 BC; so despite his arrogance, his greed, and his blatant ambition he was essentially a loyal servant of the dynasty.[10]

The end of the Syrian War in 195 BC had left plenty of clearing up to be done in the subsequent years. The king, by then fifteen or sixteen years old, beginning to exert his authority, perhaps encouraged by his newly married state, which will have changed and enlarged his court by developing a parallel section – almost a harem – for Kleopatra. The decline of Aristomenes between 196 and 192 BC, the presence of Polykrates, and the emergence of Aristonikos also indicate that changes in his court and emergence of the exercise of royal authority were under way.

This development would clearly take time. The king was, after all, still very young, and his wife younger still (she was about ten years of age at marriage). There was no possibility of her producing children for several years, and in fact it was not until 186 BC, when she was eighteen and the king twenty-four, that their first child was born. This long childless period was in effect an extension of Ptolemy V's pre-marriage state in the sense that he was still the only member of the royal family in existence until then, and it was thus necessary to ensure his health and his continued living. The alternative, if he had died, would very likely be a conflict in the court and probably in the kingdom, as pretenders of all sorts emerged to claim power.

Certain tasks had to be accomplished in the aftermath of the international war – and while the internal war continued for another ten years. The mercenaries who had been recruited in the war emergency would have the choice of returning home with their pay or being invited to settle in Egypt as cleruchs. But the continuing emergency of the rebel regime in the south will have discouraged the release of most of these mercenaries. No doubt a considerable sorting out of preferences and movements took place. The cleruchs which had been called up for the Syrian War would need to be demobilized – those who survived – to return to their homes and plots as soon as possible. The loss of Syria drastically reduced the resources of the government, so the campaign to reduce the rebel state was inevitably slower than intended.[11]

This was all complicated by the new war between Antiochos and Rome. Despite the attempt of the Ptolemaic government to interfere, the Romans kept the war to themselves; Antiochos could not ask Ptolemy for help, despite the danger to the international system of a Roman victory, because Ptolemy's price would be Syria. The war compelled Ptolemy to maintain a considerable force in the north of Egypt, if only to be prepared for any eventuality. Then, when the Treaty of Apameia (in Asia Minor) was being negotiated – or dictated – Ptolemaic interests were clearly involved. It was undoubtedly hoped that a Ptolemaic delegation could be included in the negotiations at Apameia – this after all had been the underlying purpose of offering help when the war began. The obvious intention was once again to undo some of the damage caused in the Syrian War and to recover at least some of the lost lands, but they were ignored.[12]

With Antiochos III's death in 187 BC, hopes rose once more, but without success. On the other hand, the possibility now existed, with the expiry of the peace treaty of 195 BC, that the Syrian War could be renewed. This was probably one of the purposes of Aristonikos' recruitment of mercenaries in Greece in 185 BC – the Theban War in the south was now over, so the new recruits were not needed for that problem – and two years later he commanded a small naval expedition which raided the Seleukid subject city of Arados and penetrated along the Eleutheros Valley towards Apameia-on-Orontes. This may have been an attempt to provoke a hostile response from the Seleukid king, Seleukos IV, or simply to give Ptolemy an excuse, if he wanted one, to embark on a new war; it was no longer the fashion to declare war except by the Romans, who had found deceitful ways of getting round their own religious inhibitions in the matter.

But to send a small Ptolemaic naval expedition to the Syrian coast in an attempt to gain control of Arados, the city and the island, was a sly move.[13] There is a reference to 'Apameia' in the decree which refers to this expedition but this city was the last place Aristonikos would attack, since it was the military headquarters of the Seleukid state; it may have been meant as a reference to the city of the peace treaty, or possibly simply a propaganda claim to enhance the apparent importance of the expedition. Perhaps the Ptolemaic government was arguing that the peace conference had ordered the return of some lands. The fact that the eunuch Aristonikos was commander of the expedition and had recently been the priest of

Alexander and the Deified Ptolemies (in 187/186 BC), strongly implied that the expedition was wholly official.

Aristonikos returned with quantities of loot, presumably taken from Arados, but his attack was otherwise ignored by King Seleukos. Arados was in fact a partly independent city under Seleukid suzerainty, which would give Seleukos the excuse not to become involved in a new Syrian war by ignoring the Ptolemaic raid. The Seleukid kingdom was attempting to recover, at least financially – it was being mulcted annually of a large treasure as part of the peace treaty terms – from the disasters of the recent past, and Seleukos IV carefully avoided all provocations.

Seleukos in fact more than once resisted any attempt to get him into a war; on another occasion he began a military response to a crisis in Kappadokia, even marching his army to the border before abandoning the expedition. On the other hand, he was able to ignore the kingdom's obligation to pay the annual tribute to Rome, as his brother and successor reported in 173 BC, when several years of arrears were paid over. The date when Seleukos stopped payment was probably 187/186 BC, at his accession – he had not been a party to the peace treaty and so could argue he had no personal obligation to go on paying. If he needed a further excuse, Aristonikos' raid on Arados might have provided one, allowing Seleukos to claim poverty as a result. It would not be the first such action which was turned to the benefit of the victim.

The dating of the international raid – 184/183 BC – indicates that it was not until the internal war in Egypt had been concluded that serious thought was given to an attempt to recover the lost lands. There was, however, clearly no doubt that the Ptolemaic government would, at the first opportunity, make the attempt. The Arados raid in 183 BC may have been the first move, or possibly an attempt to seize a base for further interventions. But it had all to wait until the war in Egypt ended, which it did in 185 BC, the year Aristonikos went to Greece to recruit mercenaries.

The war in the south had lasted for several more years after the conclusion of the various international peace treaties. It should have been possible to complete the reconquest fairly quickly, once the conflict with the Seleukid king had ended in 195 BC. It was, however, perhaps at this stage that the fighting degenerated into guerilla warfare. The uprising which took place at the Delta city of Lykopolis will have delayed any move southwards. If, as suggested, it took place in 197 BC, it was suppressed with some difficulty, and the Delta was hardly peaceful afterwards. The elaborate description of the siege works looks very like a careful general taking his time.

In 191 BC, a new Ptolemaic attack southwards retook the towns in the Thebais, and the Ptolemaic forces marched as far as Syene[14] – Elephantine had been held by Ptolemaic forces all through the war, but Syene had come under Nubian control for a time. Chaonnophris took refuge with the Nubian king in the face of the successful Ptolemaic offensive.[15] He returned after a time – how long is not clear – and the war revived. Little is known of this later fighting, but a papyrus dated between May and August of 187 BC details a convoy of ships sailing south along the river carrying supplies for the soldiers at Syene – supplies collected from several different parts of the Thebais; this was a considerable operation, which implies that the journey was dangerous and that the garrison at Syene was in serious need of resupply; it has been calculated, from the quantity of supplies being sent, that the garrison amounted to 4,000 men.[16] (It was still apparently impossible to get supplies from the north, since the southern Lykopolis – Asyut – remained under rebel control.) Chaonnophris' attack force now included his own people reinforced by Nubian forces. He was defeated by a Ptolemaic force commanded by Komanos, in which Aristonikos son of Aristonikos (who later commanded the raiding force against Arados), commanded the cavalry; Chaonnophris was captured in a fight on 26 August 186 BC, and his son was killed.[17] The former pharaoh was imprisoned, presumably for the rest of his life. This was almost the end of the war.[18]

It is, however at this stage that it seems best to place the siege of Lykopolis in Middle Egypt (Asyut), in which the commander of the besieging forces was poorly treated; he made his headquarters in the *chora* of the city, a little to the north along the river. The town was eventually taken but was wrecked and depopulated, and the country around the city was ravaged into uninhabitability. This condition is described in an official report on the difficulty of collecting taxation from a deserted and destroyed region.[19] Ptolemy had already published a decree of amnesty, whose aim was to encourage those who had been displaced by the fighting to return to their original homes, and Lykopolis was clearly such a place.[20] The combination of the execution of the leaders and the amnesty for the rank and file is a classic example of bringing about the end to a war. How successful it was on this occasion is not known, but the tax inspectors found the necropolis area still badly damaged some time later. This may well be typical of the condition of the country along the river south of Lykopolis, which had been fought over for the previous twenty years: parts of the Delta also suffered in the same way, including the Delta Lykopolis. It is thus likely that the financial health of the Ptolemaic kingdom generally had suffered badly not only by the loss of the empire but by the internal destruction involved; it was something which had to be considered when making plans for attacking the Seleukid conquest in Syria – but recovering Syria would also help to regenerate the Ptolemaic finances.

There followed, after the suppression of the rebellion, an extensive programme of renovation and reform, which had already been detailed in the Rosetta Stone of 196 BC (referring especially to the Delta area), and an amnesty decree aimed at persuading those who had fled from their homes in the violence to return.[21] Similar decrees and appeals were made in the south after the rebellion. This is a record in Greek, demotic Egyptian, and hieroglyphic Egyptian, of the end of the revolt and of the generosity of the king in putting things right. It included various prohibitions, such as the end of conscription into the navy, and items of generosity, such as gifts and concessions to priests – who were here recording in stone and in public what they had been awarded. The appeals for farmers to return to their lands is something which became all too frequent in Egypt. It was a process called *anachoresis*, a form of strike in which farmers moved away and refused to work, though in the aftermath of the reconquest the farmers had no doubt fled to avoid the approaching and avenging army; hence the need for an amnesty. In the south there were reforms to the government system, which had no doubt been part of the causes of the revolt. The Thebaid region was made into a governor-generalship, with the victor in the last battle, Komanos, made the first governor-general.[22] 4,000 soldiers who fought under Komanos (and perhaps under Polykrates) were allotted fifty *arouras* of farmland as cleruchs.[23] Possibly these were former mercenaries; the forces during the fighting seem to have been mainly recruited from old Greece, rather than from amongst Egyptian Greeks. Garrisons in the south were maintained, or established, all along the river from Akoris (some way south of Lykopolis) to Philai in the far south.[24] The reforms were, of course, an exercise in putting right conditions which should have been attended to decades before, but specifically in the interests of increasing the financial take from the farmers. That is, the complaints of the peasantry (and the priests) had been ignored by the bureaucracy, until they produced the revolt; the peasants' complaints were still being ignored, and no doubt their hostility to priests was not assuaged by seeing them receiving generous government handouts. This is hardly an unknown condition. The decree also notes that the government was less opulent than earlier.

The reduction in resources available to the Ptolemaic government also drastically reduced the kingdom's ability to cut a large figure in international affairs. The tentative moves in the late 180s BC towards a recovery of the lost territories did not result in anything decisive. Aristonikos had, while recruiting in Greece, renewed old Ptolemaic contacts with the Achaian League, sending gifts.[25] There were some favourable responses, but only slowly. There was evidently no enthusiasm for encouraging a return to Great Power warfare in the region. Nevertheless, a further gift was promised and a delegation to collect it, which included the young future historian Polybios, was all ready to go to Egypt in 180 BC.

From 186 BC the dynasty was increasingly safe. The first child of Ptolemy and Kleopatra was born in that year, a son, inevitably called Ptolemy; two more children were born in the next years, a second son (also Ptolemy) and a daughter (Kleopatra). Furthermore Ptolemy V was still a young man, twenty-four years of age in 186 BC. Despite his poor genetic origin (the son of full siblings), he is said to have been athletically vigorous and keen on, and skilled at, hunting. He travelled about the north of Egypt, to Memphis and other places, in the same way that earlier Ptolemies had done. But his character is said to have become increasingly tyrannical,[26] though this is perhaps the reputation gained by his final conquest of the rebel region and the execution of the rebel leaders, and the result of his poor relations with his aristocratic subjects. The treatment of those men who had commanded at Lykopolis tends to confirm this reputation, though it was more likely a well-considered political move than a mere exercise in cruelty.

There is an isolated notice which can be interpreted as indicating the Ptolemaic intentions, the difficulties in achieving them, and of the shortage of royal resources and the reluctance of the aristocracy to contribute (and shows Ptolemy's poor relations with the rich). It is an anecdote only, but revealing. Ptolemy was asked by a 'friend' (either a personal friend or a man with the rank of *philos*) when he intended to return to Coele Syria, the old Ptolemaic territory.

This encounter raises a number of topics and issues, quite apart from the point at issue, which was in fact the prospect of a new Syrian war. There is the status of the 'friend'. This was a term with two meanings in the Hellenistic courts, first in its ordinary meaning of a person one knows, meets frequently, and can talk with easily, and second as a term increasingly used as a title for a distinct set of courtiers. By the reign of Ptolemy V the court had become sorted out into a set of ranks of this sort, with *philos* (Friend) at the lowest rank. Above were First Friends, with Kinsmen at the top, with various other ranks in between. The whole system was perhaps only just becoming articulated in Ptolemy V's time, but eventually it became elaborated into seven distinct ranks, each of which had certain privileges and each of which had a different right of access to the king. That is, as the Ptolemaic kingdom became poorer and weaker the privileges of the aristocracy became more clearly and more closely defined and the court system more rigid.

A further issue raised by the king's encounter with his Friend is that the question the friend posed presupposed that it was well understood in the court, and presumably elsewhere and much wider, that the established policy of the king was that sometime soon an attempt at reconquest would be launched. It was also clearly understood that the plan was being delayed. Aristonikos' activities in recruiting mercenaries in Greece and raiding Arados only make sense if they were preparations, even justifications, for such a war, but by the time of the king's interview, in 180 BC, five years after Aristonikos' recruitment of mercenaries, still nothing had happened.

Ptolemy replied that he was giving consideration to the issue, but the friend was not satisfied with this answer, so typical of an indecisive politician, and pressed on. Perhaps Ptolemy explained that the difficulty was in financing the war or finding the forces necessary for such an expedition, but this also was probably well understood in the court. So when the friend did persist in asking where the necessary money could be found, perhaps expecting another vague answer, the king replied by pointing to others of his courtiers, all of them rich, all battening on the king and the court, and ultimately the peasantry, to increase and maintain their wealth, and replied, quoting an old saying: 'There, walking about, are my moneybags'.[27]

Here, therefore, is another item which sheds a certain light on the situation in Alexandria in 180 BC. The king could quote an old saw which, being interpreted, was that he had permitted the rich men of the city and the kingdom to acquire their riches, and in an emergency, such as a war, he had a right to expect them to hand some of their wealth back for the occasion. Similarly, it was also probably the case that the court ranks now becoming more commonly used, were temporary, certainly not hereditary and probably they could be revoked by the king at his whim. The position of an aristocrat in Alexandria, or Egypt, was thus precarious, and dependent totally on royal favour.

A final revelation within this anecdote is that in the result it was seen that the king did not have a firm grip on the loyalty of his courtiers. They clearly valued their wealth, and perhaps their court ranks, more than the person of the king, and now even the welfare of the kingdom and empire. (And if the king had become tyrannical, as Diodoros recorded, those who would suffer first and most from his irritability would be those in contact with him, the courtiers; perhaps they did not like him, as his reputation as a tyrant would suggest.) The existence of the king's three children, all flourishing, but all infants, could be seen as leaving the way open for a repeat of the situation in the childhood of the king himself – a minority in which the courtiers could scramble for wealth and position in the secure knowledge that king could do little about it for years, and yet the dynasty was safe.

If the king expected to receive contributions to his war chest, he clearly badly overestimated the willingness of the Ptolemaic aristocracy to either pay for, or involve themselves in, a war. They had no doubt done well in the early part of Ptolemy V's reign in annexing public funds to their own use; perhaps the king expected that they would return all that ill-gotten wealth for the public good. If so, he was badly mistaken. The threat of a shakedown of the wealthiest members of the population was enough to provoke a conspiracy among his 'generals', who may also have been fearful of actually having to fight a war in Syria – which they would almost certainly lose. They organized a poisoning. The king died.[28]

Chapter 10

Approaching the Sixth Syrian War

The murder of Ptolemy V had drastic effects, probably more serious than the perpetrators had expected. None of the murderers emerged as regents for the child Ptolemy VI, who was six years old at the time. Instead, Kleopatra Syra, the widow of the king and the mother of the three royal children, claimed the position as regent-guardian for the children. This was the more surprising in that she was not of Ptolemaic descent, nor even of Egyptian origin, and was in fact the daughter of the recent Seleukid enemy, and the sister of the current Seleukid king. The fact that she took the position as regent, accepted the epithet *Thea* (goddess), and was accepted by the Alexandrian court, is at first astonishing, but then also revealing.

It may be assumed that one reason for Kleopatra's success in securing this position was that there was no male member of the court who was the obvious candidate for regent. The murderers were a group of wealthy men, said to have been senior military commanders, but they were only a minority of the inhabitants of the court. Others in the court can be assumed to have been horrified at the murder, and to have been determined not to allow the killers to profit by their crime. Whether they were ever punished is unknown, but there is evidently no indication that any of them secured power, or even attempted to seize it.

One factor to be taken into account is the method of murder. Poison is not infrequently claimed as a murder weapon when it might only be that the victim fell ill with a strange or sudden disease, or had a heart attack. Ptolemy V, as noted, had a peculiar genetic origin. His father and grandfather, Ptolemies IV and III, had both died relatively young, the first at about thirty-five, the second before he was forty, an apparent genetic predisposition to early death which may have been intensified by the fact that his parents were full siblings. He was thirty years old at the time of his death and so relatively young, but that is not far off the average age of death for men in the ancient world. As king he would be given the very best of medical attention as well as adequate food, which should have secured a longer life. If there was some physiological predisposition for trouble his exhibitionism on horseback and as a hunter, both violent activities, may have aggravated his condition.[1] That is to say, without a competent medical diagnosis, the statement that Ptolemy died of poison is not corroborated, and it must remain only as a hypothesis. It may be significant that no punishments for the murders are recorded, and that no men are named as the perpetrators. The assumption that he died of poisoning may be only that, an assumption.

That Kleopatra emerged as the regent was unprecedented in a Ptolemaic state. Some hypotheses for this development suggest themselves: that Kleopatra was a master politician; or, like her later namesake, she was able to charm a bunch of greedy male politicians into accepting her; or that she manipulated the courtiers, setting them at odds with each other until she was the only possible choice because the rest would not accept anyone else – that is, she was the least bad option. Or perhaps she moved quickly enough on the news of her husband's death to foil any coup which was threatened. Or, and this is perhaps the most likely, her husband left a will in which she was named as regent, and she saw that it was accepted. But wills were tricky, and all would no doubt know of the manipulation perpetrated by Sosibios when Ptolemy III died. Kleopatra probably knew of that case also, and might have forged the will herself. (All this speculation arises because of the lack of hard information for what happened from the time itself, or even guesses later.)

Kleopatra's own origins were almost as curious and genetically dangerous as those of her husband. She was descended from three generations of marriages between first cousins. Her father Antiochos III, her grandfather Seleukos II, and her great-grandfather Antiochos II had all married first cousins (and all the wives were named Laodike). The one saving grace in this interbreeding was that there were also outside genes arriving into the mix, including those of Kleopatra's own mother, who was certainly a cousin of her father, but who was also the daughter of King Mithradates of Pontus. Ptolemy V and Kleopatra, refreshingly, had no genetic relationship to one another at all. It is not clear if the dangers of such interbreeding were understood at the time, though the scornful reaction of some to the sibling marriage of Ptolemy II and Arsinoe II suggests that some misgiving was felt. Even so the Ptolemies continued to the very end of the dynasty in marrying each other – Kleopatra VII married her brother. The purpose, of course, was to keep the political inheritance within the family, with the assumption that the husband of a Ptolemaic princess would acquire a claim to the throne. The Seleukids and the Antigonids also married their close relations – the wife of Seleukos IV married the three sons of Antiochos III in sequence, all of them her full brothers; Antigonos Gonatas was married to his niece; all in the name of political alliances.

It was perhaps an advantage to the kingdom that Kleopatra was the sister of Seleukos IV, even though she was given the derisive nickname 'Syra'. Apart from the perceived unsuitability of a woman ruling (though there had been several cases in the Hellenistic world in the previous century), it would be even more unlikely that a woman would be able to command in war. This Greek misogynistic attitude continued to prevail, however, despite several later cases (and in the succession to Alexander the Great) where women did command in war. This perceived unsuitability may have given Kleopatra a perfect excuse to avoid another Syrian war. The fact that her enemy would have been her brother may also have affected her decision, but such an explanation would not convince anyone on either side in a war; fraternal wars were hardly unknown, any more than murders within a royal family. And she had been a member of the Ptolemaic family and court for longer than she had been a Seleukid princess (as a child), so perhaps the decision for peace was hardly affected by her relationship to Seleukos.

The records of her regency are few. At least no foreign potentate attempted to take advantage of the kingdom in its apparent weakness. She appears on a coin, showing a slim young woman of very different appearance from the stouter and heavier Ptolemies. She is recorded on a few inscriptions, where her name occurs before that of her eldest son; she was 'Pharaoh Kleopatra the mother' while Ptolemy was 'the son' in Egyptian hieroglyphic inscriptions; similarly in the Greek inscriptions but with the addition that both of them were 'manifest gods'. But there is no record of any edicts or laws published in her name. This, of course, was as it should be; her function as regent was not to initiate new policies or to go to war, except in cases where the kingdom was attacked, but to maintain the kingdom in as good a condition as possible so that it would be inherited by her son when he came of age. There was no reason for her to be recorded as doing anything other than making legal judgments or approving the occasional commemorative inscription.

It was probably just as well that she was not called on to act as a commander-in-chief in a war, not because it was beyond her abilities or capacity – she had plenty of *strategoi* anxious to make names for themselves – but because the kingdom needed still more time to recover from its previous travails. It seems probable that Ptolemy V had been aiming to start a war to recover Syria when he died, though he was displaying a certain reluctance to begin, as were his court aristocrats, some of whom represented a strength of opinion opposed to a new war. This wider intention was probably in part in the belief that Seleukos IV was in an unusually weak position due to the defeat of his father and the need to conciliate Rome, while his ambivalence was perhaps due to an appreciation of the unpredictability of war. Seleukos had not reacted to the provocation of Aristonikos' raid on Arados, but not reacting might be construed as a display of patience and strength rather than weakness. Seleukos' reign is one (like Kleopatra's regency) in which few events are recorded, but to claim that he was therefore a weak king is to ignore the fact that he was an experienced commander who had been trusted by his father with an independent command during the Roman War.[2] He did have a good deal more experience of command and ruling than Ptolemy V and certainly more than his sister. In such circumstances Ptolemy V would be launching a war from a very weak position, a perfect reason for his reluctance. After all, it was only in 185 BC that the civil war had ended in his kingdom. It would take more than a few short years for Egypt to recover economically and financially from the damage caused by the rebellion and the loss of the empire, and for the inevitable subsequent internal disturbances to die down, if they ever did. Four more years of peace under Kleopatra will have helped, and, as it happened, these four years were followed by another six years of peace. That decade and a half since the end of the rebellion did not restore Ptolemaic military strength sufficiently for victory, but at least it was favourable to many of the inhabitants.

Kleopatra died in the summer of 176 BC. She was aged only twenty-five. There is no suggestion of murder in this case. This was the second unexpected royal death in less than five years, and both of them young; it may be that the palace was in an unhealthy state at the time, for she came from a fairly long-lived and robust family. The court now had to go through the process of choosing a regent once more, for King Ptolemy VI 'Philometor' – 'mother-loving' – was still only ten years old. This second time around, there were neither any Ptolemaic family members nor an obvious strongman available, so it seems, or perhaps all the most prominent men refused the post, for, as will be noted, there were plenty of important and capable men who might have applied or been appointed. Two unlikely figures emerged as joint regents: Eulaios, a eunuch and the king's *tithonos* (in Latin *nutritus*, translated as 'nurse', but clearly having a much wider application than that innocuous term – perhaps guardian-tutor might be better), was one; Lenaios the *dioiketes*, a freedman, was the other. Of these, Eulaios has been judged as having more influence with the king, not surprisingly, though this would not necessarily be the case in the government.[3]

These were unusual appointments, even more unlikely than a woman in such a position. Again, it may be that the court was riven by faction – pro- and anti-war groups can be detected, at least, and personal rivalries are to be expected. In such circumstances the influential men were unable to coalesce around any other single figure; but it may be that Kleopatra, before she died, had indicated that they should take on the task. They had held their posts at her gift while she was alive, and they will have continued to hold them after she died; their positions then left them as *de facto* regents. They would thus need to be removed before any successors were installed. They were obviously capable, despite the contempt heaped on them by the Greek historians (and many modern historians) because of their less-than-stellar origins. But a eunuch (Aristonikos) had been a prominent minister under Ptolemy V and slaves and freedmen were deliberately trained for their tasks, and were promoted on merit. Until disaster fell on the kingdom, they clearly performed their several duties well, and apparently worked well together.[4] They were probably a better choice for king and kingdom than untried greedy, incompetent aristocrats.

A consideration of the appointments of men to prominent posts would also suggest that both Kleopatra and her two successors as regents had the support of prominent men. The new post of governor-general in the Thebaid was held by Komanos, who had completed the conquest and remained to control the area, which was undoubtedly still a disturbed region. He had the rank of First Friend, and his relatives were prominent in various positions during the next two decades, at both Alexandria and at Ptolemais in the south.⁵ How long he remained as governor in the Thebaid is not known, but by September 176 BC he was no longer in post; perhaps he had died, or perhaps he was replaced by the new regents. He was succeeded by Hippalos son of Sos, who held that office at least until 172 BC; by 170 BC, the *strategos* was Noumenos son of Noumenos, but he only remained for part of that year. He had, like Hippalos, been appointed by the regents.⁶

In Cyprus, the other major viceroyalty, Ptolemy son of Agesarchos was governor from 197 to 180 BC.⁷ In that last year he was succeeded by Ptolemy Makron. He had been prominent enough to be *proxenos* at Delphi in 188/187 BC⁸, along with three of his brothers and others from Alexandria, which was a diplomatic posting presumably in part designed to repair relations with the Aitolians (who controlled Delphi) after their defeat by the Romans. Ptolemy Makron is noted by Polybios as having sent a large sum of money gathered in the island when the war against the Seleukids was imminent.⁹ This, of course, had also been done by Polykrates of Argos, who had been governor from 203 to 197 BC. (That is, he had been Ptolemy son of Agesarchos' immediate predecessor, and we therefore have a full roster of Cypriot governors from 203 to 170 BC or later). Two of these men are noted as having accumulated large sums of money to be handed over to the Alexandrian government; it would seem, therefore, that this was a normal matter, not something which was done to curry favour with the government of the king, as has been supposed.

Other officials and their families exhibit a similar career progression and avidity for offices – appointed in Ptolemy V's time, retained under Kleopatra, or appointed by her and retained under Lenaios and Euleios. There was thus a clear continuity through the three periods, and no serious administrative disruption (unless Komanos was dismissed in 176 BC). These prominent men brought with them a collection of relatives who were posted to various other official posts or in important positions, as with Ptolemy Makron;¹⁰ Kleopatra and the joint-regents who followed her were undoubtedly relying largely on a select group, possibly to the exclusion of others who might have felt entitled to such posts; it is perhaps another indication of faction in the court.

One of the first measures the joint regents undertook was to carry through two crucial ceremonies, first to promote Ptolemy VI to divine status, and his sister Kleopatra to queen (*basilissa*). The second was to marry them to each other.¹¹ The girl, had she been married to a man other than Ptolemy, would have transferred to her husband a claim to the throne; her marriage to her brother prevented that. This both protected the dynasty and solidified the authority of the two regents.

It is usual, in accounts of the reign of Ptolemy VI to jump almost directly from the marriage to the beginning of the next Syrian war in 170 BC, no doubt because of the lack of source material for that period. But this was a period of five years, and it should not be ignored in such a cavalier fashion. (The other method of many historians in working through this half-decade is to sidestep to the Seleukid kingdom, where equally odd things were happening.)¹² This therefore slides neatly to the war between the dynasties. The main excuses are that the war is more interesting, but also that the events of that five-year period are very few, at least those which are in the record. And, of course, moving directly to the outbreak of the war, or at least to its causes, enables the two regents to be roundly condemned, all too often on supposed racial or other social grounds.¹³

We know of one measure which was taken, presumably by the *dioiketes* Lenaios. The copper coinage of Egypt had been subject to inflation in relation to the value of gold and silver for the past fifty years. The exchange rate had been adjusted more than once in that time, from 1:60 to 1:120. In 173 BC it was adjusted to 1:480. The change was not due to the value of copper, but due to the increase in the value of silver. This adjustment in 173 BC was the last that was necessary in the Ptolemaic period. So it would seem that Lenaios had a certain expertise in financial affairs, or had competent advisers.¹⁴

Events in the rest of the Mediterranean pushed the Ptolemaic and Seleukid kingdoms towards war. In Macedon, Philip V died in 179 BC, and his son Perseus secured the succession. He began preparations to recover his father's position in Greece, despite Rome's insistence, by way of frequent diplomatic interventions, that Greece was the republic's own concern. In 175 BC Seleukos IV died (the year after his sister), and was succeeded, after an internal crisis, by his brother Antiochos IV. (The crisis had been an attempt to seize power by a minister, Heliodoros, a factor surely taken due note of at Alexandria; he was rumoured to have murdered Seleukos.) Antiochos had in fact made use of the Attalid kingdom in Asia Minor to get to Syria and then claimed the throne; he had been living in

Athens when the Seleukid crisis erupted and had been encouraged on his way by the Athenians, then helped by Eumenes II.[15] He therefore had a very helpful series of personal and diplomatic friendships, which his father had not had.

Antiochos was therefore immune to pressure from all the powers to the west of his kingdom – the Attalid king, Eumenes II, was a friend, as was Athens; Akhaia and Aitolia, mutually hostile, neutralized each other, and Rome and Macedon by 173 BC were clearly squaring off for a war of their own, which duly began in 172 BC. Antiochos put a good deal of effort into making friendly gestures – gifts, diplomacy, and so on – towards the Greek cities.[16] He spectacularly presented Rome with the 'arrears' of tribute his brother had not paid over – doing so in 173 BC just before a new war. Rome's conduct of this Macedonian War was very badly managed and dragged on for much longer than anyone expected. It seemed that Rome's vaunted power was less than impressive. For both Antiochos, technically regent for his nephew, and the Ptolemaic government under its regents, this was the ideal moment for another war over Syria.

There was no particular cause for this war, other than the perpetual rivalry over control of Syria, though that had always been sufficient in the past. But the stakes were this time very much greater. Antiochos III in the Fifth Syrian War had preferred to capture the Ptolemaic empire outside Egypt rather than invade that country, and had thus turned away from an invasion of Egypt to set about collecting a long series of cities along the coasts of Asia Minor, as far as the Straits and Thrace. This in fact was perhaps a mistake, though this could hardly have been foreseen, for it led directly to the war with Rome and a major defeat. On the other hand, it seems unlikely that Rome would have sat back and let him conquer Egypt. He may have partitioned it with the rebel Pharaonic regime in the south. (This was in fact Antiochos' regular method of warfare, always securing an alliance with a power in rear of his enemy.)

The union of the Hellenistic kingdoms into an empire stretching from the Aegean to India, including Egypt and Cyrenaica, would be far too much of a potential threat to Rome to be ignored. Antiochos did try to reach an agreement with the republic, but Rome used a minor dispute over the political disposition of three cities in Asia Minor as an excuse to go to war. The lesson of Rome's reaction and victory was that Rome was claiming supremacy in the whole Mediterranean, but did not do more than that so long as no threat existed from the east. The war with Perseus was a result of Perseus ignoring that condition.

But now that threat, or the unification of the two great kingdoms, might re-emerge under the course of the new Syrian War. For if the Seleukid and Ptolemaic kingdoms went to war yet again, the result this time would necessarily be the destruction of one of them. The two regents in Alexandria were under the same, or greater, pressure to make an attempt to recover Syria that Ptolemy V had been in the previous years. That pressure had not been exerted so much on Kleopatra Syra for various reasons, but it had always been there, in the background, and it had built up as a result of her clear unwillingness to launch an attack. And so the regents were not only under greater pressure from the Alexandrian court to go to war to recover Syria, and perhaps from the soldiers, but they were also in a much weaker political position, even than Kleopatra. It seems very likely that they were as reluctant to go to war as Kleopatra, or as Ptolemy V, whose ambiguous attitude may have been intended merely to keep the more warlike members of his court at his side. The regents were also probably as unsuited to command in war as Kleopatra – or Ptolemy – and given that the pressure already existed in the 180s BC they did successfully resist it for several years. In the end, however, they were pushed into war.

Part of the pressure came from the Seleukids. Seleukos IV was as reluctant to undertake a major war as any of the leading men of the Ptolemaic court, and for excellent reasons. The Seleukid kingdom needed time to recover from its defeat in the Roman War, and its financial resources had been badly strained by the payment of the indemnity mandated in the peace treaty – the initial payment amounted to over 3,000 talents, and then the annual payments were of 1,000 talents, though they were halted at some point; Seleukos' eldest son was sent as a hostage to Rome; his elephants and his largest warships were to be killed or confiscated.[17] The Seleukid kingdom was thus being systematically weakened, though it is probable that compliance with some of the terms was systematically evaded. It is clear, for example, that the prohibition on keeping war elephants was disregarded, and a clause in which five named Roman enemies were to be delivered to Rome as captives, was ignored.

The Roman aim of weakening the kingdom was hardly successful. Apart from the failure to enforce several of the clauses of the peace treaty, Rome had ignored the results of the preceding Syrian war. All the agitations from Alexandria to provide Rome with support in order to persuade the city to reverse the decision of that war were ignored. The result of that snub was that the weakening of the Seleukid kingdom was decisively lessened, and the Ptolemaic kingdom was left without any gains.

In Seleukid eyes more important than the defeat by Rome was the success in the Fifth Syrian War. From 200 BC onwards Syria had been under Seleukid control; Asia Minor, on the other hand, had only intermittently been under Seleukid control (from 281 to 241, and from 213 to 190 BC). Until 185 BC, by contrast, the Ptolemaic kingdom was mired in its own civil war, and ruled by a weak government of regents. With Syria firmly held by the Seleukids there was no possibility of recovering Syria. The death of Antiochos III in 187 BC had ended the provisions of the treaty with Rome agreed only the year before, and Antiochos IV's accession in 175 BC freed the two kingdoms for further adventures, while his friendship with the Attalids protected his western flank. Both internationally and militarily the Ptolemaic kingdom was isolated and inferior. For the Ptolemies this was clearly a dangerous condition, though it may be that many of those who agitated for war ignored these aspects, or simply did not understand them. It would be reasonable to assume that Eulaios and Lenaios did take note and did understand, however.

Antiochos IV was much more active diplomatically than his brother had been. He conciliated Rome, and clearly encouraged its intention to attack Macedon, by sending the arrears of indemnity which Seleukos had allowed to accumulate (disregarding yet another clause of the peace treaty) – at least Rome chose to regard this money as paymemt of arrears, as Livy noted, but it was in fact a gift, accepted by the Senate just as a similar gift from the Ptolemaic government had in the past been refused.[18] He sent presents to Athens and other Greek states, a recognized sign of political friendship, if not actual alliance. He sent a representative, Apollonios of Miletos, to attend a festival at Alexandria (in either 174 or 172 BC). While in the city Apollonios investigated local attitudes and came away with the strong impression of hostility to the Seleukid kingdom not only in the court, but in the general population as well.[19] (The fact that Apollonios had been governor-general of Syria for both Seleukos IV and Antiochos IV might well have been one element in the display of hostility.)[20] This same diplomat went to Rome in 173 BC with the indemnity arrears, and to remind the Senate that the peace treaty had included a clause by which Rome and Antiochos III were joined in *societas et amicitia* – alliance and friendship. This would have been dangerous, given the various infractions of the treaty by Seleukos IV, but the Romans reacted as expected, seeing a promise of neutrality, even though Perseus was married to Seleukos IV's daughter.

The Roman-Seleukid peace treaty and the friendship agreement had, of course, expired with the death of Antiochos III in 187 BC. The latter may have been renewed by Seleukos, and Rome might interpret it as still in force, as was done in a matter of the peace treaty ten years later. Even if such a relationship had been discarded, Antiochos IV was making an overtly friendly gesture in requesting its renewal. He had spent some time in Rome as a hostage and he knew many of the leading Roman politicians. All this disarmed potential Roman hostility and helped clear the way for a Romano-Macedonian war by making it clear that Antiochos was determined on neutrality in such a conflict.

Antiochos was also under a degree of pressure himself. The process by which he became king had been complex, awkward, and unpleasant. Seleukos IV was murdered by his minister Heliodoros, who then proclaimed the second son of Seleukos and his wife Laodike (who was also the king's sister) as king. This was a boy of four years or so.[21] The eldest son, Demetrios, was by this time living in Rome as a hostage, having replaced the elder Antiochos some years before; Antiochos had since then lived in Athens. This succession was thoroughly irregular in Seleukid royal practice, but excusable given that the eldest son was out of the kingdom and thus unavailable to be king.[22] And yet primogeniture had been the normal succession practice in the dynasty from the beginning. Heliodoros the minister therefore manipulated the situation, proclaiming the boy Antiochos as king in succession to his father, and his mother Laodike became his official regent, though Heliodoros, as had perhaps been his aim all along, retained the real power. It may be that his ultimate aim was to eliminate Antiochos and Laodike and make himself king, or do so by marrying Laodike, but there were too many surviving adult Seleukids out of his reach for that to be a viable objective.[23] When Antiochos IV arrived, therefore, Heliodoros' position collapsed. He was quickly executed. Antiochos IV assumed the kingship, married Laodike (her third brother-husband) and adopted the child king as his son.[24]

The question then shifted to what was Antiochos' own ultimate aim. Perhaps he intended to take the place of the child king and put the boy aside; or would he retire when the boy he had adopted, who had been proclaimed king already, came of age? And what about Demetrios in Rome, who, in terms of primogeniture, was the rightful successor to his father Seleukos? That is to say, Antiochos' position was hardly secure. And yet everyone with any knowledge of recent history could recall the actions of Antigonos III Doson of Macedon, who acted as guardian to the child King Philip V and made himself king at the insistence of the Macedonian people in arms in assembly, after successfully beating off the usual barbarian attacks from the north which came at every change of Macedonian king. His position as king was confirmed by his victory over the Spartans at Selassia six years later. He then conveniently died, just when Philip reached near-adulthood, and Philip smoothly took his place. It would be highly unlikely that such a sequence would be repeated in the Seleukid royal family, but the pressure would certainly be on Antiochos to withdraw from the kingship in favour of the rightful king, whoever it was, in, say, ten years' time – unless he waged a successful war in the meantime, in which case his position would be much firmer. The only suitable enemy was Ptolemaic Egypt, which was under a weak government, and where Apollonios had reported that there was a busy agitation in court and city for war to recover Syria.

Both sides were thus under pressure in different ways to go to war, and the only ways of postponing or stopping a war would be if Rome intervened, or one or other of the antagonists' governments were overthrown, though this was unlikely to calm the war fever, indeed it was more likely to enlarge it. But Rome was intent on a war of its own with Macedon, and the governments were firmly in power, at least so long as they promised victory. When Rome's war with Macedon began, therefore, the way was clear for a new Syrian war also to begin.

A Roman embassy roamed the eastern Mediterranean lands during 172 BC, receiving an offer of help from Ptolemy's regents, which both sides knew would not be taken up; they had a good opinion of Antiochos, not surprising after his recent monetary gift, and who also offered assistance, also not likely ever to be taken up; an envoy from Perseus had already visited him, to be rebuffed; no doubt Antiochos carefully pointed this out. From the Roman point of view the embassy was a success in reviving its inactive alliances and ensuring that nobody else would interfere. Antiochos IV and Ptolemy VI's regents were now quite certain that there would be a war in Greece.[25]

These elements in the situation were obvious to all those involved, from Rome to Babylon. Antiochos was probably convinced that his kingdom would come under attack from Egypt as soon as the Romano-Macedonian War began. He started to reinforce the defences at the southern Syrian border. This was not a preparation for a pre-emptive strike, nor was it intended to become one. He intended to wait, and let the Egyptian regents begin the war first, thus claiming the moral high ground, at least in Roman eyes.

He must have understood that the stakes in any new Syrian war were not simply the control of Syria. If Antiochos was defeated he and his kingdom would no doubt lose control of Syria, but the Ptolemaic government could not stop there. The real power of the Seleukid kingdom lay first in north Syria, with its large and loyal Macedonian and Greek population, which had always been outside the traditional Ptolemaic boundary, and second in Babylonia, which was the economic heartland and main wealth generator of the kingdom. A Ptolemaic victory in Syria would be insecure so long as these territories remained under Seleukid control; control of Syria would be no more than a half-victory (as Ptolemy III's war had shown); the Ptolemaic invasion would need to go much further, certainly to secure Babylonia, and perhaps into Iran, and would need to eliminate any Seleukids it could find.

Similarly, if Antiochos won the war it would have to involve a campaign of conquest of Egypt, since merely defeating the Ptolemaic forces would not prevent their revival and would lead to another return match. What was at stake for each side, therefore, was the existence of the kingdom, and this time a less-than-total victory would not be sufficient, since it would not guarantee peace. In addition, the lives of the Egyptian regents undoubtedly would be quickly forfeit in the event of a defeat, and that of Antiochos IV would be, if not forfeit, at least in danger, if the Seleukid forces were defeated. There would be plenty of enemies to blame him for seizing the throne so untimely once he became vulnerable. (In Greece, the same result would imperil Perseus; it might be that, if Rome was defeated by Perseus, that republic would suffer a decline, or rebellions in, say, Sicily, Africa, or southern Italy.)

Approaching the Sixth Syrian War 143

The Ptolemaic regents, like Antiochos, had been making military preparations for some time, perhaps more as a means of quietening internal pressure than intending to go to war. The assumption that the regents made no military preparations cannot be sustained. They certainly made detailed political preparations, gathering support in the court and among the Alexandrians, and when the war began they marched their army along the Sinai coast road at once – the army was clearly ready to march.

Mutual military mustering was almost certain to produce a war in the end even without any provocation by one or the other. The Ptolemaic army was presumably assembled mainly at Pelusion; it had to cross the Sinai Desert to reach the enemy. Antiochos had moved some forces into southern Syria to the border there, and he had travelled to Joppa and Jerusalem, and presumably other cities in the region, no doubt to inspect the defences and check on their garrisons. His main army, however, was concentrated in Phoenicia, well away from the border; ships were being built in the Phoenician ports to reinforce his navy.[26] This was all quite obviously, and demonstrably, intended to seem defensive. By contrast, the Ptolemaic forces concentrated at Pelusion could only be seen as offensive.[27] It was perhaps no more than a week's march from Gaza and the Seleukid border, whereas Antiochos' army in Phoenicia was at least two weeks' march away. Antiochos was casting the blame for the war, if it came, on the Ptolemaic regents.

With the armies mustered, even far apart, the stage was set for war. It only needed a decision in one of the governments to set it off. But there were still other preparations to be made in both courts. In August (170 BC) Antiochos arranged two murders. His man Andronikos had already murdered the deposed Jewish High Priest, Onias III (who had been in exile in Beroia). He was now employed to murder Antiochos' stepson, of whom Antiochos was the guardian. Antiochos then arranged the murder of Andronikos himself.

Antiochos by then had a son of his own, a boy about three years old, who had passed through the danger years of infantile illnesses by then and was healthy; the stepson was thus now dispensable. Antiochos was thereby strengthened in his political position, both by his ruthlessness, and by the elimination of the child who had been nearing his coming-of-age, and would shortly be his competitor.

In Alexandria a mass meeting of the citizens was addressed by the regents. They promised that the war would be short, and that it would result in the conquest of Syria-and-Phoenicia once more; the rest of the Seleukid empire might also be acquired.[28] Presumably the meeting indicated its approval with some enthusiasm; the crowd was very probably ignorant of affairs; they would scarcely have addressed a group of courtiers and aristocrats with such nonsense. In the palace the younger brother of King Ptolemy VI and Queen Kleopatra II was proclaimed as a joint king, Ptolemy VIII.[29] This ceremony took place in October or early November, a month or so after Antiochos' contrasting measures at Antioch. The new king was then put through his *anakleteria* to mark his coming-of-age.[30] Both governments made these reinforcing gestures more or less at the same time, exploiting the royal children for their own purposes.

Both governments sent embassies to Rome. Antiochos sent his men first, to accuse Ptolemy's regents of preparing for war. The Ptolemaic group was charged with monitoring their discussion with the Romans, to be able to answer them. Polybios assumed that the war had already begun, though that probably only happened after the envoys had set out on their journeys to Rome.[31] The three Seleukid envoys certainly complained that the Ptolemaic regents had started the war, and made the point that Syria had been taken by conquest, with the implication that Roman conquests might be equally at risk. The Ptolemaic envoys, perhaps conscious that their kingdom was the weaker of the two, despite the regents' boastfulness in the assembly, and thus the more vulnerable, attempted to negotiate a peace between Rome and Perseus – there would then be the possibility of a Roman intervention, which might save them. The *princeps senatus*, M. Aemilius Lepidus, who had experience (at Alexandria and Abydos) of Hellenistic negotiations, brushed the offer aside.[32] The Roman war with Macedon was clearly more important. But no peace with Macedon meant continuing war in Syria.

Chapter 11

The Ptolemaic Disaster: The Sixth Syrian War

The new Syrian War began at the end of 170 BC, in the winter. Who first marched to the attack is not known for certain, but the Seleukid delegates at Rome complained that the Ptolemaic army had attacked first.¹ If so, the delegates had private information rushed to them during the winter sailing season, so it may be correct. On the other hand, it is evident that the Ptolemaic army had not gone very far in its march from Pelusion towards Gaza when it met and was defeated by the Seleukid army.² Part of the main Ptolemaic army, including its commanders, with the *strategos* Eirenaios in overall command,³ and with Eulaios and Lenaios in attendance, as it were, set out from Alexandria and collected the Pelusion force on the way. They had left Alexandria with considerable publicity, carrying with them a good deal of impedimenta, such as part of the treasury – needed to finance the war and acquire supplies – precious stones, rich clothing, and even couches from the palace, for the comfort of the high command, and, so we are told, with the aim of bribing Seleukid officers to surrender the cities they garrisoned.⁴

There is some evidence that Antiochos (and perhaps his brother and his father earlier) had an active espionage system operating in Egypt. In his visit to Egypt, Apollonios of Miletos had found it remarkably easy to collect information. And in 170 BC it is clear that Antiochos was extremely well informed about Ptolemaic military movements even inside Egypt. When the Ptolemaic army, commanded by the men who had travelled from Alexandria, plus the army already accumulated at Pelusion, began its march into Syria they found that the Seleukid army, originally mainly stationed in Phoenicia, had travelled through Palestine and most of the way along the Sinai coast road, so that the two armies met at Mount Kasios, no more than 50 kilometres east from Pelusion.⁵

A Jewish source, *I Maccabees*, described Antiochos' army as including chariots, elephants, and cavalry, to which one must add infantry, both phalangites and light infantry. The author is being very general in his description – the words could apply to almost any Hellenistic army, and one would suppose that he was making the assumption that all these elements really were part of Antiochos' force, but the implication is that Antiochos' forces were decisively more powerful than Ptolemy's. On the other hand, the author also claims that Antiochos deployed a 'great fleet', which is certainly greatly exaggerated, though he did command ships; it looks to be a formula, the author reaching for a typical description without bothering with specific or accurate details.[6]

So either Antiochos had attacked first, or he knew that he was about to be attacked and resolved to stop the invasion while it was still in Ptolemaic territory. Since he had been careful to station his main army at least 200 kilometres north of Gaza originally, he had clearly been anxious to avoid the accusation of having been the first to attack, so he had to wait at least until the Ptolemaic army commenced its march from Alexandria. The main Ptolemaic army was at Pelusion, but Antiochos clearly had information about the move of the commanders from Alexandria. He began his own march as soon as he heard of the Ptolemaic army leaving the city, at which point he would have roughly the same distance to travel as his enemy. Given the baggage the Ptolemaic army appears to have carried with it, its progress was no doubt slow. Antiochos had obviously been informed by an agent when it began from Alexandria, and with information about this coming out of Egypt, Antiochos was clearly entitled to move to block the army's attack. It had been clear even before the Ptolemaic army began its march, that an attack on Seleukid Syria was intended. The agent's reports had probably announced it.

The protection of Syria against invasion was Antiochos' repeated justification for the war for the next year and more.[7] It was defence which lay behind his advance from Syria to meet the Egyptian invasion force as far from his own territories as possible, and it was also the basis of his next move. His anxiety to prevent a Ptolemaic invasion was probably the result of an appreciation that the Seleukid rule in Syria was not well liked, and that a return to Ptolemaic rule would not be unwelcome. (Not that there was a liking for Ptolemaic rule when it existed, but that's nostalgia for you.) He is said to have deliberately spared the lives of the defeated Ptolemaic soldiers, but not why. It may have been in order to make a favourable impression, but it may also have been in pursuit of recruiting the defeated soldiers, which was the traditional reason for such restraint.[8] Having won the first encounter he made an armistice with the defeated army.[9] Who exactly was in control of the Ptolemaic side is not clear, but until the battle it appears to have been the *strategos* Eirenaios, but it would be the two regents who agreed to the armistice. Antiochos insisted, apparently against the terms of the armistice (though this is quite probably Ptolemaic propaganda, and the Ptolemaic authorities certainly employed propaganda lies in this war), in taking control of Pelusion.[10] This may have technically broken the armistice terms – which are not recorded - but it was obviously understandable from the point of view of Antiochos' justification for his campaign. He is said to have employed a ruse to take the city, which was not necessarily breaking the armistice. Unless Antiochos controlled Pelusion, one of the great fortresses of the Mediterranean world, and the obvious prize after his victory, his Syrian territories were in continuing danger of attack.

If self-defence had really been Antiochos' only war aim, he could have stopped there, having destroyed the Ptolemaic invasion force, and seized its main base. Of course, after an easy victory, this was not enough, and probably, like the Ptolemaic regents, he had had much wider plans in mind from the start. For several months, while watching the regents preparing their own war plans, he had the time to work out his own aims in discussions with his council of friends. His initial public declaration that he was fighting in self-defence, as his envoys explained to the Senate during their meeting in the winter – roughly contemporary, as it happened, with the battle and its aftermath – was clearly quite acceptable. He surely understood that to go further would alarm everyone else, since to go beyond self-defence would be to move into either annexing part of the Ptolemaic kingdom – Pelusion, for example – or overthrowing the whole Ptolemaic regime. The self-defence claim could in fact be stretched to include an intention to change the Egyptian regime since it had been publicly announced by the Ptolemaic regents that their policy was to overthrow the Seleukid system.

A start had been made on internal changes in Egypt. One of the results of the defeat at the battle near Mount Kasios, and the capture of Pelusion by the Seleukid army, was the overthrow of the regency regime. Eulaios, clearly in fear of his life, escaped with King Ptolemy VI to Samothrace, a place presumably chosen because they would receive sanctuary protection there;[11] Ptolemy is said to have panicked in the battle and fled with his life.[12] Doubts have been raised over this exploit, but certain details lend the story credibility – the curious choice of destination, for example, and the fact that Eulaios, who was the young king's *tithonos* after all, was involved. (Nothing is known of Lenaios' fate.) It would seem that Ptolemy himself abandoned the plan, perhaps even before reaching Samothrace, and returned to Egypt without Eulaios. Certainly both Lenaios and Eulaios ceased to have any authority in Egypt. (Eulaios had taken a considerable treasure with him as well as the king; his ultimate intentions are not known.)

The regents were replaced by two army commanders who carried through a coup, possibly even as Eulaios was fleeing with Ptolemy. Komanos was the former governor-general of the Thebaid, the only Ptolemaic commander currently with a victory to his name (over the Egyptian rebels),[13] and Kineas son of Dositheos had been a cavalry commander in 173 BC; he was distinctly junior in military terms to Komanos.[14] Eulaios and Lenaios, in Diodoros' words (as quoted by the later Byzantine emperor Constantine VII Porphyrogenitos) went to their own destruction.[15]

The overthrow of Eulaios and Lenaios, or their desertion, could well have given Antiochos the perfect excuse to seize Pelusion in supposed violation of the armistice, since the regents had probably been the Egyptian negotiators. If they were then displaced – as Eulaios certainly was, by his flight – the agreement could be claimed to have become void, and Antiochos could move on. A further consequence of the defeat and the regents' removal was that the joint royal regime of Ptolemy VI, Kleopatra II, and Ptolemy VIII, which had been instituted by the regents as a war measure, collapsed. Their replacements, Komanos and Kineas, took power in the name of Ptolemy VI alone. He, however, in view of his regents' destruction, had thereby returned from Samothrace, and documents were being dated in his name alone by December 170 BC (though this does not necessarily mean he had returned by then). He would probably have had to be persuaded to return by clear and believable assurances given by the new men in power. He was seventeen by this time, old enough to be a political force.[16]

The details concerning Ptolemy VI rather suggest a moment of sudden adulthood overcoming him – he is said to have panicked in the battle and fled, which cannot have encouraged his soldiers (though by that time they were probably in the same state); then he was carried off to exile; but then he returned to Egypt, without Eulaios, and presumably with the intention of acting as king, only to find two more regents usurping his authority. Until this point he had been manipulated by others, but the decision to return was his own, and this was the beginning of his assumption of power on his own behalf. He would have further opportunities to do so in the next two years.

The accession to power of the two soldiers was a clear threat to Antiochos. Not only did the change of authorities in effect cancel the armistice, but it had to be presumed that Komanos and Kineas would continue the war, and probably more effectively than Eirenaios or the joint regents. Antiochos moved on from Pelusion and began to occupy the nearby parts of the Delta region.[17] There is no indication that his forces were resisted after the battle at Mount Kasios (though it is possible that the occupation of Pelusion was achieved only after a naval battle),[18] but his advance would be a slow process under any circumstances, necessitating negotiations with every town and city they had to occupy – and perhaps Antiochos moved deliberately slowly to gradually increase the pressure on the rulers, as he seems to have done the next year. He is said to have captured the fortified towns and pillaged the land, all of which would certainly take time; the lack of opposition might encourage a leisurely advance.[19] Meanwhile, Komanos and Kineas, with Ptolemy VI (evidently back from his brief exile) convened a meeting of 'the most distinguished captains'. Without delay this group decided to sue for peace.[20]

This made sense. They could easily and convincingly blame the war on the removed regents, and could at least pretend to take Antiochos' professions of acting in self-defence seriously. Another armistice would reduce the ongoing damage being inflicted by the advancing enemy. There was a flock of Greek envoys in Alexandria at the time, with varying missions to pursue. There were two pairs from the Akhaian League, one of which was specifically seeking to re-establish friendly relations with the new regime; three delegations were from Athens, one about 'a present', one concerning the Panathenaian Games, and one concerning the Mysteries (presumably the Eleusinia); and two other groups of envoys were from

Miletos and Klazomenai. These arrivals suggest that the regents' regime had been as welcoming as the preceding kings, and perhaps as generous. All these envoys were now recruited as intermediaries, or even as unofficial Ptolemaic envoys, to go to Antiochos; they were accompanied by two official envoys from Ptolemy himself. Their task was to secure a truce or even a peace.[21]

This meeting took place well away from Alexandria, where Komanos and Kineas were in control. One suggestion is that it took place at Sais, another that it was 'near Naukratis', which does not really exclude Sais – the two places were only 20 kilometres apart.[22] Polybios describes the envoys sailing to meet Antiochos 'up the river', which implies that they left from Alexandria and found the king at some distance – Sais would be a reasonable meeting place, but Naukratis is actually on the Kanopic distributary of the river not far from Alexandria.

It is calculated (by Morkholm) that the meeting did not take place until about May 169 BC.[23] This is six months after Antiochos had captured Pelusion, so if the calculated date is right, he had advanced extremely slowly, perhaps giving the Ptolemaic government time to sort itself out after the defeat and the removal of the two regents, not to mention the temporary disappearance of Ptolemy VI and his restoration. There had presumably been a degree of difficulty in Alexandria over the changes of reigning personnel, and those in the governing system (a new *dioiketes* was needed, for example) and who was in charge, and what to do. And if so, Antiochos was not yet determined on extensive and permanent conquest and annexation. Also, it had been the winter season, when armies traditionally stopped for several months to go into winter quarters – the battle had been in December. It is further clear that the Greek envoys had been coached in detail by those in Alexandria, and dutifully delivered the Ptolemaic line; this may have taken some time to arrange.

The envoys enjoyed themselves. Antiochos welcomed them with a banquet, then he heard them making a series of speeches one after the other, all on the same topic: blaming the former regents, specifically Eulaios, for the war, exonerating Ptolemy VI on account of his youth, and repeating the story which had been developed by the Ptolemaic court that Ptolemy V had been allocated Coele Syria as a dowry for Kleopatra Syra at their marriage in 195 BC. (This did not rest on any first-hand evidence, since Ptolemy V, Kleopatra Syra, and Antiochos III were all dead.)[24]

The Ptolemaic Disaster: The Sixth Syrian War 151

They met their rhetorical match in the king, who had listened patiently, and no doubt with some appreciation of the rhetorical flourishes, but surely the process of repetition became tedious. He then got his own back, and explained at great length and in elaborate detail – it served the loquacious envoys right – about his dynasty's original claim to the Syrian territory, having been defrauded by Ptolemy I, and he decried as false the dowry story.[25] These performances – all involved were professional rhetors or well trained in the art – no doubt amused everyone, but were essentially entertainment, neither information nor negotiation. The envoys had all too clearly been repeating the Ptolemaic government's line – they had no doubt been coached while in Alexandria, just as Antiochos was repeating his dynasty's justification, and nothing said at the meeting was new. But at the end the envoys professed to have been convinced by Antiochos' account, though whether this is true or they were just being polite, cannot be determined.[26] The result was that Antiochos pointed out that he had sent his own envoys to Alexandria, and he would await their report, rather undermining the self-importance of the Greeks. Meanwhile he moved his forces further onwards, first to Naukratis on the Kanopic distributary of the Nile, and then along the river towards Alexandria.[27]

What transpired when Antiochos reached Alexandria is not known – there is a gap in Polybios here, and there is little in other sources which can fill it – but some sort of agreement between Antiochos and Ptolemy VI was made. Antiochos was Ptolemy's uncle (and he was also uncle to Kleopatra II and Ptolemy VIII, a factor often ignored), and he could have exercised a deal of influence on his relations; his apparent charm and persuasiveness may well have been exercised on the adolescent Ptolemy VI with considerable effect; and yet Ptolemy had already demonstrated, in detaching himself from Eulaios at Samothrace, that he had developed a determination and a mind of his own; it may be best to assume that he knew what he was doing in making the agreement. Ptolemy left the city and moved to Memphis, where Antiochos had set up his headquarters, thereby leaving his sister and brother, and Komanos and Kineas, in charge in Alexandria, and removing himself from the generals' influence. At this point it seems probable that Antiochos' aim was to establish a personal authority over Ptolemy and thus enlist Egypt as a subsidiary kingdom.[28]

When Ptolemy VI had gone off to his brief Samothracian exile, his sister and brother had been treated as the queen and king of Egypt; on his return he had taken the post as single king, thus in effect demoting the other two; now when he left Alexandria again (where the coup leaders, Komanos and Kineas, and his brother and sister, remained) the other two were apparently returned to prominence once again, as the ruling sovereigns, but with actual authority only in the city.[29] It looks very much as though Komanos and Kineas were very reluctant to surrender the power and authority that they had usurped, and that Ptolemy VI was reluctant to accept this. But joining Antiochos, if this is what he did, while this was perhaps personally more congenial to Ptolemy, was not the answer, since he simply exchanged two domineering men for another. By going to Memphis and Antiochos he may have hoped to negotiate a peace by direct contact, but Antiochos was probably too wily to be seen to take advantage of his naivete. Ptolemy VI was still Egypt's crowned king, and the senior of the royal siblings though that would hardly alter the power relationship either in Alexandria or at Memphis. In one stray papyrus ordering the delivery of barley to the army (the Seleukid army, obviously), the king is said to have been 'with that army'; the date of the document is 17 April 169 BC.[30]

When the brother and sister were reinstated as sovereigns at Alexandria, Antiochos, acting presumably on behalf of Ptolemy VI, marched on the city; it had now thus at base become a civil war.[31] With a besieging army threatening them the government in Alexandria sent an envoy to Rome asking for help.[32] Antiochos maintained the siege for some time, but an assault failed, which might suggest that the army with Antiochos was fairly small.[33] (Some men would have been sent home when the Ptolemies' resistance ceased.)

In October (169 BC) he withdrew, and marched his army away. He also sent his own envoys to Rome. On his withdrawal, he was met by a Rhodian delegation which had come to Egypt at the behest of Q. Marcius Philippus, the Roman commander against Macedon in the war in Greece.[34] They, like the earlier Greek envoys, speechified to the king at length about the situation, on which they must have been much less well informed than Antiochos. Understandably annoyed at their ignorance and volubility, Antiochos interrupted the speeches, telling them that Ptolemy VI was the legitimate Egyptian king, and that he had made a treaty with him. The Alexandrians, he said, were willing to recall him, and he accepted that.[35]

When Antiochos withdrew he left a garrison to hold Pelusion.³⁶ Ptolemy VI was based at Memphis and probably controlled most of Egypt apart from Alexandria and Pelusion. Alexandria was held by his brother and sister, with Komanos and Kineas probably commanding the forces, and governing. To Antiochos the situation was thus quite satisfactory: he held open the gateway to Egypt, and Egypt was at odds with itself. A civil war there was almost as useful to him as direct control of the country, and events in Egypt might give him a reason to return at any moment. And yet he had probably suggested that the way forward for the three Egyptian rulers was a mutual reconciliation, as he admitted to the Rhodian embassy. He probably did not mean the suggestion to be acted on, and surely would not have expected it. His relationship with Ptolemy VI, as formed at Memphis earlier, implied that he would need to be consulted on any agreement which the Ptolemaic family reached, and he probably believed he had the power to give or withhold his agreement, based on that relationship, political, personal, and familial, with Ptolemy VI. He could be pleased with events so far, and issued a new coin in which he was described as *nikephoros* – victorious.³⁷

The envoys sent to Rome by the Alexandrian government made no progress in beseeching help. The Senate was quite determined not to become involved in Egypt so long as the Macedonian War was continuing. They did send a junior Roman official, T. Numisius Tarquiniensis, who was unable to exert any influence; indeed, he may well have not been intended to do so, but he was certainly able to find out what the situation was. He had previous experience in the Greek lands, so he was capable of understanding what was going on, no doubt seeing events in Roman eyes, and he could report back to the Senate. He was in Alexandria in mid-169 BC, while Antiochos was in Memphis, and he could explain the effective stalemate in Egypt, which would please the Senate, since it meant that they did not need to do anything.³⁸ This would be reinforced by a report from Marcius Philippus when his own envoys returned to Greece. But when the delegates from both Antiochos and the two rulers in Alexandria saw the Senate in January 168 BC, the situation had improved, with Antiochos' withdrawal and the reconciliation of the Ptolemaic siblings; again the Senate saw no need to take any action.³⁹

In Egypt meanwhile, Antiochos' urging that the Ptolemies should become reconciled, insincere as it probably was, had been acted on, possibly even while Numisius was present. Ptolemy VI was in the strongest position, controlling as he did the *chora*, the productive countryside, so that supplies to Alexandria were very restricted. Once Antiochos (and his army) had marched away, the three Ptolemies were able to see the situation much more clearly, and appreciate that Antiochos was actually their mutual enemy, his divisive tactics having been effective. But 'Egypt had separated herself from Alexandria' in the words of the priest Hor.[40]

In this situation, where it seems that the brothers were unable to agree with each other (a condition to be repeated), Kleopatra, herself with the title of *basilissa*, took the lead in arranging the reconciliation of her two crowned brothers. Ptolemy VI returned to Alexandria, his blockade of the city was ended, and Antiochos found that his suggestion, having been adopted, now left him without influence. Ptolemy VI was no longer his protege. The three Ptolemies reconstituted their joint monarchy.[41]

Antiochos was expected to react with hostility to this development. Whatever agreement he had made with Ptolemy VI was now ended, whether it was formal or informal, and he could feel betrayed.[42] It would, however, take some time for him to do anything decisive; it was winter and he still had to re-muster his campaign army. He raided the treasure held in Jerusalem to replace his funds.[43]

An embassy was sent to Rome from Alexandria to notify the Senate of the new political situation in Egypt, though probably Numisius had already done so. Probably a request also went in for Roman mediation and/or help in the continuing war with Antiochos.[44] As an inducement a supply of grain was sent to the Roman ships wintering at Chalkis in Euboia.[45] A second embassy went to the Akhaian League, and asked specifically for the loan of 1,000 infantry and 200 horse as reinforcements, to be commanded by Lykortas and Polybios, who had both had experience as envoys in Egypt. Perhaps by the same embassy, a Sikyonian, Theodorides, was commissioned to raise a regiment of 1,000 mercenary infantry; he also had been an envoy to Alexandria earlier.[46]

These requests are peculiar. An extra 2,200 soldiers would hardly make much difference to a war between the Seleukids and the Ptolemies, who could each master an army of 30,000 men instantly, and 70,000 after a fairly short time. It is likely, however, that the Ptolemaic government was by this time short of troops, though there must be another reason for the request for a minimal reinforcement, and that was presumably political.

The league was a Roman ally in the Macedonian War, so if it contributed troops to one side in the Egyptian/Syrian war, it was being drawn into that contest, and this might have been seen as a way of bringing in Roman armed help.

This request went to the league assembly for a decision. Lykortas and Polybios argued in favour, but they were opposed by a pro-Roman faction led by Kallikrates, who was able to get the decision put off to a later meeting. There, the decision, supposedly almost reached in favour of sending the troops, was sharply deflected by the Roman commander in the Macedonian War, Q. Marcius Philippus, who wrote to recommend that the league should not intervene militarily, but should attempt to mediate. Philippus was a canny politician, as well as a cunning soldier, and presumably saw through the Ptolemaic request without difficulty. The league, which had been on the verge of agreeing to send the troops, crumbled at once in the face of this Roman intervention and prohibition.[47] If the Ptolemaic aim had really been to reel in the league in order to entice in the Romans, the plot failed – it is evident that the Romans would have ignored the 'opportunity' offered.

In Rome, meanwhile, the Ptolemaic embassy informed the Senate of the new political situation, and also asked for Roman help in case Antiochos attacked again, which the family reconciliation would probably encourage him to do. This time, with a good prospect that the Macedonian War would soon be over with a Roman victory – Philippus had been busy and had organized a successful Roman advance, and a second competent soldier, L. Aemilius Paullus, had been elected as consul for the new campaign. So, in reply, the Senate nominated three senators to mediate in the Syrian War. This time the rank of the envoys made it clear that Rome was at last being serious in its policy towards the eastern kingdoms; the delegation was led by C. Popilius Laenas, a formidable ex-consul, with C. Decimius and C. Hostilius as his colleagues, both of praetorian rank. And yet, though appointed, they could not do anything decisive until the war with Macedon was over.[48] (Decimius had been praetor in 169 BC and is recorded once as acting independently of Popilius; Hostilius is effectively invisible in the activities of the envoys.)

The timing here is crucial to a proper understanding of what was going on, since, because of the limits of the source material, the Roman viewpoint tends to dominate. The Senate meeting, where it was agreed to send Laenas and his colleagues to Alexandria, was held in February 168 BC; the reconciliation of the three Ptolemaic rulers had thus taken place well before that, perhaps well before the end of 169 BC, and it was clearly one of the triggers for the Roman decision at last to intervene in Egypt. The news of that Ptolemaic reconciliation had reached Antiochos during the winter of 169/168 BC, while the Ptolemaic envoys to Rome were already on their way – another winter voyage. At about the same time also an envoy came to Antiochos from Perseus asking for an alliance, and therefore for Seleukid military assistance against Rome; Antiochos refused, but he must have been pleased to find himself in such a strong and interesting position.[49] He had experience of Rome, as a hostage there a decade before, and constantly showed he understood Roman policy and actions, and was careful to avoid any conflict.

In the spring of 168 BC the Roman army finally broke through the Macedonian defences as a result of Marcius Philippus' preparatory work and manoeuvres, and in June under the command of Aemilius Paullus, Perseus was finally defeated in battle at Pydna. It is only when this had happened that Popilius Laenas and his colleagues, who had spent the spring at Delos, were able to make their move to Egypt; that is, Popilius was waiting until he could, metaphorically, arrive in Egypt with the victorious Roman army at his back. At more or less the same time, Antiochos also launched his forces against the Ptolemaic regime in Alexandria.

Antiochos had begun his new campaign with a new policy, a systematic process of conquest. He had first sent a naval expedition against the Ptolemaic island of Cyprus. This was still governed by Ptolemy Makron, who had held the office for some ten years. After the naval fight, which the Ptolemaic ships lost, and a defeat on land, presumably by a force of soldiers landed from the fleet, he invaded the island. It is unclear what sort of force he had to hand, but the island was usually well garrisoned; being at a considerable distance from Egypt it needed to be able to defend itself. Part of the garrison might have been withdrawn, however, to help with resisting Antiochos' invasion of Egypt, or possibly to fight in the brief civil war. Usually Ptolemy Makron is indicted as the weak link, for having deliberately failed to make a successful resistance.[50] He was a long-standing Ptolemaic official, and had proved his loyalty to Ptolemy VI and to his mother, so incompetence seems fairly unlikely, unless he had no, or inadequate, forces, which is perhaps the best reason for his defeat (and for Antiochos' opportunistic invasion). He will have known what would result for him in Egypt when he surrendered, and therefore transferred his services to Antiochos.[51] (This was by now almost the normal reaction by prominent Ptolemaic commanders – as in both the Fourth and Fifth Syrian Wars.)

The main Seleukid army will have mustered at Apameia, the Seleukid military base, and marched through Syria to attack Egypt directly, once again. Antiochos was met at Rhinokoloura, which was a village just west of Gaza on the Sinai coast road, by a delegation from the kings in Alexandria. By that time the Seleukid fleet had already sailed against Egypt and it was patrolling the Pelusiac mouth of the Nile, Pelusion being already in Antiochos' hands from the previous campaign; Livy, in a misplaced item, suggests that there was a naval battle, but this was more likely to have been during his first march through, the year before.[52] The envoys disregarded Ptolemy VI's desertion of the friendship (or alliance) which he had made with Antiochos the year before and which had clearly subsisted until a few weeks earlier; instead they conveyed Ptolemy's thanks for Antiochos' restoration of him (which Antiochos had only suggested, not assisted in), and expressed a wish that Antiochos should explain the terms he required for a return to an alliance with Ptolemy.[53] This was a good confusing explanation of events which had happened the year before, and which the Ptolemies clearly now interpreted in a way designed for consumption by subjects and foreigners.

Antiochos' terms were the acknowledgement that Cyprus and Pelusion should be annexed to the Seleukid empire, and that the 'land around Pelusion' and the Pelusiac mouth of the Nile be added to it. This last was not defined, perhaps deliberately, so as to provide some room for negotiation, unless the territory of Pelusion city was what was meant.[54] Antiochos required an answer – that is, acceptance – from the two kings by a certain date. Until then he would observe a truce. No answer was received by the time he stated, nor was there even an attempt to delay Antiochos further by discussion. But by not answering, or even discussing, these terms, they were clearly rejected.

Antiochos marched his army along the traditional invasion route into Egypt, past (or through) Pelusion and then along the Pelusiac branch of the river on the 'Arabian desert' side. At Memphis he was met by the people of the city, and presumably the city authorities, and received the submission of other Egyptians.⁵⁵ There was no resistance so far as we can see. The Ptolemaic army apparently remained out of sight and inactive, permitting Antiochos to go where he willed. This was, no doubt, because he had arrived in overwhelming strength, and so the Ptolemaic army would certainly have been defeated. It looked very much as though he would be able to secure full control of Egypt without fighting, at least until he reached Alexandria, which is possibly where the Ptolemaic armed forces had been concentrated. It had been shown during the past year that to retain control of Alexandria would do several things – it would prevent too much fighting in the *chora*, it would prevent morale-damaging defeats (which would be expected, given Antiochos' military superiority); the city would therefore act as the citadel of the country, and if the city was properly defended, it would then be available as the base for recovering the *chora* when the invader retreated. (In the event of a Roman intervention, diplomatic or naval/military, the city and the harbour would be available as a safe landing place.) But a successful defence of the city was absolutely essential; if it was taken, the whole country was lost.

Antiochos' march to Memphis from Pelusion was 200 kilometres and more, and would take his army at least a fortnight, not counting crossing rivers, but he stayed in Egypt for several months. The stay at Memphis must have taken up most of that time. Delegates from the rest of Egypt had to come to the city and make their submission, and this would take time. He certainly extended his authority to the far south. In the Fayum, there is some evidence, at Moeris, of violence and damage to a temple of Ammon, which had to be repaired after the Seleukid troops had left.⁵⁶ There was also fighting elsewhere in the Fayum, which is hardly surprising since it was thickly settled by Ptolemaic cleruchs, though Antiochos also gave orders to those cleruchs, an action normally reserved to the king, which suggests that whatever trouble there had been had died away.⁵⁷ Graffiti at Elephantine at the southern Egyptian border are evidence that Antiochos' authority, in the persons of some of his soldiers, reached the far end of the country.⁵⁸

By giving orders to settled cleruchs, Antiochos was assuming the authority of the king of Egypt in place of the Ptolemies. He also appointed a governor for Memphis, a man called Kleon.⁵⁹ It may have been on this visit that he had himself crowned as king, 'following the Egyptian custom', according to Porphyry.⁶⁰ This would mean a coronation ceremony in a temple of Ptah at Memphis.

Altogether Antiochos' actions, plus the publicity given to his campaign showed that he took the position of Egyptian king, and that his forces had established control from Pelusion to Elephantine. He might justify his assumption of the kingship by pointing to the betrayal by Ptolemy VI and the inability of the siblings to rule, though this would be a weak defence; straightforward conquests, such as the Romans indulged in, would be much more convincing. His actions were thus a clear indication that he was intent on conquest and the annexation of the whole kingdom. From Memphis, probably after whatever resistance that occurred had been put down, the Seleukid army travelled towards Alexandria along the Kanopic branch of the river 'by short marches'.⁶¹ This will have taken as long as the march from Pelusion to Memphis, perhaps longer, if 'short marches' means a deliberately slow pace, but the time cannot be stretched by much more than a week, one would have thought; perhaps a total of three weeks would suffice.

The whole procedure was evidently leisurely, but thorough. It seems clear that Antiochos expected no serious opposition, nor any intervention – by Rome, that is – at least until he reached Alexandria. He probably knew that the recruitment of Akhaian and Sikyonian troops had failed, and perhaps he understood that it had been Roman intervention which stopped the process. He had refused to help Perseus against Rome, and this refusal may have been publicized, so as to set his policies in as good a light as possible as far as Rome was concerned. This may well have persuaded him that Rome had been reciprocally persuaded not to intervene to save the Ptolemies. But he had acted as, and had taken measures as, king in Egypt, even if the story of his coronation is only a rumour or an assumption; Rome, he must have known, would not ignore that, since it implied the unification of Ptolemaic Egypt and the Seleukid empire, and had to react.

Antiochos' army eventually arrived close to Alexandria and camped nearby at Eleusis, only 1,500 metres from the Kanopos Gate. He had thus this time secured control of the *chora*, the rest of Egypt, and he was clearly now intent on capturing the city to complete his conquest. It was now summer, so Antiochos had spent four months on his campaign, beginning probably in February; well over half of that time had been spent at Memphis. Meanwhile, Popilius Laenas and his colleagues had been waiting for the right moment to commence their intervention in the Egyptian war. Until Antiochos approached the neighbourhood of Alexandria there was no point in the Romans leaving Delos, where they were based; they would not wish to spend time chasing after the Seleukid army in the Delta or in the Egyptian desert. They had travelled through Greece, stayed for a time at the Roman naval base at Chalkis, and then had moved to Delos, which may well have been a better centre for news than the Greek mainland. They spent their time at Delos attempting, probably without much success, to supervise a Roman and Attalid naval campaign to clear the Aegean of Macedonian warships.[62] Finally everything came together. The defeat of Perseus at Pydna in late June brought the Macedonian War close to an end; and news arrived (so we must assume) that Antiochos' campaign had brought him to Eleusis, near to Alexandria.

The next series of events are always told from the Roman perspective, leading to the dramatic – actually low-key – meeting of Antiochos and Popilius at Eleusis. This provides a distorted view of these events, for, by following the Romans, the story quietly ignores both Antiochos and his army and, above all, the Ptolemies in Alexandria, who were obviously concerned as much as anyone. But there was a whole series of events which had been happening almost simultaneously – Aemilius Paullus and the war with Macedon, which was being fought out in Thessaly even after the battle, and then in Macedon itself; the Roman delegation which arrived in the Aegean in the spring and lingered for several months, first at Chalkis and then at Delos; the Seleukid army which in that same time conquered Cyprus and Egypt, except for Alexandria; and the Ptolemaic kings and the population who were blockaded, and later besieged, in Alexandria. All of these need to be considered in this account, though it has to be said that there is precious little information about this last group, and not a great deal about Antiochos and his army. Nevertheless, it is necessary to attempt to keep in mind that these separate groups also existed and were concerned in what was going on. It is, however, possible to work out what they were all doing, and in this process a different set of circumstances and sequences emerges.[63]

The Roman naval campaign commanded from Delos, such as it was, was at once abandoned when the news of the defeat of Perseus arrived.[64]

As an excuse it was thus clearly seen to have been fabricated, but the seas were still unsafe, for the battle of Pydna did not actually end the war. The delegation no doubt travelled in one or more Roman warships, quinqueremes for preference. Whether the battle at Pydna was decisive for the delegation's plans was equally uncertain. The war was by no means over with the battle. Aemilius Paullus spent several more weeks, possibly months, after winning the battle, campaigning into Macedon and searching for Perseus; only when the king had been captured by C. Octavius at Samothrace (when the Roman soldiers were preparing to invade the island) could the war be said to have ended.[65]

Dating of anything here is partly guesswork, except for the date of the Pydna battle, 22 June. It seems much more likely that it was Antiochos' tardy arrival outside Alexandria which finally compelled Popilius to sail to Egypt. The Roman delegation stopped for five days in Rhodes on the way, where Popilius made at least one ferocious speech castigating Rhodian actions in the war,[66] after which the Rhodian politician Simmias made a slightly more conciliatory one, but it may be that calling at Rhodes was for the purpose of receiving news for it was an even more useful place to receive news from Egypt than Delos had been. It cannot be ignored that it was at Rhodes that Popilius will have received information of Antiochos' presence so close to Alexandria, which had perhaps been only rumoured while they were at Delos. It is noticeable that the naval excuse had been so thin that he is not commended for risking the sea voyage. With the Macedonian war still on, Macedonian ships – if there really were any roaming the sea – would be as dangerous as ever.

The Battle of Pydna was fought on 22 June. If, as is usually supposed, it was the news of this victory which propelled Popilius into action, it will have taken several days for the news of the battle to travel to Delos – perhaps a day or two by land, then two days by sea to Delos, with a day of preparation first – and this would be followed by time for preparation at Delos, perhaps two more days, minimum. A day at least, possibly two, would be spent sailing from Delos to Rhodes, and then they spent five days on that island. The news of the battle will have reached Rhodes well before them, and it was this which induced the Rhodians to insist on the delegation visiting the city.[67] This adds up to at least a fortnight after the battle, and the delegation was still only at Rhodes. It is this stay at Rhodes which is the most puzzling part of the journey. It implies that the mission to Egypt was not in fact all that urgent, and the best explanation is that they were waiting for news from Alexandria, and only when they knew that the city was about to be besieged did the Romans move on to Egypt. From Rhodes the news that Popilius and his colleagues were sailing to Alexandria would spread widely – the Romans were riding to the rescue of the Ptolemies. The final part of their journey from Rhodes to Alexandria would take some days, perhaps up to a week, depending on the winds. We cannot expect the Romans to have arrived in Egypt before the second, even the third, week in July.[68]

How long Antiochos had been camped at Eleusis before Popilius arrived is one of the many unknown details in this encounter. He had deliberately marched from Memphis 'by short stages', which could have been a means of exerting slow pressure on the Ptolemaic government in Alexandria, but it could also be that he was expecting a Roman intervention, and would prefer to arrive well after the Romans. If he was besieging, or at least blockading, Alexandria when the Romans arrived to put their oar in, he would be compelled to break off; still worse would be the case if he had already captured the city, for the Romans would then compel him, on pain of a Roman war, to evacuate his conquest, which would be even more humiliating. Far better would it be for him to meet the Romans while in his army's camp, not fighting, not besieging, but perhaps blockading the city, surrounded by his own soldiers, and able to accept Roman terms (or instructions) as a settlement of the war without argument or fuss. That is, just as the Romans, at Delos and at Rhodes, will have had accurate information of Antiochos' march towards the city, so Antiochos will have had accurate information about the Roman activities in Greece and the Aegean, and will have had time to anticipate the Roman demands and to prepare his response. If news of the battle reached Rhodes before Popilius and his colleagues had arrived from Delos, the stay of five days they spent there would certainly give enough time for the news to reach Alexandria and Antiochos. So when Popilius and his colleagues arrived at Alexandria, the king will have known exactly where the Roman delegation was, when it had left Delos, possibly even when it had left Rhodes, and he could make a good estimate of what the Roman achievement and intentions were. Whether Popilius and friends understood this is not clear, but they could certainly do the calculations, and probably established exactly where Antiochos and his army were before they sailed from Rhodes. If they landed at Alexandria, as is most likely, they could then be briefed by the Ptolemies, so what was known at Alexandria would be told to them – but it would also be known in the Seleukid army camp.

In other words, the encounter at Eleusis was not a surprise to either party. Popilius certainly knew where the king's army was and he came prepared to issue his ultimatum (he had a copy of the Senate's instructions in his hand at his meeting with Antiochos). When and where the Romans landed is not known, but it was probably at Alexandria, but possibly at one of the places along the Egyptian coast east of the city – Kanopos, for example. It must be admitted, however, that a proud – over-proud – Roman ex-consul such as Popilius would hardly be pleased at being made to land anywhere but at the great city, and he would certainly have wished to consult with the Ptolemaic government before seeing Antiochos.

What the two sides expected of the meeting is not obvious. Popilius, carrying a copy of the *senatus consultum*, clearly intended to use it in his discussions. Antiochos expected to have discussions with him and approached the meeting as one between friends, holding out his hand in greeting. He had a group of friends – advisers – with him, just as Popilius had his colleagues with him, and probably more men as well to bulk out his entourage. Antiochos must have expected that the Romans would insist that he withdraw from Egypt, but he will have hoped to come away with some territorial gains – Cyprus, perhaps, at least. Whether there was also a Ptolemaic delegation in attendance is not mentioned, but it seems unlikely. It was an encounter between Roman and Seleukid; despite the subject under discussion, the Ptolemies were ignored.

It may be pointed out that the stakes were actually very high. If the discussions became bogged down in detail and could not be resolved by an agreement, or if the Romans made demands which Antiochos could not accept – such as the evacuation not just of Egypt, but of all or part of Syria and its return to the Ptolemies – or if Antiochos insisted that his military (and naval) victories entitled him to certain rewards, such as Cyprus and Pelusion or more, and perhaps an indemnity (on the pattern of the Roman terms of the Apameia treaty), the issue would almost certainly be war. And there was a victorious Roman army in Macedon which would be able to march unhindered to Antiochos' northern border with the enthusiastic assistance of the states of Asia Minor along the way.

(Antiochos' friendship with the Attalid King Eumenes would not survive Roman demands for rights to march through his kingdom.)

For Rome, on the other hand, the three delegates will have known that Antiochos had developed a wide set of friends in Greece, the Aegean, and Asia Minor, and that Rome was now thoroughly disliked by most Greek states, especially in view of the barely competent conduct of the Macedonian War by many of the Roman commanders, and the deeply unpleasant behaviour of several of them when in occupation of parts of Greece. Popilius' treatment of Rhodes only a few days before was similarly not calculated to win friends. A war between Romans and Seleukids might well have to be fought in Greece and the Aegean, just as the war in Antiochos III's time had been, but this time with an aggrieved Macedon weighing in. It had taken five years to beat Macedon alone. The Roman citizenry might not accept yet another war, which might find Roman armies having to fight and campaign as far east as Iran. Both states were thus looking for a peaceful settlement; neither much cared if the Ptolemaic kingdom was trampled underfoot in the process, hence the absence of a Ptolemaic delegation, though it is certain a Ptolemaic official was in attendance and taking notes.

Both Popilius and Antiochos will have been aware of the risks involved in this meeting, but the behaviour of both men was the result of their upbringing and character. When Popilius marched towards the king, he was the representative of the most powerful state and army in the Eurasian world, excepting only perhaps the Han Empire in China (whose existence was at last becoming known for certain in the West by this time); he was confident that the Romans could defeat any enemy, but he must also have been aware that the Roman citizens were weary of war, that many of the senatorial commanders had displayed outstanding incompetence in the recent war against Macedon, and that the city and the state required peace.

Antiochos was probably much less confident. His army had been victorious in battle against the Ptolemaic forces, but it had been defeated in war against Rome once already. He was aware that Rome was adamantly opposed to the unification of the Seleukid and Ptolemaic empires, which would produce a state of such wealth, size, and power that Rome might well be unable to defeat it. Antiochos could assure himself that his aim in invading Egypt had been achieved, whatever that aim had been; the

The Ptolemaic Disaster: The Sixth Syrian War 165

Seleukid kingdom's main enemy had been humbled and punished, and its kings were quarrelling with each other. That is, Popilius arrived at the meeting full of arrogant confidence, whereas Antiochos lacked that quality, and was prepared to accept Rome's terms unless they were too outrageous.

The result was that when Popilius handed over the *senatus consultum* to the king and marked a circle around him, demanding an instant answer – that is, instant compliance – neither was really surprised, though Popilius had probably acted as he did on the spur of the moment.[69] But Antiochos knew even before his meeting with Popilius that he had no choice but to accept the Roman terms; he could not afford a Roman war. After only a moment he accepted – and that brief hesitation was more the result of Popilius' unexpectedly insulting behaviour than the terms – to which he then agreed. He then immediately – after shaking Popilius' hand in a gesture of personal friendship, thus emphasizing Popilius' boorishness – ordered his army to begin the withdrawal from Egypt.[70]

Whatever the personal or political reasons for Popilius' behaviour, his actions cut short what might have become a long process of discussion and negotiation. And that negotiation could only end in hard words and mutual blaming between the two powers, and if it got down to details, possible war. Popilius' boorishness was typically Roman (and recalled with relish by later Romans just as it was widely reported), but it paradoxically saved the day, a factor which Antiochos, with his quick intelligence, clearly understood.

The evacuation of the Seleukid forces took some time, the king himself leaving Egypt on 30 July, but this timing was not important.[71] The Seleukid army had to recall its widely spread units, from as far away as Elephantine, in addition, it seems to have looted its way home, which would usefully weaken the Ptolemaic kingdom still further. The gains which Antiochos had aimed for – Cyprus and Pelusion – were not permitted him; a Roman naval force went to Cyprus to insist that it be evacuated too (so implying that Popilius had arrived at Alexandria with a considerable naval strength).[72] The Ptolemaic kingdom, its lands, its appurtenances, and its defences, were thus restored. Antiochos could reasonably claim a military victory, and his troops had certainly loaded themselves with loot.

The real result of the war was that nothing had been settled. The hostility between the two great surviving Hellenistic kingdoms continued, and further wars were likely, though only when the Ptolemaic kingdom had recovered some strength. The Romans fully understood this, and will have angled their policy to maintain the division and the mutual hostility. The Ptolemaic government had been left divided and uncertain. There were still three sovereigns, and the two boys were already at odds with each other, both having had a taste of the untrammelled power of the Ptolemaic monarchy. Popilius apparently made a perfunctory attempt to moderate this, but here again, division was in the Roman interest, and he was scarcely the man to be diplomatic and conciliatory. Similarly, Kleopatra was now a power in the kingdom herself. Their future arguments contributed to continued Egyptian weakness in the next decade, and to its continued subjection to Rome's policy, when Rome could be bothered to notice.

Chapter 12

The Aftermath of War: Division and Rebellion

Having been invaded and conquered twice in two years, suffered several changes of ruler in that same period, been thoroughly looted by the retreating conquerors, and having had to be rescued from those invaders by foreign forces in the person of a single Roman politician, Egypt was in a very reduced and damaged state by July 168 BC, when the Seleukid forces withdrew. For the next several years Ptolemy VI worked to return the country to a peaceful and prosperous condition. In this project he had to contend with open rebellions, disputes with and disloyalty from his brother, and widespread strikes by the peasantry. And yet amid all this he continually maintained an intention to make another attempt to recover Syria. He was hardly helped by Rome, which had certainly assisted in expelling the Seleukid invaders, but not for the benefit of the Ptolemies, or the Egyptians – Rome was as big an obstacle to an Egyptian recovery as any other of his difficulties.

The first tasks after the 'day of Eleusis' were to remove from Egypt both the three Roman emissaries, and the Seleukid king and his army. Popilius was probably as anxious to leave Egypt as the Ptolemies were to see him go. He is said to have made an effort to get the brothers Ptolemy VI and Ptolemy VIII to work together, but it cannot have been more than a perfunctory effort.[1] He did ask that two Greeks, Polyaratos of Rhodes and Menalkidas of Sparta, be released from protective detention in Egypt, the first to be sent to Rome, presumably for some sort of punishment for voicing his anti-Roman sentiments; Ptolemy sent Menalkidas to Sparta, but Polyaratos was allowed to go to Rhodes in freedom.[2] Popilius' reaction to this, if any, is not known. He did not really care whether the kings were reconciled or not, and this indifference was perhaps at the root of Ptolemy's failure to accede to the deportation of Polyaratos; he may also have felt it necessary to display some independence. Like Antiochos in the last couple of years, Popilius will have seen that discord in the Ptolemaic family was a quite acceptable condition for Rome, rendering the kingdom essentially powerless. Popilius could sail home to applause and admiration – both of which he was, being who he was, anxious to receive – and take his seat in the Senate once more as an elder statesman.

There is no indication that a formal peace treaty was agreed between the Ptolemaic kings and Antiochos. The Romans by their method had in effect put themselves in a position to protect Ptolemaic Egypt from further attacks by the Seleukid empire. At the same time, this meant that the Seleukid empire was similarly protected, at least to a degree, from Ptolemaic attack, since it was highly unlikely that the Roman Senate would agree to a Ptolemaic invasion of Syria, which in the circumstances would require Roman involvement, since quite certainly the Ptolemaic army would be beaten. Not that a Ptolemaic attempt on Syria was likely for some time yet, and Antiochos IV, from his activities in the next several years, was clearly confident that no such attack would take place; Egypt was in such a mess after he left it that it was in no position to launch any attack. And yet, the agreement for peace was still only tacit, and, like other peace treaties, oral or written, it would last during the lifetimes of the two kings involved; when one of them died, the agreement ended, and both sides were free of any obligations. From all these uncertainties no new Syrian War was in prospect.

Antiochos left Egypt on 30 July, which is probably only three weeks or so after the meeting at Eleusis. An officer called, in Hor's papyrus documents, Tynys, and in Greek probably Deinias, went to Pelusion; probably he had the mission of checking that Antiochos and his troops really did leave Egypt.[3] (Popilius had already left; it is doubtful if the Romans bothered about any Seleukid movements directly, leaving it to the Ptolemaic government.) The date may be the deadline set by Popilius, but it is unlikely that all the Seleukid soldiers, who had spread as far south as Elephantine, were able to get to Pelusion in time. For their own journey, they had to be informed and given orders to return north – a joint distance of about 1,300 kilometres; this would take quite some time, even if they sailed along the river,, and it seems unlikely that the men sent as far south as Elephantine would be able to return to the north by 30 July. Antiochos, in fact, as recorded by Hor, left by sea, which probably means from Pelusion. The king would wish to supervise the evacuation of his soldiers as far as possible, in accordance with the deadline, and we know from Livy's ambiguous notice that he had brought ships to Egypt, and particularly to Pelusion. No doubt other ships had arrived at Kanopos when the king reached Eleusis.

The governor Kleon remained for a time in Memphis, according to notices in Hor's documents, again probably in order to supervise the evacuation. It would be some days before he knew what his orders were, and still longer before he would be able to move. We must also assume that Kleon was only one of several Seleukid governors who had been placed in Egyptian posts – a governor in the Thebaid would be almost essential – and such men may well have been very reluctant to leave their comfortable situations, and might take some convincing that the orders they received were authentic. The Seleukid evacuation, that is to say, was complicated, slow, and took a good deal of time.

Hor, a priest, had badgered the general Eirenaios with his dreams and predictions, but the general had remained sensibly sceptical until Antiochos actually left on 30 July. (Hor in fact showed himself all along to be fully alert to changes and developments, and his 'predictions' were clearly made in the knowledge of what the kings and generals aimed to do. It would not have been difficult to find out the date at which Antiochos had to leave Egypt, and then to incorporate the date, at first perhaps approximate, into his next 'dream'.) This could then be taken as validating Hor's messages. Once Eirenaios was convinced, Hor was taken to Alexandria under the escort of another commander called Totytts (The Egyptian version of Diodotos), though it was not until 29 August that he was received in audience in the Serapeion in the city. It was, in fact, probably during a celebration of thanksgiving for the 'salvation of Alexandria and every man within it' that he was received.[4] The king and queen were both present. The celebrations had been held a month after the date set – presumably by Popilius – for the evacuation, no doubt to make sure it had actually happened. After all, the Romans may have given orders, but no Romans were any longer present, so far as we know, to enforce them, and it may be that Kleon was still in Memphis at the time.

A number of necessary measures then followed the celebration. The former governor-general of the Thebaid, Noumenios, headed a delegation which was sent to Rome with a message of gratitude. He had held his office at Thebes in 170–169 BC, and had presumably been ousted by whoever Antiochos had appointed in his place. He was a major figure in the Ptolemaic government, and had been for some time, under the two previous regents and probably also in the resistance to the Seleukids. As with Komanos and others of a similar rank, his daughters were priestesses of the deified queens in Alexandria. He was certainly as distinguished a figure as any who could be sent on such a diplomatic mission, and Popilius and his colleagues would probably be able to vouch for his eminence in the Ptolemaic court.[5]

Ptolemy VI himself went to Memphis, joined there by Kleopatra. The prolonged residence there of Kleon, and Antiochos before him, will have persuaded the king to visit the ancestral capital of the country in order to re-establish his own authority; this was perhaps fuzzy in the city after the varying royal and governing personalities who had been in and out of the city over the past year or so. The city may well have been disturbed, and the royal hand in calming the situation would be helpful.[6]

That such a measure was the minimum that would be needed is illustrated by two letters written from the Serapeion in Memphis on the same day as the thanksgiving celebration took place in Alexandria. In this the writer refers to the hard times they are enduring.[7] If the Serapeion in Memphis, surely one of the wealthiest institutions in Egypt, could be said to be enduring 'such times as these', the rest of the country was surely suffering a good deal worse. The withdrawal of the loot-laden Seleukid forces was no doubt one of the reasons, but the dislocation of the city's administration was also no doubt an upsetting factor. Tax collection had presumably failed during the past years, and maybe planting and harvesting had been interrupted. The disruption, however, may have permitted the peasants, well accustomed to hiding part of their produce from the tax inspectors, to have concealed even more when those inspectors' work had been interrupted.

The kingdom, after the withdrawal of Antiochos and his army, and the departure of Popilius and his colleagues, was then left under the joint government of the three siblings, 'the King, the Queen and the Brother', an arrangement with an unfortunate origin in the emergency measures taken by the joint regents when they began the war, and which had been disbanded and resuscitated more than once since. But this time the joint rule of the three had been organized between them in 168 BC as a means of defence against Antiochos' pretentions and invasion; it could hardly be dissolved once he had been expelled from the country. Ptolemy VI was certainly the senior and elder of the three, and Kleopatra was his wife – she had given birth, in 168 or 167 BC, to a son – which left Ptolemy VIII rather isolated. And Ptolemy VIII had had a period of active kingship without his brother – assuming Kleopatra could be disregarded – for a time during the war, while Ptolemy VI was in Memphis, and had apparently enjoyed it and wished to return to that condition.

The triple kingship was therefore by no means a happy situation. The brothers were constantly at odds. Kleopatra on one occasion had reconciled them, but this was no more than a temporary measure, and it was notorious, and known as far as Rome and the Seleukid kingdom, throughout Alexandria, and no doubt in the rest of Egypt, that they disagreed with each other on most issues. They were capable of appearing in public with a display of, if not unity and amity, at least an absence of open enmity. Ptolemy VI and Kleopatra appeared together at the Alexandrian Sarapeion, when Hor made his report, and it seems likely that Ptolemy VIII was there as well; certainly the three were together at Memphis later that year.

For the next two years there is no information about either Egypt or the situation in the royal family; one can only assume that the enmity of the brothers grew steadily worse. In the *chora* there is no indication that social and economic conditions improved in any serious way. After the destruction and damage of the past two or three years the short period since the withdrawal of the invaders would hardly be enough time to do more than make a start on recovery. And whatever progress had been accomplished was to be cancelled by further internal troubles in 165–163 BC, again set off by the intra-royal enmities.

This was the general situation – continuing local disorder, lack of confidence in government, division amongst the rulers – which was the condition favouring a new outbreak of trouble. That it came from a member of the Ptolemaic elite, a Friend (*philos*) of the king, was perhaps the only surprise, the previous disturbances had come from similar people.[8] The events which followed amounted to a new civil war, and included the overthrow of the government.

The originator was a man called Dionysios, with the surname Petosarapis, names which make him a Greek with strong Egyptian connections – though 'Petosarapis' does not necessarily make him an Egyptian except in his domicile.⁹ He was described as a most senior man in the court, though this may be an exaggeration to build up the seriousness of his actions. He was clearly disgusted at the quarrelling within the royal family, but chose a curious way of expressing that disgust, by calling a public meeting in the stadium in Alexandria to explain his feelings. He claimed he had been approached by Ptolemy VI to help in a plot against the king's brother and he wanted to announce this disgraceful proposition to the audience. He succeeded in rousing the crowd to fury, almost to the point where Ptolemy VI might be assassinated.

How much of Dionysios' allegations were invented, as Diodoros claimed, or was authentic, as Dionysios was proclaiming, cannot now be decided. But the general atmosphere in the court, as understood by outsiders, evidently appeared to be such that a plot was quite feasible, or at least would not be unexpected. It does seem, in view of the character of Ptolemy VI which is given by the historians, that he was unlikely to have produced such a plan. On the other hand, that character of peacefulness and generosity seems thoroughly unlikely in a king who had schemed and dodged his way through the last two years, abandoning his tutor, abandoning his wife and brother, and betraying his uncle. And yet, it must be admitted that removing Ptolemy VIII would probably have been a benefit to Ptolemy VI, to Egypt and to the Ptolemaic dynasty. He was a thoroughly unpleasant character, in marked contrast to that ascribed to Ptolemy VI.

What was Dionysios' main aim is not clear. Rousing the mob of Alexandrians suggests he aimed for an attack on the palace with an unofficial army with the aim of a comprehensive royal assassination, and Diodoros certainly assumed he was aiming to seize power, or the throne. But his complaint to the crowd was of a plot inside the royal family, which implies that he aimed to foil such a plot by naming Ptolemy VI, who he said was its author. On the surface, Dionysios was speaking on behalf of Ptolemy VIII, and one must entertain the possibility that he had been put up to his speech by 'the Brother'. Whatever his original aim, once he had begun, Dionysios could hardly stop before attempting to seize the government and kill all but Ptolemy VIII among the royals; the alternative would be his own death.

Ptolemy VI cleverly extricated himself from the threats of the crowd, by calling in his brother, swearing that he had planned no plot against him. He persuaded him to appear in public before the angry crowd with a display of unity and friendship. Ptolemy VIII acceded to this display, even though it was his open ambition to displace his brother, and was probably even then in the throes of planning a coup of his own. Clearly it was not in his interest to be seen as a fratricide-cum-regicide – though benefiting from someone else's coup would be acceptable. He could therefore participate in the brotherly display with mental reservations – which were probably shared by his brother. But being compelled to do so no doubt irked him sufficiently to confirm him in his own adventurous intentions.

Dionysios did not give up. He contacted those soldiers who were most aggrieved, though what their complaints were is not specified, and left the city to camp at Eleusis, where more men joined him until he had 4,000 under command. His position was strong, for he could probably count on a considerable number of supporters inside the city, those who had been convinced by his words, and the 4,000 soldiers, some extracted from the city garrisons, would be a useful force. But again, Ptolemy VI unexpectedly foiled him. The king was a less than militant ruler, more a politician – as his defusing of the crowd in the city had showed. Now Dionysios and his soldiers found that he had been wrong about the king again, for Ptolemy came out with his own loyal force, and in a battle at Eleusis he defeated Dionysios' forces, and forced him to disappear 'among the Egyptians'.

It is tempting to link Dionysios' attempted coup with subsequent disturbances in other parts of Egypt, but other than that they all seem to have been concentrated into a couple of years (165–163 BC), no direct connections can be made. Dionysios certainly, when he was 'among the Egyptians', attempted to raise them in rebellion in the Delta area but this plot does not seem to have lasted very long; at least we know no more about it, though in the absence of source material this is not definitive. The fact that a whole series of other disturbances did take place in these few years is, however, a clear indication that something had gone wrong in the Ptolemaic state, which is best blamed on the aftermath of the Syrian War. We should perhaps therefore put the countrywide disturbances first, and Dionysios' attempt at a coup as a consequence of that situation. On the other hand, Dionysios' attempts may be simply the first of these disturbances, and perhaps the most spectacular uprising, and was the one which set off the rest by example.

Other incidents at the time include references to revolts and wars in other texts, whether the references are a means of explaining actions or locating them in time. Most references are imprecise as to when or even where the revolts were. The cleruchic temple of Ammon at Moeris in the Fayum which had been damaged in Antiochos' war was systematically destroyed and looted by 'rebels', defined as Egyptians. This has all the appearance of a local dispute, possibly over taxes or work schedules. The dispute appears above all to have been between the Greek cleruchs and Egyptian peasants. The overseer of the temple, who wrote a report on the incident to the governor, described the assailants as 'rebels', in the same way that modern affronted governments flourish the term 'terrorists' at any opposition. The systematic process and thoroughness of the destruction is remarkable – the temple was stripped of its valuables and dismantled, and the stones broken up or carried off – which rather suggests that the repairs which took place after the war with Antiochos had ended up being paid for by the peasants/rebels, even though it was a Greek temple.[10]

A papyrus from Soknapaiou Nesos, also in the Fayum, mentions a 'revolt', but only incidentally in connection with the dispute being described.[11] Another from Herakleopolis mentions the disturbed times but only to date the theft being discussed, and the reference is too general to indicate more than it says.[12] Again, a papyrus from the Serapeion in Memphis referring to the recluse Ptolemaios dates his death at the time of 'the revolt', and another document places the man's death in October 164 BC. No details of the action or causes of the 'revolt' are mentioned, but it is a reasonable conjecture that it was the trouble in the Thebaid.[13] None of these incidents can be connected with Dionysios Petosarapis' attempted coup, other than approximately by date, despite attempts to do so. Referring to 'rebels' and a 'revolt' in Alexandria while writing in Memphis or the Fayum might mean only rumours of disturbances elsewhere. Dionysios' activities, and the man himself, seem to have faded away quickly, after his defeat, if Diodoros' reference to his disappearance 'among the Egyptians' means anything.

Trouble caused by Dionysios Petoserapis may be best classed as an attempted coup, since it was clearly aimed at the royals. On the other hand, the problem in the south was a real revolt of some duration. Unlike Dionysios' affair, it required the extended attention of Ptolemy VI in person, and because of its location in the Thebaid in Upper Egypt, it would be more likely than Dionysios' attempt to be referred to as a 'revolt'. For the Thebaid was exactly the place which had been the centre of the great movement for Egyptian independence which had ended only twenty years before.

This is described by Diodoros specifically as a popular uprising. Apart from Dionysios' adventures and those incidents which can plausibly be connected with them, probably the most serious revolt occurred in the Thebaid. This, of course, had been the rebel centre of the pharaonic regime twenty years before, and had been occupied by Seleukid forces during the Syrian War. 'An urge to revolt swept over the populace', Diodoros says, which looks serious, but is notably unspecific. It was, however, threatening enough to bring Ptolemy VI and an army south on campaign. Most of the rebellion was put down easily, probably as soon as the king and his army arrived in the region, but the hardliners gathered at the city of Panopolis (Ackhmin), halfway between Thebes and Asyut, in old rebel territory. There they stood a siege which lasted for some time (again, no timing is available), but Ptolemy was successful in the end.[14]

All this can perhaps be connected to the activities of Dionysios, but only by way of example – the two events were several hundred kilometres apart, but news travelled reasonably quickly through Egypt. Diodoros says that when Dionysios escaped from Ptolemy VI's pursuit he went away 'among the Egyptians' and began persuading them to rise.[15] The two events were however clearly separate, for Ptolemy had dealt with Dionysios before he took a large enough army south to the Thebaid to crush the revolt there quickly, except for the group 'of the most active of the rebels' who took refuge in the fortified mound at Panopolis, and had to be ground down by the lengthy siege.

This conflict therefore turned into a determined defence of the strong Panopolis position, and it took the Ptolemaic army some time to capture it. But, given the place and time, it was necessary for this particular king to command here and with success. His reputation was hardly of the highest, and his army was no longer as strong and numerous as during his grandfather's time. But if he succeeded at Panopolis, as well as defeating Dionysios' coup attempt, he would grow in political stature and would surely quieten the various areas of discontent in the country. He did in the end succeed in capturing the place, and 'punished the ringleaders'.

Ptolemy returned north after his victory and we know he was at Memphis in October 164 BC.[16] The Apis bull had died in April.[17] This was a significant event not only for the priests who attended him (and for the bull himself) but for Ptolemy VI, who was calculated to have been born about the same time as the bull.[18] He was therefore linked in his fortunes with the life of that particular bull. It was buried in June 164 BC while he was fighting and winning in the Thebaid. Depending on how superstitious the king was, the series of troubles in Egypt in the past year or so could be said to have culminated in the bull's death, and perhaps that was an end. But his troubles were not over yet.

When he visited Memphis in October 164 BC, Ptolemy was accompanied by his sister/wife Queen Kleopatra. The visit was to celebrate the Egyptian New Year. At some point between then and December, Ptolemy VIII, 'the Brother', succeeded in ousting Ptolemy VI from power.[19] Exactly how this was accomplished is not described, but it was clearly a *coup d'état* which had probably been in preparation for some time, notably no doubt while Ptolemy VI was away from Alexandria in the Thebaid fighting the rebels. Ptolemy VIII must have spent that time gathering a set of supporters, including at least part of the army – the Alexandrian garrison, for preference – which must have taken some time; he then seized the moment when his brother was politically vulnerable. None of this is visible in the record, but Ptolemy VI turned to Rome for help in recovering his throne. So it may be going too far to credit Ptolemy VIII with provoking the revolt in the south as a distraction for his brother, but it is surely not going too far to see Dionysios' attempted rising as a movement on behalf of Ptolemy VIII, and Ptolemy's coup at the time of the southern revolt as successful opportunism. It seems difficult to disconnect Dionysios' attempt and the success of Ptolemy VIII.

The absence of any indication of how and why the southern revolt took place compels a search for possible reasons. The timing may well be connected with events in the north, again opportunistically, but it is also possible that it was connected with a recent attempt by Ptolemy VI to deal with the grievous agricultural situation in the country, an attempt which had led to considerable trouble for him – quite apart from his siblings. In his travels from Memphis to the Thebaid in the mid-160s BC he had surely seen the condition of the Egyptian countryside. There were deserted villages where the people had left in the Egyptian version of a strike, *anachoresis*; there were areas, perhaps particularly in the south, where the damage caused in the war for independence and its suppression was probably not yet repaired, partly no doubt because of the Seleukid occupation, which probably caused further damage. The casual vandalism which occupying armies tend to inflict on the land, and the looting the soldiers had indulged in, particularly on their retreat, can be cited. And in all this there were disputes over ownership; there are several legal cases known concerning this, typically where the original owner has left for a time for various reasons, only to find a new 'owner' in occupation of house and land when he returned – that at Herakleopolis noted earlier is an example.

Ptolemy VI's solution to this problem was typical of a ruler who was an autocrat, and scarcely understood what he was dealing with. He issued a *prostagma*, that is an ordinance, which is now simply entitled *On Agriculture*.[20] It began by describing the ruin of parts of the country, and also the water shortage after a series of low Niles, then came the king's solution to these problems: farmers with land which was not being cultivated were to be compelled to lease it out at a lower price than they hoped to charge; some royal land which was being neglected was to be cultivated by compulsion; farmers with livestock – cattle and other animals used to plough and harvest and in transport, and probably to turn waterwheels, these animals being evidently scarce as well – were to allow them to be used on the royal land. Payment was not mentioned.

The scope for abuse is obvious, and complaints flooded into the office of the *dioiketes* Heroides in Alexandria, especially about the way in which those officials charged with administering – or enforcing – the new laws were doing their job. The complaints eventually had their effect. In response Heroides amended the order in the autumn of 164 BC, changing the method of allotments of land, and, significantly, exempting the *machimoi*, the armed militia mainly composed of native Egyptians, from the leasing provisions.[21] *Machimoi* had formed the backbone of the great revolt, and had perhaps participated in the Panopolis siege. It made sense to conciliate them. The modifications were the result of the political strength of those who objected, notably the *machimoi*, who were also part of the royal guard, and who enlisted help in their complaints from the *naukleromachimoi*, the river police who were also both an armed and organized group. And yet, after these modifications, the essential basis of the order remained. It was the first attempt to compel the farmers to do the government's bidding, and was the preliminary move in reducing the free farmers to a sort of serfdom.

The revolt in the south had occurred in part because the population of Greeks and Macedonians in the area had been much less than in, for example, the Fayum. There had been garrisons, of course, but quite likely many of the personnel had been *machimoi*; there were also some cleruchs in the area, such as those who had settled on Agathokles' allocation after about 220 BC. But the cleruchs had probably been driven out or killed during the revolt. After 185 BC there was, therefore, land available for new settlers. A land survey in the Edfu region in the late second century reveals evidence of the planting of settlers in 170 and 164 BC and later, that is, before and after the revolt.[22] This was no doubt one of the measures taken by Ptolemy VI as a means of enforcing royal control. In fact, it is probable that the governor-general of the Thebaid, a new office, would be responsible for supervising the work of settlement.

The problem of abandoned land was large enough to bring about the establishment of a special government department, the *Idios Logos* ('special account') to deal with it. This was to take over the lands which had been state owned but which were not being cultivated. They had probably been deserted or abandoned or in some cases were only marginal to begin with. Probably deserted lands were fairly common in the south, deserted either because the tenants had been driven away, or had left to save their lives during the revolt. The new department carried out the necessary surveys to determine which lands it was responsible for. (This, of course, entailed the employment of more bureaucrats, and so increased the costs to the government.) It then was to seek ways to cultivate the land, and find peasants to work it. The aim was to increase food production and to profit from the land, and claim more taxes. Again, it was a process in which compulsion would gradually be extended, and where it was only a simple bureaucratic step to compel peasants to work such land and to reduce those peasants to serfdom. It does not appear to have occurred to anyone involved that any incentive other than compulsion would produce results.

This measure and the disruption it was causing clearly angered many people, notably those already wealthy, who were therefore almost as influential as the armed soldiers. It was probably one of the elements which persuaded Ptolemy VIII that the opportunity had come to unseat his brother, whose popularity, such as it was, had clearly suffered from the reaction. (There is no evidence that Ptolemy VIII rescinded it.) But Ptolemy VIII's coup was unstable for three reasons: Ptolemy VI's effective response, Kleopatra's refusal to accept his action, and Ptolemy VIII's unpleasant nature.

Ptolemy VI decided to appeal to Rome for help. The basis for this curious step was presumably the work Popilius had achieved in removing Antiochos IV and his army, and later in attempting to reconcile the two brothers. This had put the Ptolemies in a subordinate, even protected, relationship towards Rome, even more decisively than earlier. This was generally ignored by both Rome and the Ptolemies most of the time, but was becoming important in that very year, 164 BC, in view of the military successes of Antiochos IV in his campaign into Iran. (He died in the process of the war, in that year, but this was not known until late in the year.) An increase in the power of the Seleukid king would not be welcome to Rome, which was still sensitive to changes in the balance of Eastern affairs: probably the Senate feared that Ptolemy VI might resort to asking Antiochos for his assistance, thus linking the two monarchies together once more. Ptolemy VI had always gravitated to a protector – his mother, his *tithonos* Eulaios, Antiochos IV, possibly Kleopatra II, and now Rome. In fact his appeal was probably unnecessary, since Ptolemy VIII made himself so thoroughly disliked in Alexandria in the four or five months he was sole king, that the Alexandrians turned against him.

Ptolemy VI went to Rome personally and put on a show for the Roman Senate. He arrived with only four attendants, a eunuch and three slaves. He was dressed in old and worn garments – where did he get them? How did he reach Italy? He had to have travelled by sea, and presumably he had done so as the king, only temporarily deposed. The clothes could have come from the minimal possessions of the sailors. (It was becoming traditional to dress down deliberately like this in appealing to and appearing before the Senate.) Where he landed in Italy is also not known, Ostia perhaps, or more likely Puteoli.[23] He walked towards the city in his non-disguise – for he was recognized, and the word reached the Seleukid prince Demetrios, who was still a hostage in Rome, while Ptolemy was some distance away from the city, said to be twenty miles. Demetrios was, of course, Ptolemy's cousin as well as a fellow royal. And if Demetrios had heard of his arrival, so had the Senate.

Demetrios was quicker off the mark than the Senate, which could simply wait for Ptolemy to arrive. He met Ptolemy on the road and offered support, including more suitable clothes, suitable for a king, that is. Ptolemy refused them; he had his scenario fully planned out.[24] The Senate sent messengers to him, apologizing for their remissness in not meeting him and not sending a quaestor to escort him, as was the custom. No matter, Ptolemy replied, and when he reached Rome he took up lodgings with a Greek painter of his acquaintance.[25]

All this was a splendid performance, of course. It attracted the Senate's full attention, and so in this it was successful. It is probable that the Senate already knew that he had been overthrown, and was in two minds (at least) whether to do anything about it. Ptolemy's arrival in beggar's clothing showed that he was acting in the same way as other Hellenistic messengers who came to Rome to ask for assistance, and they usually turned up in a similar guise.

Perhaps it was too theatrical, for the Senate did not, as Ptolemy surely hoped, immediately send to Alexandria to insist that his brother reinstate him. He was able to speak to the Senate, but no immediate decisions were reached. But some arrangement was certainly made. A pair of envoys – suggested to have been L. Canuleius and Q. Marcius[26] – is known to have reached Alexandria soon after this, apparently charged with reconciling the two kings. This was unlikely to have much effect on Ptolemy VIII now that he had managed to gain sole control of the country; he was unlikely to give up his seized position easily.

Ptolemy did not insist on actual help, presumably realizing he would not get it, but soon he left Italy and sailed to Cyprus, where, it seems probable, his wife Kleopatra had gone, as much to avoid the Brother as to prepare a base for Ptolemy VI. (Ptolemy VIII's name alone is on documents from this period, without his sister's.[27]) There Ptolemy waited. The senatorial delegation in Alexandria made apparently little progress in pursuing a new royal reconciliation, but in the end it was not needed. The Alexandrians very quickly tired of Ptolemy VIII – 'Physkon', they called him, 'fatty' – and soon demanded that Ptolemy VI return.[28] He was in Alexandria by mid-August.

Ptolemy VIII was the type of autocrat who was brutal and insensitive, despite being an intelligent, cultured, and well-educated man.[29] But he was up against his brother who was a much more skilful politician, and

The Aftermath of War: Division and Rebellion 181

who had apparently gained some understanding of the mentality of the Greeks of Egypt, and particularly those of Alexandria, in the past few years. In addition, he had with him in Cyprus his wife Kleopatra, who had more than once already taken decisive action to bring about internal peace in the royal family. She apparently had been the natural heir in a political sense to her mother, Kleopatra I, in this, and was as prominent in public affairs, such as in the regular royal visits to Memphis, as her husband. Ptolemy VI had apparently decided that all he had to do was wait; sure enough, the Alexandrians summoned him back.

In a highly successful and significant move, Ptolemy VI then arranged the fraternal reconciliation which the Senate had been unable to achieve. The brothers divided the kingdom between them, Ptolemy VI taking Egypt and Cyprus, Ptolemy VIII Cyrenaica.[30] Not that Ptolemy VIII was ever satisfied with his portion, but his unpopularity (in Cyrenaica as well as in Alexandria) restricted the scope of his actions. He continued to agitate for more, nonetheless.

So much for Rome's position as supervisory authority and protector. Ptolemy VI was in fact, by ignoring the Senate after it and its envoys failed to provide effective assistance, declaring his independence, and hoping that the new arrangement would satisfy his brother, who would have a kingdom and would possibly learn to discipline his unpleasant nature. It was an object lesson in recovering from an apparently decisive setback to achieve long-term goals and a more stable political position, a classic set of political manoeuvres.

The period from 170 BC, when the Syrian war began, and 163/162 BC, when Ptolemy VI was finally seated more or less firmly on his throne, had seen invasion, rebellion, *coups d'etat*, and shifting royal authority, in Egypt, with the result that serious disturbances had been caused throughout the country. It is difficult to avoid the conclusion that it was all brought on the Egyptians by themselves, and above all by the disputes at the government level. Furthermore, the basic issue of who ruled the country had not yet been settled and would not be for the rest of the Ptolemaic period. The difficulty of governing the country can of course be traced all the way back to before Alexander the Great, but the behaviour of the Ptolemaic family and its ministers had undoubtedly made everything worse. Those who suffered, of course, as always, were the Egyptian population. It has to be said that their condition has not improved since.

Chapter 13

Ptolemy VI at Peace

The political settlement between the Ptolemies in summer 163 BC was, if not definitive, then at least it lasted for almost a decade. From the next ten years, Ptolemy VI was king in Egypt and Cyprus; Ptolemy VIII ruled in Cyrenaica while attempting, three times, to overthrow his brother once more, but without success. This was close enough to stability, especially after the various conflicts of earlier years. Kleopatra II returned to Egypt along with her brother-husband in 163 BC, and she is regularly named in official documents with him as joint ruler from then on. She produced four children in the next ten years. Ptolemy VI had been king from 180 BC, when his father died, until his own death in 145 BC, one of the longest of Ptolemaic reigns, but it was only from 163 to 152 BC that he was the complete master of Egypt without serious distractions, and able to govern.

He began with a series of measures clearly designed to reward and conciliate all the various elements of the population in Egypt which had collectively restored him to the throne and rejected his brother. An amnesty decree, apparently produced by mid-August 163 BC, pardoned a number of crimes and offences which had been committed by their perpetrators before 17 August.[1] This manoeuvre was clearly aimed at blocking any attempts at revenge and subsequent feuds, and to quieten the general population. That it needed to be done and enforced was evident in a letter Ptolemy sent to the *strategos* Dionysios of the Memphite district telling him of the decree and that he was instructed to enforce it;[2] it is evident that the enforcement of such measures was not always bureaucratically automatic. In October, once again, the king and queen were at Memphis for the Egyptian New Year.[3]

This event, as well as earlier (and later) visits, was aimed particularly at the native Egyptian population, and above all at the Egyptian priesthood, who could claim to be the leaders of Egyptian opinion, though many in the south had opposed the revolt, and were seen as allies of the Ptolemaic regime – which, of course, they actually were. Ptolemy received petitions, through a window in the temple wall, visited and made offerings at several temples in Memphis and stayed in the Serapeion; that is, he generally acted as a pharaoh more than as a Hellenistic king.[4]

Ptolemy VIII did not accept his new situation with any good grace. He nursed his resentment for a short time, then resorted to the same tactic as his brother had used: he went to complain at Rome. He was, however, in a less convincing situation, since it was unlikely that the Senate saw him as a dependent, as it had probably regarded Ptolemy VI. On the other hand, if he was obligated to the Senate for a favour such as acceding to his new request, this would make him a dependent, and meanwhile Ptolemy VI was manifesting disturbing symptoms of independence. Both sides clearly understood this. Ptolemy VIII asked the Senate to alter the partition agreement which he had accepted, with solemn oaths, claiming to have agreed to it unwillingly and under compulsion. He suggested an improvement in the partition by which he could keep Cyrenaica, but also take over Cyprus. This was accepted by the Senate despite the objections raised by Ptolemy VI's envoy Menyllos, who could point to the sacred oaths sworn by both brothers.[5]

Polybios explains the Senate's agreement to this scheme as being likely to further weaken the Ptolemaic kingdom, and this is convincing. Cyprus, of course, was in a strategic position and was a major source of minerals, wood and sailors. In Ptolemy VIII's hands it would become a base from which he could interfere in Egypt, even invade it. The initial success of Ptolemy VI in settling affairs inside Egypt would be likely to produce an economic and military revival of the kingdom, which the Senate, always nervous about the Eastern kingdoms, would not wish to see. A constant threat from Cyprus would distract Ptolemy VI very nicely. An embassy went to Syria at about this time to investigate the situation in the Seleukid kingdom after Antiochos IV's death. The envoys used the situation to demand that the obsolete terms of disarmament – the Seleukid elephants and warships – set out in the Apameia treaty of 188 BC (three Seleukid reigns ago) be enforced, and the regency government of the kingdom felt unable to refuse. But the agony of the hamstrung elephants as they died infuriated the population, and the chief Roman envoy, C. Octavius, was murdered.[6] It is significant that the Senate did not react to this, thereby implying that Octavius had well exceeded his remit. (He had been a brutal naval commander in the Macedonian war, and maybe he carried this attitude into Roman politics, and his diplomatic manners.)

Having agreed to Ptolemy VIII's new partition scheme, the Senate was not at all keen to get involved in enforcing it. An embassy was organized which would go to Egypt to announce the Senate's decision, but it was only to exercise diplomatic pressure, not use threats of violence. It was also to set about reconciling the royal brothers, though we may assume that this was purely formulaic, since it was obvious from the events of the previous decade that no such reconciliation had ever worked, nor would it ever.[7]

The envoys to Egypt separated, T. Manlius Torquatus to deliver the message to Ptolemy VI (Philometor), the other, Cn. Cornelius Merula, accompanied Ptolemy VIII (Euergetes). Ptolemy VI flatly refused to accept the Roman partition, though he took his time about responding, hoping no doubt to discover what his brother was doing, to delay him, and so confound his purpose. He clearly discovered that the envoys had no instructions to use force. Ptolemy VIII recruited a band of Greek mercenaries, and a professional commander, Damasippos, and had camped in the Rhodian *peraia* in preparation for an attempt on Cyprus and then sailed on to Side in Pamphylia. The Roman envoy who was with him, Cn. Cornelius Merula, persuaded him not to go ahead with an invasion, but to go back to Africa and wait for the result of the discussions in Egypt. Clearly the prohibition on using force applied to the Ptolemies as well as the Roman envoys, but with rather greater effect. Ptolemy VIII's ploys all failed, since Ptolemy VI, visited by T. Manlius Torquatus, did not give way, especially no doubt when he discovered that his brother had been persuaded to disband his mercenary force. Then, as he waited on the Libyan border of Philometor's kingdom, Ptolemy VIII found that in his rear the Cyrenians had staged a revolt, since they were as annoyed at his unpleasantness and tyranny as the Alexandrians had been, and just reacted even more quickly;[8] one might expect an investment by Ptolemy VI in this sudden retreat by the Cyrenians.

The revolt in Cyrene had been joined by Ptolemy Sympetesis, who had been left as governor by Ptolemy VIII.[9] Ptolemy turned away from Egypt and marched his force back towards Cyrene. He found that the Cyrenians were in occupation of 'the great slope', which is probably Sollum. Ptolemy gambled, and sent half his force – he only had a thousand men – by sea to outflank the rebels. The joint attack then succeeded. Ptolemy marched his force through the desert and met the Cyrenian army, which vastly outnumbered his; he was defeated. The next we hear of him, he was once more in office as king, and receiving Roman envoys. It must be assumed that he had negotiated his return despite, or perhaps because of, his defeat, probably promising to be less oppressive, and perhaps with the assistance of the Romans.[10]

Ptolemy's ability in this crisis of his affairs rather contradicts the reputation he is too often given of grossness and mere cruelty. He displayed a degree of military ability and an apparent diplomatic flexibility in conciliating the Cyrenian rebels, which is at odds with stories of his tyranny and gluttony. This in fact should not be too surprising. He was still a young man, in his 20s; he had had a good education, and he displayed persistence all the time in his dealings with both the Romans and his brother.

He tried again. He appealed again to the Roman Senate, which, presumably annoyed at the failure of its envoys in both Syria and Egypt – and in Cyrenaica and Cyprus – agreed to issue a decree that Ptolemy's cause had been accepted. Nothing more was done. The words of the Senate were useless without force to back them up, and no force was provided. Ptolemy VIII recruited soldiers again, but it appears that he was unsuccessful in whatever he attempted.[11] For several years he had to be content with misgoverning Cyrenaica.

Ptolemy VIII's harassment of his brother ceased for some years after the failure of 162 BC, perhaps as a result of the compromise he had evidently reached with the Cyrenians. In those years, Ptolemy VI was busy within Egypt, though his activity then is badly recorded. One action that can be seen is that during his reign there was a resumption of the sponsored building activity. This had more or less come to a halt since his grandfather's reign and the great revolt, with only a few records of building under Ptolemy V. There are in fact no more than two or three dated buildings over the previous forty or more years before Ptolemy VI's resumption of his sole rule in 163 BC. Then, after 152 BC, the king was busy with his absorbing task of attempting to recover Syria, into which project much of his resources had to be devoted (Chapter 14). It is therefore convenient, if not necessarily entirely chronologically accurate, to consolidate the building activity of Ptolemy VI into this distinct period of 163–152 BC.

Geographically Ptolemy VI's building activity is not, as in the previous century, spread throughout the country, but is concentrated in the south, the Thebaid and neighbourhood. One unusual item is the foundation of a new Jewish temple at Leontopolis in the Delta. There was a long history of Jewish migration from Judaea into Egypt, as far back as a garrison of Jewish soldiers on the southern frontier in the fifth century BC, and even, if you will, to the time of Moses. This migration had continued, even increased, during the early Ptolemaic period, when both Judaea and Egypt were under Ptolemaic rule. There was therefore a substantial Jewish community in Egypt, probably spread throughout the country, by the early second century, but with a large number of them in Alexandria, and this became substantially increased by refugees from the troubles in Judaea in the time of Antiochos IV and after.

The combination of problems in Judaea had sparked this migration. There was a conflict within the Jewish community over how much of Hellenic culture to accept, if any.[12] At least one high priest had been exiled – Onias III – and was then murdered by Antiochos IV's paid assassin.[13] And Antiochos IV himself had raided the temple in Jerusalem in 169 BC to replenish his own treasury in the midst of the Egyptian war. This was followed by a rising led by the Maccabbee brothers in reaction to both of these factors – Hellenization and royal oppression – but it was directed as much against enemies within the Jewish community in Judaea as against the Seleukid state. The result of the rising was a successful Seleukid reconquest, and this pushed even more Jews out of Judaea.[14] Egypt was the obvious place for them to go; often they could be received by relatives already in that country.

One of the casualties of the Judaean rebellion was the Jerusalem temple, which was desecrated by its use for Greek sacrifices – the 'abomination of desolation' for the author of *I Maccabees*.[15] The refugees in Egypt, deprived of access to the traditional temple, petitioned Ptolemy VI for the right to establish their own new temple in Egypt.[16] For a variety of reasons Ptolemy was pleased to agree. First, the Jews were a valued part of the Egyptian population, diligent and busy on the whole. Some of them had risen high in the government system, and the considerable concentration of them in Alexandria could provide support in that volatile city. Second, they were a connection to Syria, the lost Ptolemaic province which the dynasty constantly hoped to recover; the Jews in Judaea, conquered by the

Seleukids after their rebellion, could thus be seen as a community which would welcome a Ptolemaic reconquest. Third, by generosity to Jews in Egypt, Ptolemy might find that the Jews in Judaea would be a helpful fifth column; he might be able to use Jews in Egypt as a propaganda vehicle against the Seleukid rule in Judaea.

In the 160s BC a son of the murdered Onias III, Onias IV, arrived with an extra-large contingent of Jewish refugees seeking refuge in Egypt.[17] Onias was the petitioner, seeking permission to build a new temple, perhaps believing that he and his flock would never be able to return to Judaea, or have access to Jerusalem. They were allocated a disused pharaonic temple at Leontopolis which they could rebuild and convert into a temple to the Jewish Yahweh. (The place retains the name Tell el-Yehudiya to this day.)[18]

There was little room in Egypt for new colonial settlements, even if there had been the available populations to occupy them. The dynasty had always been reluctant to develop new urban centres on Hellenic lines, so that only two Hellenic cities (*poleis*), Alexandria and Ptolemais, both essentially government centres, had even been established – neither were typical of the run of Greek cities. Leontopolis, from its name, may have been another one, but it is not recorded as a *polis* in any legal terms, though it probably had the usual self-governing system of any Egyptian community, enhanced by the fact that it was under Jewish rule. It was probably allocated to Onias and his people because it had been damaged during the wars – the temple they were given is expressly said to have been damaged and abandoned.

There were always buildings which needed improvement and repair, like that abandoned temple, and others which needed to be built anew. In the reign of Ptolemy VI the vast majority of the building work was of this sort, and it happened in Upper Egypt. Again, it is likely that the repeated troubles in the south – the independence war in 207–185 BC, and the rebellion in 165/164 BC – were responsible for the damage to many buildings, as well as the likely abandonment of much maintenance and renovation. At the temple of Horus at Edfu, begun under Ptolemy III, work had ceased during the revolt, and only resumed under Ptolemy V. Also, Greek-style buildings dedicated to Greek deities may well have been the targets for nationalistic rebels, as in the case of the temple of Ammon – or perhaps Zeus Ammon – at Moeris in the Fayum, which was systematically destroyed and dismantled by an angry native Egyptian group; it had been damaged in the wars earlier, and then repaired, and now dismantled, and its materials removed, presumably to prevent its reconstruction.[19]

Very little was actually done at Thebes, though some repairs, particularly to gates, at the temples of Harpre and Ptah were carried out.[20] It is possible that Thebes, which was no doubt the government centre for the rebel regime, had not suffered in the way that other places did, and in fact an account dated 180 BC notes the good condition of the temple of Amun (so probably it had been taken care of by the rebels).[21] A temple for Khnum was built under Ptolemy VI.[22] Across the river at Deir el-Medina, on the other hand, the temple had a new antechamber constructed, and the temple of Hu was redecorated.[23] The other major religious centre, in a region which was held by Ptolemaic forces throughout the independence war, and which was the southern frontier of the kingdom for much of the dynasty's time, was at Elephantine and Philai. This was a little to the south at the First Cataract, a natural choke-point on the river. At Elephantine new work was done at the temple of Setat,[24] but at Philai, a favoured place for the dynasty, at the temple of Isis pylons and a hypostyle were built.[25] This was part of a long and systematically continuing project of construction; also the temples of Hathor and Arensnuphis received extra buildings – the latter a Meroitic god.[26]

Work was done and recorded at a string of places along the Nile north of Elephantine, about as far as Asyut, again implying that this was usually repairs to damage caused in the fighting in the independence war. At Antaeopolis (Qau el-Kebir) the temple of Nemti received a pronaos; at Tentyra (Dendera) a columned hall was added to the temple of Isis; at Nag el-Medamad a temple to the god Month was begun; at Esna the temple of Khnum had a naos added; at Kom Ombo also a naos was added to the double temple of Haroeris and Sobek.[27] There is a clear concentration on improving and repairing temples of the Egyptian gods, often locally important gods rather than the national ones. At the same time, some of the favourites of the dynasty received attention, notably Isis at Philai and at Tentyra. Many of these buildings were completed in Ptolemy VI's time, or were still unfinished under Ptolemy VI and were completed under his brother and successor, who could claim that distinction in his inscriptions, though no doubt he would not appreciate such a minor role in this affair.

Two places beyond or south of Philai also received attention in Ptolemy VI's reign. This was the region of northern Nubia, always a contested frontier area in which the power of Nubian and Egyptian authorities fluctuated and alternated.[28] There is evidence that Nubian kings had some influence, if not control, at Philai during the Egyptian independence war; Nubian kings had left their names on inscriptions at Philai.[29] It has been suggested that the Nubian king Adikhalamani, a contemporary of Ptolemy III and IV, took the side of the Ptolemies in the great revolt.[30] On the other hand, Pharaoh Chaonnphris at one point took refuge with the Nubians, and received Nubian assistance in returning to the fight. Both of these interpretations could be true, of course; it was normal for such kings to interfere in and influence such events, switching sides as they felt necessary. Before that, Ptolemy II had invaded the region, apparently with the main object of gaining control of the product of the gold mines in the Wadi Allaqi.

The region in question was essentially that between the First and Second Cataracts, and was divided into two sections, the Dodekaschoinos – the 'twelve-mile' section – which stretched south from Philai, and the Triakontoschoenos – the 'thirty-mile' section – south of that. The first of these sections reached from Philai to the junction of the Wadi Allaqi with the main river; the second stretched from there to the Second Cataract.

The purposes of controlling these areas were different. If access to the gold in the Wadi Allaqi was the main aim, the shorter region would suffice; there was a settlement of sorts near the source of the gold, called Berenike Panchrysos (Berenike the Golden) which was only occupied intermittently since, if the Nubians controlled the Dodeskaschoinos, they ultimately controlled the gold.[31] If control of the river and hence access towards the centre of Nubian power at Napata or Meroe were required, then the army would garrison the forts along the Triakontoschoenos.

Under Ptolemy VI there is evidence for Ptolemaic control of just the first, northernmost, of these sections. His building activity can be seen at Dabod, about 20 kilometres south of Philai, but also at el-Dakka, called Pselchis by the Greeks, which is situated where the Wadi Allaqi joins the Nile.

It would seem therefore that Ptolemy VI was initially aiming for the gold source in the Wadi Allaqi. It is possible that he could be called the founder of Berenike Panchrysos, but it is more likely that he took over whatever settlement already existed (which may in fact have been founded long before the Ptolemaic period, and occupied intermittently ever since early Pharaonic times). His Ptolemaic predecessors such as Ptolemy II and Ptolemy III had earlier exploited the sources, and Ptolemy III is most usually identified as the founder of the place. But the gold mine clearly existed much earlier than the Ptolemaic dynasty; all that the Ptolemies did was to seize, exploit, and revive the work, and then abandon the settlement, which, as with other parts of northern Nubia, was only ever occupied by anyone intermittently.

This appears to be the situation in the period of peace until 152 BC. The work in the Dodekaschoenos is recorded in an inscription, dated 157 BC, from Philai, inscribed on a stele placed in front of Ptolemy VI's pylon at the temple of Isis. It is the record of a grant of revenues from the Dodekaschoenos region to the temple, which makes it clear that by that date Ptolemy was in control of the region south of Philai. (This was in fact a confirmation of a grant which originally was made by Ptolemy II: it had to be repeatedly confirmed for centuries.)[32]

Later, between 152 and 149 BC, the *strategos* of the Thebaid, Boethos, claimed in another inscription to be the founder of two 'cities' called Philometoris and Kleopatra in the Triakontoschoenos. Boethos was certainly an important man with responsibilities for relations south of Philai in the reigns of both Ptolemy VI and Ptolemy VIII, but to claim to have 'founded' such 'cities' is as misleading as any Ptolemaic claim to have 'founded' Berenike Panchrysos – in other words, he had certainly occupied the Triakontoschoenos and had imposed garrisons in at least two places, which he had renamed in honour of the king and queen, but no more, though no doubt rebuilding was necessary.[33] Nor is it clear how long the garrisons remained in those sites. Since Ptolemy VI, soon after Boethos inscription, became involved in war in Syria, it is very likely that any speculative expansion and distant garrisons would be withdrawn. The precise sites and territories of the cities are not known, but Qasr Ibrim was probably one of them – it is the necessary basis for power by which to hold this part of the river. The suggestion that el-Dakka was the second cannot be accepted, since we know that its name was Pselchis; possibly Buhen was the second. Qasr Ibrim and Buhen were always the places seized and fortified by every Egyptian expeditionary force seeking to control the region, from the earliest pharaohs to the Ottomans; there is no clear evidence of their occupation in the second century BC, but Boethos' claim may nevertheless be accepted.

Ptolemy VIII settled into ruling Cyrenaica after his second attempt at expanding his kingdom had failed. His behaviour and his tyranny had not, it seems, changed, despite his return to the kingdom, possibly on terms. In 155 BC he claimed to have suffered an assassination attempt, and a Cyrenian may be blamed, or assumed.[34] But his reaction was such that some doubts have been raised as to the authenticity of the attempt. He used the attack to mount another attempt to expand his kingdom, and it is the measures he took to exploit the attack which have rendered his claim suspect.

He made a will, dated 155 BC, leaving his kingdom to the Roman people if he died without heirs, and had the gist of it inscribed on a stele and set up in the temple of Apollo in Cyrene.[35] Whether he publicized it further is not clear, and certainly Rome paid no attention (and Polybios, busy as ever, does not seem to have known about it).[36] So the target of the threat was probably the Cyrenians who detested him, suggesting he believed they were responsible for the attempt, and the existence of the will was a warning of what might happen if the assassins persisted. That Rome could be used as threat in this way gives some indication of the city's general unsavoury reputation among the Greeks. Ptolemy VIII also went again to Rome (next year, 154 BC) and explained that the attack had been inspired, or organized, by his brother in Egypt, so contradicting the implications of the will. In a typical theatrical gesture (worthy of his brother), he displayed the scars he had suffered.[37]

Whether the Senate believed him or not is not known, though some senators will have naïvely voiced their support, but the Senate as a whole was prepared to give him equally theatrical support for his claims. Verbal support, yes, but effective support was still not forthcoming. Five senatorial legates were provided to support him, and five quinqueremes allocated to carry them.[38] But none of these would be any use in the face of Ptolemy VI's continued obduracy. So, if force was needed the claimant must find it for himself, and finance it himself. No doubt he could draw on the accumulated revenues of Cyrenaica, but Ptolemy VI could find and fund a much bigger force to meet any attack his brother might make.

The island of Cyprus may have seemed vulnerable at that moment, for a year before (in 155 BC) the governor, Archias, had been detected in a plot to let in a force sent by Demetrios I of the Seleukid kingdom, who would then annex the island.³⁹ (It is evident that Rome's unwillingness to be involved in such matters had been fully appreciated.) Archias had probably been with Ptolemy VI when he returned from Cyprus to Alexandria in 163 BC, and will have been governor since then. He committed suicide on being discovered; some Cypriots had probably welcomed his plan – until his death, at least. So Ptolemy VIII's little expedition may have been expecting local support.

Ptolemy VIII had sailed to Cyprus and landed with his force of Greek mercenaries at Lapethos on the north coast of the island.⁴⁰ Support did not appear, if it had ever existed. Instead, an army loyal to Ptolemy VI arrived and besieged him in the town. Internationally the Cretan *koinon* of cities announced support for Ptolemy VI,⁴¹ while Demetrios I, who might have interfered, was unable to do anything after the fiasco the year before. Rome was seen to be helpless and useless, despite the five quinqueremes. Ptolemy VIII quickly saw the helplessness of his position and surrendered. His brother, who must have had enough of his brother's antics by this time, and had plenty of precedents in his and other Hellenistic royal families for drastic action against him, instead kept him in prison for a time and then let him go, supposedly as a favour to Rome. He also promised him his daughter in marriage, but not yet.⁴²

The king's forbearance at last worked. Ptolemy VIII returned to Cyrenaica and set about enjoying being king there. He gave lavish feasts, paid for out of Cyrenian revenues of course, and kept the threat of Rome inheriting his kingdom hanging over his Cyrenian subjects/opponents. His acceptance of the situation is suggested by the construction of the monster tomb for himself just outside of Ptolemais.⁴³ Ptolemy VI's problem brother seemed to have been tamed.

The real revelation from Ptolemy VIII's antics was the continuing indifference of Rome, and that city's ineffectiveness in Eastern affairs. In addition, besides waging a continuing colonial war in Spain, the republic was very probably heading towards a new Carthaginian War, for tensions over the situation in Africa were rising. So long as these difficulties existed Rome was unlikely to concern itself with the East. The message spread widely, and in the next several years this resulted in wars in Greece, Macedonia, Syria, and Asia Minor – all at first without Roman interference, since the new war with Carthage preoccupied the Romans.

Even before the African situation broke into war, that in Syria had done so. The reign of Ptolemy VI from 152 BC onwards was then dominated by what became the Seventh Syrian War. His expertise had always been in politics and intrigue, and warfare he had left to be conducted by his commanders – Boethos in Nubia, for example – which in fact was the traditional method of the dynasty ever since Ptolemy II. His dynastic dynamic, however, required him to take advantage of any Seleukid crisis to make an effort to recover Syria. A slow-burn Seleukid crisis began in 152 BC.

Chapter 14

Victory and Death: The Seventh Syrian War

The royal succession in the Hellenistic dynasties was a haphazard matter. In theory, the eldest son succeeded a ruling king: in fact, every king had to make special arrangements to ensure this. Thus Ptolemy VI in 152 BC made his eldest son, Ptolemy Eupator, joint king at about the age of fourteen.[1] A number of purposes can be discerned in this decision. One was to make the succession clear, so that when he died the next king would take office at once; the second was to exclude his brother Ptolemy VIII; the third was to train the boy to kingship; and a fourth was to be able to use him as his royal representative in times and places which he himself could not go. There was also a danger in appointing a successor – more than one king had been murdered so that a chosen successor could hurry a succession along, and there was a tradition of royal murder in all dynasties.

Nevertheless, naming a successor was standard procedure in every Hellenistic kingdom. The Seleukid kingdom's succession problems, which became especially difficult at exactly the time when Ptolemy Eupator was being promoted, were an object lesson in how not to go about arranging who would succeed. It would not surprise anyone if the sight of the succession in the Seleukid kingdom sinking gradually deeper and deeper into the mire of conflict in the late 150s BC was a fifth reason for promoting the boy Ptolemy in a formal and public manner. And, of course, the Seleukid succession dispute spilled over into the Ptolemaic family. The two were related after all, by the marriage of Ptolemy V and Kleopatra I; but this was actually largely because Ptolemy VI deliberately involved himself in it.

It may also be relevant that Rome, by far the most powerful political force in the Mediterranean despite its recent self-withdrawal from involvement in the East, was about to find itself involved once more in affairs from Spain to Africa and Greece. But this had the result of confirming the Roman indifference about matters further east, a general

Victory and Death: The Seventh Syrian War 195

indifference which had been obvious since the city's victory in the Macedonian War. It went to war in Africa, and then in Macedonia and Greece in the period 149 – 146 BC, so, with Rome thoroughly involved in the West, the kingdoms of the East did not, so they clearly thought, need to worry about any force from the West. This may be one factor in the new war which developed in Syria.

The Seleukid succession in the 160s BC had become unclear. In 175 BC Seleukos IV had died unexpectedly, probably murdered by his minister, Heliodoros, who, along with the queen, Laodike, put forward the child Antiochos, son of Seleukos IV, as the new king.[2] The process was distasteful, and the ambition of the minister, Heliodoros, may have been to marry the queen and make himself king. Certainly, to have a child as king looked to be a danger to the kingdom, and to the king himself, as was illustrated in the Ptolemaic kingdom at the same time. Seleukos IV's brother, Antiochos, rode to the rescue, killed Heliodoros, married Laodike the queen and made himself king, at first as regent for the young Antiochos. But the newly married royals soon had a son of their own, another Antiochos, who survived childhood, and Seleukos' son was killed to clear the way for his half-brother.[3]

Ignored in all this was Seleukos' other, and eldest, son, Demetrios, who had been held hostage in Rome since 176 BC, and was refused permission by the Senate to go to Syria to claim the throne.[4] His claim to the Seleukid kingship was based on being Seleukos' eldest son, so he had been denied his rights, as he might have put it, four times: first when his younger brother Antiochos was made king after Seleukos was killed; second when the Senate kept him in Italy; third when his uncle Antiochos (IV) usurped the throne, and the fourth time when Antiochos IV died in 164 BC and Antiochos' son by Laodike was made king as Antiochos V.

The Roman Senate, according to Polybios, did not want a strong king on the throne, nor did certain powerful people in Syria, who, as with Ptolemy V in Alexandria, would find their wings clipped if Demetrios succeeded. There seems no doubt also that the Senate refused Demetrios permission to leave Italy to claim the kingship as much as a means of sowing confusion in the Seleukid kingdom as to hold on to their hostage. It was exactly the sort of interfering non-intervention which had been the Senate's policy in Greece and Egypt at the time.

Demetrios, who by 164 BC was in his 20s, finally decided to take advantage of senatorial laxity and Seleukid confusion. He escaped from Italy, laying an elaborate false trail to fool the Senate (not a difficult task) and sailed to Syria.[5] On landing in Syria he publicly claimed the kingdom, and arranged that the regent Lysias was arrested, and that he and his ward, the child Antiochos V, were both then killed. He was thus king with, so it seemed, no rivals.[6]

In fact, the royal confusion in the Seleukid house was as profound as it was with the Ptolemies. Demetrios in Italy had befriended Ptolemy VI on his visit in rags in 164 BC, and he was perhaps inspired by the latter's success in regaining his throne next year, despite senatorial objections and arrogance, by way of Cyprus. It was the year after that, 162 BC, when Demetrios escaped from Italy, incidentally assisted in this by, amongst others, Ptolemy VI's envoy to Rome, Menyllos, and the historian Polybios. He was also helped by the second attempt to gain control of Cyprus by Ptolemy VIII, and which happened at more or less the same time as his escape, which seems to have foxed the Senate.

Demetrios' succession, in fact, upset others besides Rome. Antiochos IV had constructed a new international system in which he was allied, or at least very friendly, with the Attalid king in Asia Minor, who until then had been a Seleukid enemy, but who had assisted his journey from his exile in Athens to Syria. He also went out of his way to develop friendly relations with several of the Greek states, which was traditionally a Ptolemaic project. Demetrios' accession, and the killing by Demetrios' order of Antiochos IV's son, reversed that system. The Attalid king, Eumenes II until 160, and then his brother Attalos II, broke off the Seleukid alliance, leaving Demetrios internationally isolated. And then there emerged, hardly by chance, a pair of young people who claimed they were the children of Antiochos IV by a concubine. They were called Alexander and Laodike.[7]

Attalos II became king in the midst of the Roman political withdrawal from Eastern affairs. In the decade and more after the end of the Macedonian War, the Attalid state had enjoyed a period of autonomy and authority, and Eumenes II had used it to establish a near-hegemony in Asia Minor, assisted by his friendship with Antiochos IV, which had the effect of guarding his eastern flank. Attalos II had lost that connection with the arrival of Demetrios, and had no scruples about supporting the two

Seleukid pretenders. They were apparently living in his territory, possibly the children of a concubine called Antiochis, to whom Antiochos IV is known to have assigned substantial revenues generated in Kilikia.[8] He, or at least other members of his family, also later supported a pretender to the Macedonian kingdom, Andriskos, which was a direct attack on the Roman domination of the Balkans. This policy of supporting these contentious pretenders could only be pursued while Rome was looking elsewhere.

For the moment Rome was amenable to supporting the pretensions of Alexander and Laodike, though, of course, not to the extent of actually doing anything. But when they appeared in the Senate in 157 BC, sent by Attalos, they created a good impression.[9] Annoyance at Demetrios' absconding from Italy continued, so any policy which struck at Demetrios as king, and yet did not make Rome do anything active was acceptable. So Alexander and Laodike returned to Asia Minor to plan and organize an action to supplant and remove Demetrios.

An agent, Herakleides, who had been minister under Antiochos IV, had continuing contacts in Syria. His brother, Timarchos, had attempted a rebellion, but was defeated by Demetrios; Herakleides sought revenge. He could explain the political situation in the Seleukid kingdom, and identify possible sources of support.[10] Alexander (Laodike was not involved in this part) maintained his pretensions, and became well known throughout the region. Demetrios became involved in a Judaean war, and forfeited any Ptolemaic sympathy by that (there were many Jews in Egypt, constituting a valuable constituency), and by his unsuccessful attempt to seize Cyprus from Ptolemy's governor Archias. Alexander therefore had support from Attalos II, approval from Rome, and the favour of Ptolemy VI. This last was crucial, for it meant that Demetrios was even more decisively isolated. These elements of the plot were in place by the end of 153 BC.

For Alexander to attack Syria with any hope of success, however, he needed Ptolemy's armed support, and an entry port, which, without a force of his own, meant a group of supporters being already in place there. This was evidently arranged during 153/152 BC. In 152 BC Alexander landed at Ptolemais-Ake, the chief city of Palestine, probably by pre-arrangement with local supporters, though it is highly unlikely he arrived alone. He was able to count on Demetrios' governor in Palestine, Apollonios Taos, who had pledged his support earlier, obviously secretly, and had kept his position as a means of providing Alexander with an early and secure base. Demetrios will have arrived with a force of mercenaries, recruited probably in Greece and Asia Minor, and carried in ships provided by Attalos, probably by way of Attaleia, Attalos' own new port in southern Asia Minor. The combination of Alexander's recruits and Apollonios' garrisons in Palestine gave him a substantial force, and above all, a convincing extent of territory as a geographical base. Given that, he also had support from Ptolemy VI, which would have consisted of ships and finance, the former to transport his soldiers, the latter to support them.

Once ashore and installed at Ptolemais-Ake (as king), Alexander very quickly made contact with the Judaean leader Jonathan Maccabee, who offered his support, including troops, at a meeting in October 152 BC. This was one of the results of Jonathan having been attacked recently by Demetrios. In other words Demetrios had collected an inordinate number of enemies in his very short reign, who were collectively and individually annoyed enough to combine to overthrow him; his own policies had contributed to this disaster.

With a firm geographical and military base, Alexander, called 'Balas' (apparently a Syrian term), was able to recruit a larger mercenary army, as well as collecting local supporters, and, as he had done with Jonathan, he could conduct diplomatic activities. The support he received from Ptolemy VI included the promise of a wife, Ptolemy's second daughter Kleopatra Thea, who was fourteen or fifteen years of age at the time – just about the normal marriageable age for girls.

At this time, however, Ptolemy VI's dynastic plans went awry, for his eldest son Ptolemy Eupator, recently made joint king, suddenly died in the late summer of 152 BC, while Alexander was busy setting up at Ptolemais-Ake. Ptolemy VI and Kleopatra II had another son, but he was the youngest of their children and too young yet to be promoted as a new joint king. Also named Ptolemy, he has hardly been recorded anywhere.

The gift of a Ptolemaic daughter to a foreign king was highly unusual; the only other time this had happened was in 252 BC, when Ptolemy II's daughter Berenike was given to Antiochos II as part of a peace treaty; this had turned out to be disastrous, both for her and for the Seleukid kingdom. The rarity of the process was due to the value of the princesses which was placed on them by the dynastic system in Egypt, since anyone marrying a princess would acquire a claim to the throne; the answer was either not to let them get married at all, to kill them all off, or for them to marry an existing king, as Ptolemy VI had married Kleopatra II, his sister, thus keeping their eligibility within the family. This also meant that usually the Ptolemaic kings did not marry foreign princesses – Kleopatra Syra had been the first one since Ptolemy I's multiple marriages.

Ptolemy VI's eldest daughter, Kleopatra III, had thus been carefully hoarded. Kleopatra Thea, a younger daughter, had been promised to Ptolemy VIII, but Ptolemy VI broke that promise. Ptolemy VIII is not recorded as complaining, but equally he had not yet himself married. The dynastic events of 152 BC certainly improved his chances of inheriting the Ptolemaic kingship. No doubt he was keeping count – only Ptolemy VI's last son, very young, was now between him and the throne.

Alexander secured military and naval support from Ptolemy, and expanded his control through Palestine and Phoenicia – significantly, this was the former Ptolemaic province, and it seems likely that residual nostalgia for Ptolemaic rule was at work assisting him. Demetrios was unusually slow at mustering his forces and making a counter-attack; the earlier challenge, by Timarchos, had been countered relatively swiftly and successfully. It may be that a threat from Attalos II pinned Demetrios down in the north; for a time Alexander had operated as a mountain guerilla in association with a chieftain called Zenophanes in the Taurus, and this may well have been part of the northern threat against Demetrios.[11]

There were also diplomatic contacts by the rival kings, each seeking the support of Jonathan and the Maccabee army. They each offered him a variety of inducements: Alexander eventually succeeded by offering him the vacant post of high priest in Jerusalem, at which point Jonathan, having gained a concrete advantage, which Demetrios did not offer, declared for Alexander.[12] This allowed Alexander to leave Palestine in safety without fearing attack from Judaea. Jonathan was skilfully exploiting his strategic position on Alexander's flank.

In 150 BC Alexander marched north, perhaps tired of waiting, but also having received reinforcements from Ptolemy and the alliance of Jonathan. He turned out to have a reasonable gift for command, or perhaps he had been sensible enough to hire a professional commander. He met Demetrios in battle near Antioch – which means that Alexander was invading north Syria, the old Seleukid province, and he had apparently had no difficulty in marching through Phoenicia, where he was able to have coins minted at Tyre, Sidon, Berytos, and Ashkelon as well as at Ptolemais-Ake.[13] The two armies are said, in Justin, to have fought twice, in which Demetrios was victorious in the first, and Alexander in the second. When their armies met in the second (or perhaps only) battle (Justin is probably wrong) it was a typical exercise in Hellenistic warfare: Demetrios' left wing was victorious, but so was Alexander's left wing. The decision came when Demetrios was cut off from his forces and surrounded; he was unhorsed in a swamp and killed.[14]

Demetrios had clearly feared defeat, and had sent his sons, Demetrios and Antiochos, for refuge to Greece before the final battle.[15] Alexander, through his minister Ammonios, who judging by his name was probably an Egyptian Greek, one of Ptolemy's gifts to the new king, arranged the killing of Demetrios' widow, Laodike, and of the one son of Demetrios, a boy called Antigonos, whom he could capture. (Note the Macedonian dynasty names of Demetrios and Antigonus, a further indication of the closeness of the two dynasties.) So sending the other boys away had been a sensible move. Alexander was now king, and he asked for Ptolemy's daughter in marriage as promised. The marriage therefore duly cemented the alliance of Ptolemy VI and the new Seleukid king.

The origin of Alexander is disputed. It is widely assumed that he and Laodike were 'of low birth', as Holbl put it, but if so their acceptance as legitimate pretenders for the Seleukid kingship is unusual.[16] If they were not 'legitimate' by birth, the mother of the two, Antiochis, may have been a concubine, or possibly a second wife of Antiochos IV; there were no rules about monogamy in these dynasties, anymore than there were recognized decrees within which marriage was not permitted. The Roman Senate, Attalos II, and Ptolemy VI, all highly conscious of class distinctions, had accepted them as genuine Seleukids; the girl, Laodike, eventually married the Pontic King Mithradates V (and became the mother of Mithradates VI the Great). Alexander was accepted by the Seleukid Syrian population as king, if perhaps not with enthusiasm, but then they had not accepted Demetrios with enthusiasm either.

Both of these men had succeeded in making themselves kings by means of military victory, and this was an alternative legitimizing method, apart from being a king's first-born. Since so many contemporaries, albeit if all of them carrying their own agendas, accepted the two as proper Seleukid family members, perhaps it is time modern historians put aside their own class (and religious) prejudices and did the same. The disparagement of the two is typical of the propaganda to be expected – it was an argument displayed against other pretenders at the time, including Andriskos (Philip VI), Alexander Zabeinas, and Eumenes III.

Alexander's victory was a clear triumph for all of his allies, but probably mostly for Ptolemy VI, who had established a clear ascendancy over the new king, assisted by his new wife and his minister. Ptolemaic coins were copied by Seleukid mints, Kleopatra Thea soon produced a son to succeed Alexander (called Antiochos), and Ptolemaic influence was strong in the Seleukid kingdom. On the other hand, Demetrios I's final action in sending his sons for refuge in Greece (actually at Knidos, close to Rhodes) had turned out also to be decisive. By 147 BC the eldest son, Demetrios II, who was about fifteen by then, was seeking support for an expedition to recover the Seleukid throne for his line of the family. By 145 he was campaigning with an army inside Syria against the joint armies of Alexander and Ptolemy VI.

Alexander had proved to be a lazy king, at least in stories preserved in the later histories.[17] He was not popular in Antioch, and his allegiance to the Ptolemaic king and his Ptolemaic wife was demonstrated all too well by making his normal residence at Ptolemais-Ake in Palestine, which would hardly assist him in recovering his authority in Antioch. It also left him vulnerable: Ptolemais-Ake was tucked away in a corner of the kingdom, a long way from the troubled frontiers, and he was unable to supervise or counter the steady crumbling of his Iranian dominions. Ptolemy thus may have been due to return to Egypt, but with the threat of Demetrios ever present, he would obviously find it difficult to leave Syria in Alexander's inefficient hands. Demetrios II, from his base at Knidos in Karia had collected a substantial force of mercenaries and a professional commander in the Cretan Lasthenes. This force landed in Kilikia in 147 BC.[18]

Alexander, presumably leaving his wife Kleopatra Thea at Ptolemais-Ake, headed north on hearing the news. Apollonios Taos was left in command in Palestine, controlling what the author of *I Maccabees* regarded as a 'powerful force', which probably consisted of parts of the combined garrisons in the Palestinian towns, since there was no need for a large field force in Palestine, other than one to watch the situation in Judaea, where Jonathan Maccabee was still an ally of Alexander.[19] Once Alexander was in the north, however, Apollonios collected his forces together and came out in support of Demetrios, having been previously persuaded.[20] He was (like Archias in Cyprus ten years earlier), acting in the tradition of traitorous Ptolemaic governors of the region seen repeatedly over the last century.

This set off a subsidiary war in Palestine, Apollonios against Jonathan Maccabee. Apollonios gathered his forces at Jamneia, and then marched south, no doubt with the intention of blocking any intrusion which might come from Egypt. Jonathan, his way unexpectedly opened for him, came out of Judaea and attacked Joppa, crossing behind Apollonios. Joppa swiftly succumbed, presumably because Jonathan claimed to be acting for Alexander.[21] Apollonios in fact had had to choose between blocking Jonathan and the prospect of an attack out of Egypt. He was now an enemy of Alexander, and Ptolemy was Alexander's ally, as was Jonathan; either way, Apollonios was likely to be caught between them.

Apollonios was at Azotos (Ashdod), intending to block Ptolemy's advance when it came. Ptolemy had to cross Sinai, and probably had to bring forward forces from various parts of Egypt, so his arrival would take some time. Apollonios presumably believed that he could occupy Gaza in time to block the Ptolemaic army and confine it to Sinai. But he discovered that Jonathan, after taking Joppa, had turned south to tackle Apollonios at Azotos, who was thus in danger of being attacked from two sides; he turned to attack the weaker of these two enemies. The numbers of the two armies were roughly equal, with probably an advantage to the Jewish forces, but it was a battle between trained soldiers on Apollonios' side and a large but irregular army of mainly light infantry on the Jewish side. They each laid a trap for the other by holding out a reserve force. The battle lasted all day, but Apollonios' cavalry (his reserve – the Jews had no cavalry) failed to break the Jewish infantry, which then advanced, reinforced by its (infantry) reserve, which was commanded by Simon Maccabee, Jonathan's younger brother. Apollonios' cavalry had become separated from the infantry during the fight, and was apparently reduced in number, worn down by its previous failed charges. Apollonios' force was thus defeated in the last phase of the battle, and Jonathan's men captured and sacked Azotos. It seems that Apollonios did not survive.[22]

Alexander sent orders that his forces in Palestine – some had presumably held aloof from Apollonios' change of loyalty, and he would include Jonathan in this – to welcome Ptolemy's force when they arrived. He therefore knew that the Ptolemaic force was on its way (perhaps he had actually told Apollonios this). Jonathan returned with his army to Judaea, having marched as far south as Ashkelon. It appears that Gaza, the main fortress barring the advance of an army out of Egypt, was not held. Apollonios had surely reinforced it, which may have been one of the reasons his army was outnumbered in the battle, but his defeat had no doubt persuaded those of his forces who survived to lay low, or to surrender and join the apparently winning side. Ptolemy marched his army without hindrance through southern Palestine to take up residence at Ptolemais-Ake, where he was visited by Jonathan, this time without his army. Jonathan's withdrawal into Judaea had included, it seems, taking his forces from Joppa, because Ptolemy managed to install a garrison of his own in the town.[23]

Ptolemy in fact installed garrisons in many of the cities in Palestine as he marched north. Alexander rewarded Jonathan by making him a 'Kinsman', and, more practically, by handing over to him the town of Ekron (Accaron) 'and all its district', which was an important extension of his Jewish principality, perhaps in exchange for his abandonment of Joppa.[24] Ptolemy VI, meanwhile, had occupied many of the cities along the coast, carefully thereby avoiding any clash with Jonathan's forces. Then together Ptolemy and Jonathan moved northwards, dropping off garrisons in the coastal cities of Palestine and Phoenicia along the way.

This was a distinct increase in Ptolemaic influence in these areas, for this had been an area which had been part of the Ptolemaic kingdom until fifty years before, and had produced coins influenced by Ptolemaic currency during the previous year, including money minted on the weights used in Egypt.[25] Probably these coins were made in this weight so as to be available to pay the Ptolemaic soldiers, but to the Seleukid king and his supporters, it was a disturbing indication of Ptolemaic influence and probably of the ambition of Ptolemy VI. It was an advance notice of the price Ptolemy would exact for his help. Another indication of this came when Ptolemy arrived at the Eleutheros River, the old frontier between Ptolemaic and Seleukid parts of Syria; there Jonathan turned back to return to Judaea – or was sent back by Ptolemy.[26] It was, to those accustomed to interpreting such events, a clear sign that Ptolemy was serious about establishing his authority in the traditional Ptolemaic province.

There were, when Ptolemy arrived at Seleukeia-in-Pieria, three armies in north Syria. Ptolemy camped at Seleukeia, the port seized and held by his great-grandfather at the start of the Third Syrian War, another pointed gesture.[27] The choice of Seleukeia may have been deliberately nostalgic, a reminder that the Ptolemaic empire had for a generation held that city, and for a time had even controlled Seleukid Syria. By that time he had established control by way of his garrisons all along the coast from Gaza to Seleukeia, though not so much, apparently, in the inland areas; this was perhaps designed to avoid any clash with Jonathan, but also to economize on his forces. Antioch had declared for Demetrios II when he arrived, but then when Alexander came from the south, he had gained control. The attitude of the citizens clearly wavered between the contestants; Alexander had installed his man Ammonios as *strategos* of the city, and as his own minister. Demetrios II, with his mercenary army, plus no doubt supporters who had been recruited in Syria since he had arrived, was camped somewhere to the north of Antioch, and presumably also he controlled Kilikia, where he had landed.

Ptolemy's purpose in this expedition had been, so it seems and perhaps so he had announced, to support his son-in-law in securing control of his kingdom against invaders and rebels, or at least the Syrian part of it; there seems to have been no Ptolemaic intention of mounting an expedition into the East, where territory was currently being lost to the Parthians. By planting Ptolemaic garrisons along the coast, Ptolemy had clearly gone beyond any such minimal assistance to Alexander, and this had raised suspicions that he was aiming to revive the Ptolemaic empire in Syria (which he surely was). Then, while in Seleukeia, Ptolemy suddenly announced that he had survived an assassination attempt when he had been at Ptolemais-Ake; he blamed Ammonios, Alexander's minister who was in control of Antioch, for the deed.[28]

The authenticity of this assassination attempt is by no means certain. It appears in only one surviving source, Josephus, and it is completely ignored by the author of *I Maccabees*. These are the only two extant sources. Nor is it in Polybios or Diodoros, though their accounts are very scrappy at this point. Ptolemy may have been taking a leaf out of his brother's book, who had used a (supposed) assassination attempt ten years before as an excuse to demand an extension of his own territory, and then to make the will in which he threatened to leave his kingdom to Rome. One item which certainly suggests doubt in this new assassination story is that Ptolemy waited until he was at Seleukeia before announcing it, and

Jonathan Maccabee seems to have known nothing of it though he was in Ptolemais-Ake at the time of the supposed attempt. It is best to assume that it did not happen and that Ptolemy VI invented it for purposes of his own, one of which was to get rid of Ammonios.

Ptolemy demanded that Ammonios be handed over to him for punishment. And here is another curious element in this incident, for, judging by his name, Ammonios was probably an Egyptian Greek, possibly handed over to Alexander by Ptolemy as a skilled administrator (the government system in the former Ptolemaic province still operated on Ptolemaic lines, and Ammonios was perhaps familiar with the system and able to make it work); he may also have been intended as a Ptolemaic agent within the Seleukid high administration. So perhaps Ptolemy had perceived that Ammonios had transferred his allegiance, for whatever reason, to Alexander.

Alexander refused to hand Ammonios over, which was the honourable stance to take;[29] to have acceded to Ptolemy's demand might have indicated Alexander's own complicity in the assassination attempt, and it would certainly soon lead to Ammonios' killing. This contretemps between Ptolemy and Alexander was not the real quarrel between them, however, for Ptolemy on being refused Ammonios, announced that he was dissolving his daughter's marriage to Alexander and was transferring her to Demetrios.[30] The accusation against Ammonios was therefore probably either a means of forcing a break with Alexander, or, if he agreed to betray him, to reinforce Ptolemy's dominance over his son-in-law.

This was an extraordinary decision, overriding whatever feelings his daughter had for her husband, if any, and proposing to hand her over to a new husband, a teenage boy she had never met. The sudden announcement about delivering her to Demetrios also implies that Ptolemy had been in negotiations with Demetrios for some time before his announcement – Kleopatra may have been part of the price that Ptolemy had to pay for the agreement, and there would be no point in announcing the change if Demetrios did not know about it and had agreed to it.

Here is where Ptolemy's purpose in intervening in this campaign becomes clearer. His own price for betraying Alexander and handing his daughter over to her new husband was the old Ptolemaic province of Koile Syria, which, of course, he had already secured with his own forces. It is a sign of Demetrios' essential weakness that he agreed to this. Demetrios had enough strength to insist on payment for ceding the old province, but Ptolemy was clearly in overall control. The catch was that Alexander had to be beaten in battle before this new agreement could be implemented.

Alexander had already, before any of these negotiations and betrayals occurred, sent his son by Kleopatra, unsurprisingly called Antiochos, to foster care with a friendly Arab chieftain called Diokles/Zabdiel.[31] Alexander had evidently either heard of the negotiations, or had been generally suspicious, which after the accusation against Ammonios, would not be surprising. Kleopatra had probably been left at Ptolemais-Ake when Alexander headed north to confront Demetrios, and there she fell under her father's control, but it is clear that Alexander had taken the child with him; it does not seem that this married couple had much trust in each other, though it is difficult to estimate Kleopatra's feelings in all this; she was being used as a commodity, and she cannot have enjoyed these events. Alexander's action was, of course, copied from Demetrios I's decision to send Demetrios II and his brother to Greece when Alexander invaded.

Ptolemy had, therefore, by his clandestine campaigning and his diplomatic double-dealing, succeeded in recovering the territory which his father and grandfather had lost. And he had done so without fighting – Jonathan and Apollonios, Alexander and Demetrios had fought each other, Ptolemy had not yet had to fight anyone. Perhaps he judged that whatever he had lost in his diplomatic dealings and in the terms of the negotiation, he had made up for in not causing military casualties. The problem was that defeat in battle tended to impose a certain finality on the peace terms which followed, whereas double-dealing was more likely to produce anger in those who were betrayed. No doubt Demetrios was now considered to be under the sway of his new father-in-law. Alexander campaigned into the north, probably seeking to defeat Demetrios before turning to deal with Ptolemy. He penetrated into Kilikia, where Demetrios had originally landed, which suggests that he was being successful.[32]

It would make sense to attack one enemy at a time. Alexander could also portray Ptolemy as an oath-breaker, and Demetrios as a dupe and a traitor to his Seleukid family. And perhaps more to the point for the Seleukid subjects, the civil war between Alexander and Demetrios had become transformed into a new Seleukid-Ptolemaic War, the Seventh Syrian War, which would be a familiar, and perhaps more comfortable, condition for many in Syria. There will have been men in north Syria who were veterans of Antiochos IV's Egyptian campaigns; they would not be pleased to see the gains of that successful war, and the previous one by Antiochos III, handed back so easily, and without a fight.

Ptolemy moved on Antioch while Alexander was away on campaign. He was only a short day's march from the city when in Seleukeia, and, given the confusion in north Syria over 'who was king, who was not king?', he was able to get control of the city without difficulty.[33] Ammonios, reasonably enough, fled as he arrived, but made the mistake of doing so disguised in women's clothing, and was detected and killed.[34] He was thus unable to deny in public what he had denied in private, and proclaim that he had nothing to do with the assassination accusation. Ptolemy, or perhaps technically it was Demetrios, installed two men to replace Ammonios, Diodotos of Kasiana, a Syrian Greek, and Hierax, an Egyptian Greek, evidently a carefully chosen pair to imply an alliance.[35]

Ptolemy by this time had gained control, either through his own garrisons, or through his ally Jonathan Maccabee, and now by his alliance with Demetrios, of the whole Ptolemaic province of Koile Syria, plus Seleukeia and Antioch. Now that he held Antioch, this included the political heartland of the Seleukid empire, which was in the cities of Seleukid Syria. He was in much the same situation as Ptolemy III in 246 BC, just a century before. But Ptolemy VI's ambition went even higher than his great-grandfather, and having gained control of the administrative centre of the Seleukid state, he put the next stage of his plan into effect, though it is probable that it was only as a result of the success so far that he now went further than occupation and annexation.

Ptolemy had installed the two men, Diodotos and Hierax, as governors of the city, though they were technically agents of Demetrios. Their joint control of the city in effect prepared the way for the next step taken by Ptolemy. They themselves, in theory still acting as agents of Demetrios, put forward the suggestion that Ptolemy should accept the kingship of the Seleukid state in addition to his own kingdom. So much for Ptolemy's alliance with his son-in-law. This, of course, was not a spontaneous action, nor was it merely a suggestion, but was a carefully planned and choreographed *coup d'état*, and the suggestion had been Ptolemy's. Diodotos and Hierax even gathered a crowd of Antiochenes to express their support for the suggestion.

There was precedent for this process. Over a century and a half earlier, Antigonos I was hailed as king, a process which was similarly carefully prepared and choreographed, and followed a victory. In fact, it had taken place in almost exactly the same place as Ptolemy VI's new proclamation, at the entrance to Antigonos' new palace in his new city of Antigoneia, which had later been dismantled by Seleukos I after his own victory over Antigonos, and Antioch was then built in its stead. More immediately, the same sort of ceremony had been staged by Sosibios and Agathokles in 204 BC on the death of Ptolemy IV, a ceremony as stage-managed and phoney as that of Antigonos I. It was also enacted more than once in the Macedonian kingdom, but there at least they gathered the men of the army in some numbers for the ceremony. In addition, it was traditional for new kings to feign reluctance (as it was to be for usurping Roman emperors), and to require to be persuaded by a political assembly of sorts, though nobody was ever fooled by this. Ptolemy, no doubt with a ritual display of reluctance, complied with the generous suggestion of his subjects.[36]

He was hailed as 'King of Egypt and King of Asia', and he wore two diadems to signify this, while documents began to use a new dating formula, 'the 36th year which is also the first' – thirty-six years as king of Egypt, and the first as king in Asia.[37] This was the second time that Ptolemy VI's dating had been adjusted in this way, for in 168 BC it had been 'the twelfth year which is also the first', after the retreat of Antiochos IV from Egypt and the reassembly of the joint kingships of Ptolemy, Ptolemy VIII and Kleopatra II.[38] The use of the new dating formula suggests that a reasonable length of time elapsed while Ptolemy acted as double-king; it also suggests he was aiming at a permanent union of the two kingdoms.

This was a policy – uniting the two surviving Hellenistic empires – which might have occurred to Ptolemy III when he had captured North Syria a century before, and to Antiochos IV when he had overrun most of Egypt a quarter of a century before, but both of these kings were still being actively opposed by their opponents and were fairly quickly driven out of their conquests. Their pretensions were thus foiled, the first by rapid military defeat – he had lost control of Antioch within a few months – the second by Rome, in the person of Popilius Laenas, and by his own repeated failure to capture the city of Alexandria. Perhaps Ptolemy VI felt he could bring the Seleukid population into accepting him as their king – he was the son of a Seleukid princess, after all, and the succession in the Seleukid house had been thoroughly scrambled since 150 BC, and he might be able to put forward a reasonable claim. Perhaps Ptolemy had become so confident after his easy successes so far that he felt he could carry it off. Perhaps, by making the gesture of uniting the two empires by proclamation, he felt that he had actually achieved it.[39]

There were, of course, immediate problems, objections, and difficulties which stood as obstacles. In the immediate situation he still faced his two rival claimants, both in arms, and neither willing to accept less than a crown and their independence of action. Demetrios, when he heard of Ptolemy's self-proclamation as king of 'Asia', surely felt as betrayed as Alexander had been; he was demoted at least, or possibly deposed. Having succeeded so far by diplomatic means – he had not had to fight once on this campaign – Ptolemy will have hoped to achieve his further goals by negotiation and conciliation. But there were wider objections to his claims than simply the two rivals who were his immediate problem. It is doubtful, to pick out just one detail, if Jonathan Maccabee was pleased to find that his overlord would now be able to deploy so much extra military manpower; the last three Seleukid kings had been his and his family's active opponents; it would not be surprising to him if Ptolemy became his opponent also; he had, after all, betrayed his successive sons-in-law, and if he succeeded in his aim of ruling all Syria, Jonathan was likely to be his next victim. Then the Seleukid citizens could well object also, not having been consulted in any serious way; after all, it was the custom in Macedonian monarchies to convene the army or at least a large section of it to give assent to a royal accession, particularly a disputed succession; the selected crowd shouting support in this way was even less convincing than usual. If the population did object, Ptolemy might well have to contemplate the slow conquest of the Seleukid empire, city by city, and all those cities were fortified, held by garrisons, and contained trained military personnel. These were all issues which he had probably not even considered so far. And there was one other problem he had not faced either.

This was the problem, the overwhelming problem, of what would be Rome's reaction. The complicated events in Syria between 152 and 145 BC occurred at the same time as the next group of Roman wars – the Third Punic War (149–146 BC), the Macedonian and Greek Wars (148–146 BC) – which resulted in the physical destruction of the ancient and wealthy cities of Carthage and Corinth, the annexation of the Carthaginian territory and Macedon to the Roman Republic, and the definitive Roman domination of Greece. After these wars had been settled, only the continuing fighting in Spain could distract the Roman Senate from events in the East. And there had been a full year in which these events could be assimilated, and the implications absorbed. Further, Roman territory now reached as far east as the Hellespont and the Aegean Sea, and Rome had a large fleet. Roman behaviour in those wars had been a step up in savagery even from that which had taken place in Greece and Macedon twenty years before.

In fact, by this time, the only hope for the continued independence of the Greek East lay in Roman forbearance, or in Greek unity. Unity of the two great monarchies might produce sufficient strength to deter further Roman aggression eastwards. But it was unlikely that Rome would forbear from intervening in the large, rich, and military empires of the Seleukids and Ptolemies, if these were formed into a single state; such a combination of wealth and power might be sufficiently deterring, even to Rome. In the fighting in Macedon in 148 BC, a single Macedonian force under a pretender (Andriskos, calling himself Philip VI) who had never been any more than a private soldier, had defeated a Roman legion under a praetor, who had been killed.[40] Consider how difficult it would be to achieve a Roman victory if their armies were faced by the combined forces of the whole East; in the Battle of Raphia, sixty years before, the combined total of the two armies had been 140,000 men.[41] (And that battle had been fought at about the same time as the Roman defeat at Cannae.)

Ptolemy, wearing his two diadems, and occupying the city of Antioch, may not have considered this problem at first, though this is unlikely, but it would have soon been brought to his attention, once the Romans had settled affairs in Macedonia and Greece and Africa. He could hardly avoid considering Roman reactions, given his contacts with Rome in the past, when even the possibility of unification of no more than the Ptolemaic territories had already provoked repeated Roman interference. How much more determined the Senate would be to disrupt his plans if the prospect was the actual unification of the whole Eastern territories.[42]

This, of all the problems Ptolemy's latest plan had produced, was the real stopper. He attempted to solve it by renouncing the Seleukid kingship. He convened a new assembly of Antiochenes as a substitute for a general assembly of the kingdom or of the army, and announced his renunciation; then he persuaded them to accept Demetrios, his new son-in-law, as king.[43] No doubt the assembly was as carefully selected as the earlier one organized by Diodotos and Hierax, and no doubt also there were armed soldiers supervising the meeting (as Demetrios Poliorketes, the son of Antigonos I, had done in Athens in the same year that his father made himself king).

There is no evidence, other than this phoney assembly, that the people of Antioch were at all enthusiastic about Demetrios, but they clearly had no choice, though they may well have been relieved not to have become Ptolemaic subjects in this way. All the evidence is that they had come to prefer Alexander as their king, but in all cases their preferences were not seriously considered. And when it became clear that the new peace treaty concluded by Ptolemy and his protege Demetrios II, the new Seleukid king, included the cession to the former of Koile Syria, there can be no doubt that Demetrios' approval rating in the city, and in the Seleukid kingdom generally, sank to zero.

Ptolemy's new settlement in the end did not last for very long. Alexander had gathered a considerable army and came to challenge the new allies. At last Ptolemy was compelled to fight for his all-too-easily-achieved conquests. The three kings met in battle a little to the north of Antioch, at the River Oenoparos. The combined armies of Ptolemy and Demetrios, with the advantage of professional commanders such as Lasthenes, defeated Alexander's force, which had only recently been recruited.[44] Alexander himself escaped from the battlefield, aiming to take refuge with Diokles/Zabdiel, his son's fosterer, but he was murdered by two of his officers on the way.[45] They had accepted the offer of a pardon from Demetrios in exchange for murdering Alexander. They cut off his head and sent it to Ptolemy (not, apparently, to Demetrios).

Ptolemy had also survived the battle, but only briefly. He had been thrown from his horse, possibly at the trumpeting of an elephant – elephants had probably been discontinued in use in the Ptolemaic army, so Egyptian horses had not been trained to be accustomed to them. Ptolemy hit his head as he fell and his skull was fractured; the doctors could do nothing. The severed head of Alexander was shown to him before he died, and he is said to have expressed satisfaction.[46] Therefore Demetrios was unexpectedly a king without a challenger, and the Ptolemaic kingdom was without a king, and Ptolemy's son was only a child. Trouble ahead. At least Rome did not have to do anything.

Conclusion

Ptolemy VI's death led to the unravelling of all his elaborate schemes for Syria. His armies and garrisons were recalled to Egypt, and Demetrios II reoccupied Koile Syria for the Seleukids, gaining prestige by doing nothing, very much in Ptolemy's mode. In Egypt Ptolemy was succeeded at first by his son, the child Ptolemy VII, with Kleopatra II as regent, but Ptolemy VIII arrived from Cyrenaica (by way of Cyprus), and was summoned by the Alexandrians to take power. The times were dangerous and a capable ruler was needed, even one rejected by those same Alexandrians in the past. He swiftly disposed of the king, and married Kleopatra, his elder sister. Everything Ptolemy VI had worked for – his own posterity to inherit, foiling his brother, recovering Koile Syria – was lost or reversed. And yet he is described by Polybios in admiring terms, and he has been followed in this by modern historians.

Yet while he was king he could be said to have been 'successful', though it was all founded on sand, as became clear as soon as he died. He may have been admirable as a person, but this was clearly not enough to succeed as a king. No Ptolemaic ruler since Ptolemy III could be said to have been successful, except in beating down a major rebellion. And even that took twenty years.

Of course, Ptolemy VI's failure was not entirely his own fault; it was a result of the whole Ptolemaic system, excessively centralized and autocratic, which therefore became vulnerable to disturbances at the top, by infant inheritances, by vicious court intrigues, by army coups which only encouraged later army coups. Excessive taxation and wasteful expenditure (Ptolemy IV's ship, the huge 'forty', is a prime example, but this started with Ptolemy I's palace in Alexandria) brought peasant enmity, desertion, and rebellions.

Ptolemy III had brought the kingdom to a pitch of power, if it is in terms of possession of territory that power is to be judged. But, as with his father, the possession of distant lands was illusory. Overstretch is the precise term, and is illustrated by the hollowing out of the empire outside Egypt in the reign of Ptolemy IV. The victory at Raphia in 217 BC was, in retrospect, a Ptolemaic disaster, since it clearly gave the Ptolemaic government a false sense of confidence in its resources and strength which it could not support. The contrast with the reaction in the Seleukid empire is instructive: Antiochos III set about recovering lost territories in Asia Minor and the far East and came back after fifteen years to renew the struggle with the Ptolemies, this time victoriously. The fifty years after the Raphia victory produced, for the Ptolemies, complacency, followed by rebellion, defeat, loss of territory and, to cap it all, much dynastic confusion, murders and usurpations.

This last is unusual in the Ptolemies, but the kingdom, like that of the Seleukids and the Attalids, existed only as a dynastic construct. The dynasty was not, and never became, Egyptian. The Attalids, by contrast, were clearly natives of Asia Minor; the Seleukids established a network of cities, inhabited by Greeks and Macedonians and Syrians, and celebrated and conciliated their economic powerhouse in Babylonia so that its people remained loyal throughout Seleukid rule. But the Ptolemies seem to have been scared of Egypt and Egyptians. They made gestures towards the conciliation of elements of the Egyptian population, notably the priests in particular, by which they prised apart the relationship between priests and peasants, but essentially they relied on the Greek population they had imported and rewarded with grants of land. This produced a social division which was a source of weakness from the start.

This was the origin of the great rebellion of 207–185 BC, and of further rebellions in the following century. But the disaffection and rebelliousness of the Egyptian 'native' population had not established a solidarity amongst the outnumbered Greeks, despite, or perhaps because, they lived lives separate from the Egyptians. The fact that there were no more than two Greek cities, perhaps three, in the country meant that the Greeks were concentrated in Alexandria, a non-Egyptian city, and in military settlements such as the Fayum, and in garrisons, perpetuating and emphasizing the social division of the whole population.

The divisions in the dynasty, the weaknesses of the kings and regents and ministers, will certainly have reduced the respect of both Greeks and Egyptians for their rulers. Usurpation may have been rare in the first Ptolemaic century, but it continually threatened until resort was had to the Ottoman solution, of killing off unwanted brothers as the first task of a new king. But this produced further instability. From 220 BC onwards, no king (or queen) could act decisively, even if they had the ability to do so, because there were too many special interests involved – Greeks, Egyptian priests, the army, the *machimoi*, the farmers, the bureaucrats, the landowners, the wealthy aristocracy – most of whom were either unenthusiastic or hostile. And so a decisive Ptolemy became a threat, as with Ptolemy V, murdered by his aristocrats when he proposed a means of recovering the lost Syrian province, which had become the essential policy goal of the dynasty. The antics of Ptolemy VI and Ptolemy VIII were further illustrations of the inefficient dynasty.

When Ptolemy VI, after an effective reign of no more than ten years, having been hampered in the 160s BC by his brother, attempted an intrigue-ridden campaign to recover Syria, the whole process was unconvincing, founded on nothing but an erratic diplomacy and dishonoured promises – he serially betrayed all his allies – and resulted once more in a new imperial overstretch, based on fewer resources than Ptolemy III and Ptolemy IV had disposed, and this time in a royal death on the battlefield. Hence his empire collapsed as soon as he was dead. It was to be the last serious imperial recovery by the dynasty, and it had lasted only half a decade.

Appendix I

The Ptolemaic Descent

```
Ptolemy III = Berenike II
(246 - 222) |  (M 221)
     ┌───────────┼────────────┬────────────┐
Arsinoe III = Ptolemy IV    Magas      Lysimachos
(M 204)   |   (221 - 204)   (M 204)     (M 204)
          |
        Ptolemy V  =  Kleopatra I
       (204 - 180, M) | (Regent 180 - 176
            ┌─────────┴─────┬──────────────┐
       Ptolemy VI = Kleopatra II      Ptolemy VIII
        (180 - 164, |                  (164 - 163,
        163 - 145, K)                   145 - 116)
                   |               (Cyrenaica 163 - 116)
            ┌──────┴──────┐
         Ptolemy       Ptolemy VII
         (D 152)        (M 145)
```

D - Died
K - Killed in battle
M - Murdered

Bibliography

Abbreviations
Austin – M.M. Austin, *The Hellenistic World from Alexander to the Roman Conquest*, 2nd ed.
FGrH – *Die Fragmente der griechischen Historiker*
I. Crete – *Inscriptiones Cretae*
IG – *Inscriptiones Graecae*
JEA – *Journal of Egyptian Archaeology*
OGIS – *Orientis graeci Inscriptiones selectae*
Ptol. Pros. – *Ptolemaica Prosopographia*
SEG – *Supplementum Epigraphicum Graecum*
ZPE – *Zeitshcrift fur Papyrologie und Eipgraphik*

Bibliography
Abel, Karlhans 'Det Tod des Ptolemaios IV Philopator bei Polybios; Eine historisch-textgeschichte Studie', *Hermes*, 95 (1967), pp 72–90.
Alliott, M, 'La fin de la resistance Egyptienne dans le Sud sous Epiphane', *REA* (1952), pp 18–26.
Amantini, Luigi Santi 'Tolemei VI Filometore re di Siria?', *Istituto Lombardo (Rend. Lett.) Storia Antico*, 108 (1974), pp 511–529.
Aymard, A, *Les Assemblees de la confederatin achaienne* (Paris, 1938).
Aymard, A. 'Autour de l'avenement d'Antiochos IV', *Historia*, 2 (1993), pp 49–73.
Bagnall, R.S, 'Archagathas son of Agathokles, *epistates* of Libya', *Philologos*, 120 (1976), pp 195–209.
Bagnall, R.S, *The Administration of the Ptolemaic Possessions outside Egypt* (Leiden, 1976).
Bar-Kochva, B, *The Seleukid Army, Organisation and Tactics in the Great Campaigns* (Cambridge, 1970), pp 124–127.
Bennett, C, 'Theoxena', internet article.
Bennett, C, 'The Children of Ptolemy III and the date of the Exedra of Thermos', *ZPE*, 138 (2002), pp 141–145.
Bernard, M, *La Delta egyptien apres les textes grecs: I, les confines libyques* (Cairo, 1970).
Billows, Richard A, *Kings and Colonists, Aspects of Macedonian Imperialism* (Leiden, 1995).
Bowersock, G.W, *The Throne of Adulis* (Oxford, 2013).
Bulow-Jacobsen, A, 'O. Haun 6, a new look at the original', *ZPE*, 36 (1979), pp 91–96.
Burstein, S.M (trans. and ed), *Agatharchides, On the Erythraean Sea* (Hakluyt Society, 1989).
Casanova, G, 'Una datazione tardiva de Tolomeo IV e it banchiere Portos de Crocodilopolis', *Aegyptus*, 68 (1988), pp 13–18.
Cauville, S, and D. Devonchelle, 'Le temple d'Edfou, etappes de la construction, nouvelle donnees historique', *Revue Egyptien*, 35 (1984), pp 31–55 and 36.
Chapman, Dee L, *Berenike II and the Golden Age of Alexandria* (Oxford, 2014).
Chauveux, M, 'Un Ete 145', *BIFAO*, 90 (1990), pp 135–168, and 91, 1991, 129–134.
Christensen, Thorolf, Dorothy J. Thomson and Katelijn Vandorpe, *Land and Taxes in Ptolemaic Egypt, an Edition, Translation and Commentary for the Edfu Land Survey* (Cambridge, 2017).

Clarysse, Willy 'The Great Revolt of the Egyptians (204–186 BCE)' on the Berkeley website, 2004.
Clarysse, W. and G. Van der Veken, *Eponymous Priests of Ptolemaic Egypt* (Leiden, 1983).
Clarysse, W. 'Ptolemaic Papyri from Lycopolis', *Actes du XVe Congres Internationale de Papyrologie* (Brussels, 1979), pp 101–106.
Clarysse, Willy, 'The Ptolemies visiting the Egyptian Chora', in L. Mooren (ed), *Politics, Administration, and Society in the Hellenistic and Roman World, Studia Hellenistica,* 36 (Leuven, 2000), pp 29–50.
Clarysse, W, 'Hakoris, an Egyptian Nobleman and his Family', *Ancient History*, 22 (1991), pp 235–243.
Cohen, G.M, *The Hellenistic Settlements in Syria, the Red Sea Basin and North Africa* (Berkeley and Los Angeles, 2006).
Daressy, G, 'Un decret de l'an XXIII de Ptolemee Epiphane', *Receuil de Travaux relatifs a la philologie et a l'archeologie egyptienne et assyrien*, 32 (1911), pp 1–8 and 38 (1916/1917), pp 175–179.
Debevoise, N, *A Political History of Parthia* (Chicago, 1938).
de Witt, C, *Les Inscriptions du temple d'Opet a Karnak* (Brussels, 1958–1968).
Duryat, F, *Arados hellenistique, Etude historique et Monetaire* (Beirut, 2005).
Farid, Adel, 'The Stela of Andikhalamani found at Philai', *Mitteilungern Deutschen Archeologischen Instituts, Ableitung Kairo*, 34 (1978), pp 53–56.
Feyel, M, *Continuation a l'epigraphie beotienne* (Le Puy, 1942).
Fischer-Bovet, Christelle, *Army and Society in Ptolemaic Egypt* (Cambridge, 2014).
Fraser, P.M, *Ptolemaic Alexandria* (Oxford, 1972).
Fraser, P.M, *Samothrace* II.1 (Oxford, 1960).
Gera, D, 'Ptolemy son of Thraseas and the Fifth Syrian War', *Ancient Society*, 18 (1987), pp 63–73.
Goudriaan, K, *Ethnicity in Ptolemaic Egypt* (Amsterdam, 1988).
Grainger, John D, *Hellenistic Phoenicia* (Oxford, 1991).
Grainger, John D, *The League of the Aitolians* (Leiden, 1999).
Grainger, John D, *The Syrian Wars* (Leiden, 2010).
Grainger, John D, *The Roman War of Antiochos the Great* (Leiden, 2001).
Grainger, John D, 'The Campaign of C. Manlius Vulso in Asia Minor', *Anatolian Studies*, 45 (1995, 23–42).
Grainger, John D, *Diplomacy in the Hellenistic World* (London, 2020).
Grainger, John D, *The Wars of the Maccabees* (Barnsley 2012).
Green, Peter (ed. and trans.), Apollonius of Rhodes, *Argonautica* (Berkeley and Los Angeles, 1997).
Gruen, E.S, *The Hellenistic World and the Rise of Rome* (Berkeley and Los Angeles, 1984).
Habicht, C, 'Bemerkungen zur P. Haun 6', *ZPE*, 39 (1980), pp 1–5.
Habicht, Christian, *Studien zur Geschichte Athens in Hellenistische Zeit* (Gottingen, 1982).
Habicht, Christian, *Athens from Alexander to Anthony* (Cambridge MA, 1999).
Haery, G, 'A Short Architectural History of Philae', *BIFAO*, 86 (1985), pp 197–233.
Hammond, N.G.L, and F.W. Walbank, *A History of Macedonia*, vol. 3 (Oxford, 1988).
Hanson, A, and P.J. Sijperstein, 'The Dossier of Euphron: three Ptolemaic letters from the Princeton University Collection', *Ancient History* 20 (1989), pp 133–147.
Hayward, Robert, 'The Jewish Temple at Leontopolis: A Reconsideration', *Journal of Jewish Studies*, 33 (1982), pp 429–443.
Hendrick, Philip, *Libya Architectural Guide, Cyrenaica* (London, 2013).
Hengel, M, *Judaism and Hellenism* (London, 1980).
Hill, Sir George, *History of Cyprus* (Cambridge, 1940), Vol. I.

Holleaux, M. 'Etudes d'Histoire Hellenistique; la chronologie de la cinquieme Guerre de Syrie', *Klio*, 8 (1908), pp 267–280.
Houghton, A, and C. Lorber, *Seleukid Coins, A Comprehensive Catalogue*, Part I, *Seleucus I through Antiochus III*, 2 vols (New York, 2002).
Huss, W, 'Eine Revolt de Aegypter in der Zeit der 3 Syrische Krieg', *Aegyptus*, 58 (1976), pp 151–156.
Huss, W, 'Eine ptolemaische Expedition nach Kleinasien', *Ancient Society*, 8 (1977), pp 187–193.
Jacob, Christian, and Francois de Polignac, *Alexandria third century BC* (Alexandria, 2014).
Johstono, Paul A, *The Army of Ptolemaic Egypt, 323–304 BC, an Institutional and Operational History* (Barnsley, 2020).
Jones, C.P, and C. Habicht, 'A Hellenistic Inscription from Arsinoe in Cilicia', *Phoenix*, 43 (1989), pp 317–345.
Lampela, Anssi *Rome and the Ptolemies of Egypt, The Development of their Political Relations, 273–80 BC* (Helsinki, 1998).
Lanciers, E, 'Die Vergottlichung und die Ehe des Ptolemaios IV und Arsinoe III', *Arch AE*, 34 (1988), pp 405–433.
Lanciers, E, 'Die Agyptische Tempelbauten zur Zeit des Ptolemaios Epiphanes (204–180 B.C,)' *Mitteilungern Deutschen Archeologischen Instituts, Ableitung Kairo*, 53 (1986), pp 81–99 and 43 (1987), pp 173–182.
Landau, Y.H, 'A Greek Inscription found near Hefzibah', *Israel Exploration Journal*, 16 (1966), pp 54–70.
Ma, John, *Antiochos III and the Cities of Western Asia Minor* (Oxford, 1999).
Maas, P, 'Sosibios als pseudipetropos ses Ptolemaios Epiphanes', *Memoire Henri Gregoire*, pp 443–448.
McGing, Brian C, 'Revolt Egyptian style: internal opposition to Ptolemaic Rule', *Archiv fur Papyrusforschung* 43 (1987), pp 273–314;
Mooren, L. 'The Governors General of the Thebais in the Second Century A.D.', *Ancient Society*, 4 (1973), pp 115–132, and 5 (1974), pp 137–152.
Morgan, W. Gwyn 'The Perils of Schematism: Polybius, Antiochus Epiphanes, and the "Day of Eleusis"', *Historia*, 39 (1990), pp 37–76.
Morkholm, O, 'Eulaeus and Lenaeus', *Classica at Medievalia*, 22 (1961), pp 32–45.
Morkholm, O, *Antiochos IV of Syria* (Copenhagen, 1966).
Morkholm, O, 'The Accession of Antiochos IV of Syria', *ASMNM*, 11 (1964), pp 63–70.
Newell, E.T, *Late Seleucid Mints at Ptolemais-Ake and Damascus* (New York, 1939).
Ogden, D, *Polygamy, Prostitution and Death* (London, 1999).
Oikonomides, A.N, 'Opron and the sea battle off Andros, a note in Ptolemaic History and Prosopography', *ZPE* 56 (1984), pp 151–152.
Paltiel, E, 'Antiochos Epiphanes and Roman *Politics*', *Latomus*, 41 (1982), pp 229–254.
Peremans, W. 'Sur le domestic seditio de Justin XXVII.1.9', *Antiquite Classique*, 50 (1981), pp 28–36.
Pestman, P.W, *Chronologie egyptiens d'apres les textes demotiques* (Leiden, 1967).
Pestman, P.W, 'Haronnophris and Chaonnophris, two Indigenous Pharaohs in Ptolemaic Egypt' in S.P. Vleeming (ed), *Hundred-Gated Thebes* (Leuven, 1995), pp 101–138.
Pestman, P.W, et al, *Receuil des textes demotique et bilingue* (Leiden, 1977).
Piejko, F. 'Episodes from the Third Syrian War in a Gurob Papyrus, 246 BC', *Archiv fur Papyrusforschungen*, 36 (1990), pp 13–27.
Porter, B. and R.L.B. Moss, *Topographical Bibliography of Ancient Egyptian Hieroglyphic Texts* (Oxford, 1927–1952).
Ray, J.D, *The Archive of Hor* (Leiden, 1976).

Bibliography 219

Ray, J.D. 'Observations on the Archive of Hor', *Journal of Egyptian Archaeology*, 64, (1978), pp 113–120.
Reekmans, Tony, 'Economic and Social Repercussions of the Ptolemaic Copper Inflation', *Chronique d'Egypte*, 24 (1949), pp 324–342.
Reger, Gary 'The Political History of the Kyklades, 260–200 BC', *Historia*, 54 (1994), pp 32–69.
Roberts, M. and B. Bennett, *Twilight of the Hellenistic World* (Barnsley, 2012).
Roztovtzeff, M.I, *Social and Economic History of the Hellenistic World*, vol. II (Oxford, 1941).
Sachs A.J, and H. Hunger, *Astronomical Diaries and related texts from Babylonia*, Vol 1 (Vienna, 1988).
Salame-Sarkis, Hassan 'Inscription au Nom de Ptolemee IV Philopator trouvee dans le Nord de la Beqa', *Berytus*, 34 (1986), pp 207–209.
Schmitt, H.H, *Die Staatsvertrage des Altertums*, vol 3 (Munich, 1969), p 492.
Seyrig, H, *Tresors du Levant, anciens et nouveaux* (Paris, 1973).
Sherk, R.K (ed and trans), *Rome and the Greek East to the Death of Augustus*, Translated Documents of Greece and Rome (Cambridge, 1984).
Shore, A. F, and H.S. Smith, 'Two Unpublished Demotic Documents from the Asyut Archive', *JEA*, 46 (1959), pp 52–60.
Skeat, T.C, *The Reigns of the Ptolemies* (Munich, 1969).
Skeat, T.C, 'Notes on Ptolemaic Chronology: II, The Twelfth Year which is also the First: The Invasion of Egypt by Antiochos Epiphanes', *Journal of Egyptian Archaeology*, 47 (1971), pp 107–112.
Swain, J.W, 'Antiochus Epiphanes and Egypt', *Classical Philology*, 34 (1944), pp 73–94.
Thiers, C, 'Civils et Militaires dans les temples. Occupation illicite et expulsion', *BIAO*, 99 (1999), pp 493–516.
Thompson, Dorothy J, *Memphis under the Ptolemies*, 2nd ed (Princeton NJ, 2012).
Thompson, Dorothy J, 'Ptolemaic State Barges' in Costas Buraselis et al (eds), *The Ptolemies, the Sea, and the Nile, Studies in Waterborne Power* (Cambridge, 2013).
Torok, Laszlo, 'To the History of the Dodekaschoenos between c.250 BC and 298 A.D.', *ZAS*, 107 (1980), pp 76–86.
Turfa, Jean MacIntosh, and Alwin G. Steinmayer Jr, 'The *Syracusia* year as a giant cargo vessel', *International Journal of Nautical Archaeology*, 28 (1999), pp 105–125.
Viesse, Anne-Emmanuelle, *Les revoltes egyptiens, recherches sur les troubles interieurs en Egypte du regne de Ptoleme III, a la conquete romain* (Leuven, 2004).
von Reden, Sitta, *Money in Ptolemaic Egypt from the Macedonian Conquest to the End of the Third Century BC* (Cambridge, 2007).
Walbank, F.W, *Aratos of Sicyon* (Cambridge, 1933).
Walbank, F.W, 'The Accession of Ptolemy Epiphanes; a Problem in chronology', *JEA* (1936), pp 20–34.
Walbank, F.W, *Philip V of Macedon* (Cambridge, 1940; reprinted by Archon Books, USA, 1967).
Welsby, Derek A, *The Kingdom of Kush* (London, 1996), pp 66–67.
Whigley, Peter (trans), *Catullus, the Poems* (London, 1966).
Whitehorne, John, *Cleopatras* (London, 1994).
Will, Edouard, *Histoire Politique du monde Hellenistique* (Nancy, 1982).
Winniki, J.K, 'Die letzten Erengenisse des vierten syrischen Krieges. Eine Neudeutung des Raphiadecretes', *JJP*, 31 (2001), pp 133–145.
Wolski, J, 'The Decay of the Iranian Empire of the Seleukids and the Chronology of Parthian Beginnings', *Berytus*, 12 (1956–1958), pp 35–52.

Notes

Introduction
1. This description is a brief summary of the previous book in this series, *The Rise of the Ptolemaic Dynasty, 323–246* (Barnsley, 2022).
2. Justin 26.3.2–8; Dee L. Chapman, *Berenike II and the Golden Age of Alexandria* (Oxford, 2014), pp 39–40.
3. Plutarch, *Philopoimen* 1.3–4; Polybios 10.22.2–3.
4. Paul Johstono, *The Army of Ptolemaic Egypt, 323 – 204 BC, an Institutional and Operational History* (Barnsley, 2020), Chapter 4; Christelle Fischer-Bovet, *Army and Society in Ptolemaic Egypt* (Cambridge, 2014), Chapter 5.
5. Polybios 2.37–43.
6. Gary Reger, 'The Political History of the Kyklades, 260–200 BC', *Historia*, 43 (1994), pp 32–69.

Chapter 1
1. The date of this battle is disputed, either 246 or 245 BC; Gary Reger, 'The Political History of the Kyklades, 260 – 200 BC', *Historia*, 54 (1994), pp 32–69, favoured the former date, as here; see also A. Bylow-Jacobsen, 'O. Haun 6, a new look at the original', *ZPE*, 36 (1979), pp 91–96; A.N. Oikonomides, 'Opron and the sea battle off Andros, a note in Ptolemaic History and Prosopography', *ZPE*, 56 (1984), pp 151–152.
2. Austin 265 = *I. Crete* III, 83–85, no. 4.
3. Appian, *Syriake* 65; Phylarchos *FGrH* 81 F 24, claims Antiochos was poisoned by Laodike.
4. A.J. Sachs and H. Hunger, *Astronomical Diaries and related texts from Babylonia*, vol 1 (Vienna, 1988), '-246' and '-245'; the diarist had the news in 'Month IV', and marked his next cuneiform tablet of Months V-VI as 'King Seleukos; month VI is roughly August; it would take a month at least for the news to travel from Ephesus to Babylon.
5. P. Gurob = Austin 266; F. Piejko, 'Episodes from the Third Syrian War in a Gurob Papyrus, 246 BC', *Archiv fur Papyrusforschungen*, 36 (1990), pp 13–27.
6. Austin 267.
7. *Ptol. Pros.* 5288 and 17243; Walbank, *Commentary*, p 487; Tlepolemos was of Iranian descent, his family powerful in Lykia, and now in Alexandria.
8. The sources for these events are a curious mixture. *P. Gurob* (Austin 267) appears to have been an official Ptolemaic report, though its chatty language might suggest a letter home – Ptolemy himself has been supposed to be the author; the biblical book of *Daniel*, 11.6 – 4, with Porphyry, *FGrH* 260 F 43, which is a comment on the text in *Daniel*; Justin 27; an inscription from Adulis in Eritrea, copied by the voyager Cosmas Indikopleustes in the sixth century AD (*OGIS* 54 = Austin 268).
9. *OGIS* 54 = Austin 268.
10. *Ibid.*
11. Baktria: Adulis inscription (*OGIS* 54); India: Polyainos 8.50.
12. Sachs and Hunger, *Astronomical Diaries*, vol 2, -245.
13. Kallimachos, *Berenice's Lock*, translated into Latin by Catullus, and reprinted in English in Chapman, *Berenice II*, pp 187–189.

Notes 221

14. Justin 27.1.9; Porphyry *FGrH* 260 F 43; Holbl, *Ptolemaic Empire*, p 49; W. Huss, 'Eine Revolt de Aegypter in der Zeit der 3 Syrische Krieg', *Aegyptus*, 58 (1976), pp 151–156; W. Peremans, 'Sur le domestic seditio de Justin XXVII.1.9', *Antiquite Classique*, 50 (1981), pp 28–836; Brian C. McGing, 'Revolt Egyptian Style: Internal Opposition to Ptolemaic Rule', *Archiv fur Papyrusforschung*, 43 (1987), pp 273–314; Anne-Emmanuelle Viesse, *Les revoltes egyptiens, recherches sur les troubles interieurs en Egypte du regne de Ptoleme III, a la conquete romain* (Leuven, 2004), pp 3–5.
15. Canopus decree: M. Bernard, *La Delta egyptien apres les textes grecs: I, les confines libyques* (Cairo, 1970), pp 990–994.
16. Johstono, *Army of Ptolemaic Egypt*, pp 162–226.
17. Jerome, *In Danielem*, 11.7–9.
18. For Ptolemy Andromachou: *P. Haun* 6; Polybios 5.35.11; Athenaios 13.593 a-b; Holbl, *Ptolemaic Empire*, p 50; see also the references in note 1; N.G.L. Hammond and F.W. Walbank, *A History of Macedonia*, vol. 3 (Oxford, 1988), pp 587–595.
19. Justin 27.2.2.
20. *OGIS* 229 = Austin 174 = H.H. Schmitt, *Die Staatsvertrage des Altertums*, vol 3 (Munich, 1969), p 492.
21. A. Houghton and C. Lorber, *Seleukid Coins, A Comprehensive Catalogue*, Part I, *Seleucus I through Antiochus III*, 2 vols (New York, 2002), p 229.
22. *Chronicon Pascale* I.330
23. Austin 269; P.M. Fraser, *Samothrace* II.1 (Oxford, 1960), p 69; R.S. Bagnall, *The Administration of the Ptolemaic Possessions outside Egypt* (Leiden, 1976), pp 159–168.
24. Plutarch, *Aratos*, 4.4.
25. *P. Haun* 6; Bulow-Jacobsen, p 161 and note 4.
26. F. Duryat, *Arados hellenistique, Etude historique et Monetairei* (Beirut, 2005), pp 229–232.
27. Strabo 16.2.14; John D. Grainger, *Hellenistic Phoenicia* (Oxford, 1991), pp 83–89.
28. Eusebios, *Chronographia*, 1.251.
29. *Ibid*.
30. Strabo 11.92–93; Justin 41; N. Debevoise, *A Political History of Parthia* (Chicago, 1938); J. Wolski, 'The Decay of the Iranian Empire of the Seleukids and the Chronology of Parthian Beginnings', *Berytus*, 12 (1956–1958), pp 35–52.

Chapter 2
1. *Pap. L. Bat.* 15; P.W. Pestman, *Chronologie egyptiens d'apres les textes demotiques* (Leiden 1967), p 134.
2. *OGIS* 56; Clayman, *Berenice II*, p 124.
3. Aelian, *Varia Historia*, 14.42.
4. Clayman, *Berenice II*, p 171; *IG* IX.1.I.56; C. Bennett, 'The Children of Ptolemy III and the date of the Exedra of Thermos', *ZPE*, 138 (2002), pp 141–145.
5. Hyginus, *Astronomica* 2.24.
6. *Ptol. Pros.* 2272, 14631; P. Maas, 'Sosibios als pseudipetropos ses Ptolemaios Epiphanes', *Memoire Henri Gregoire*, pp 443–448.
7. He is rarely discussed in modern accounts; the records are virtually non-existent: Clayman, *Berenice II*, p 172; Holbl, *Ptolemaic Empire*, p 128.
8. Justin, *Epitome* 23.2.6.
9. C. Bennett in his internet article on 'Theoxena'.
10. *SEG*, XVIII, 626; R.S. Bagnall, 'Archagathas son of Agathokles, *epistates* of Libya', *Philologos* 120 (1976), pp 195–209.
11. Clayman, *Berenice II*, pp 175–177.
12. *P. Cairo Zen.* III 59340; *P. Petrie* IV 376; Austin 267.
13. *Pros. Ptol.* III/IX 5040.
14. Agatharchides, *On the Erythraean Sea*, trans. and ed. S.M. Burstein (Hakluyt Society, 1989), pp 78–79; G.W. Bowersock, *The Throne of Adulis* (Oxford, 2013).

15. Eutropius 3.1.
16. Austin 273.
17. Plutarch, *Aratos*, 41.5; F.W. Walbank, *Aratos of Sicyon* (Cambridge, 1933).
18. *IG* IX.1.I.202; cf. Bennett (note 4).
19. Christian Habicht, *Athens from Alexander to Anthony* (Cambridge MA, 1999), pp 163–166.
20. Plutarch, *Life of Agis* (IV).
21. Habicht, *Athens* 173; id, *Studien zur Geschichte Athens in Hellenistische Zeit* (Gottingen, 1982), pp 79–83.
22. This is obvious from the extravagant honours to Ptolemy voted by the city later.
23. Frontinus, *Stratagems*, 2.6.5.
24. Plutarch, *Life of Kleomenes*, 14–16.
25. Schmitt, *Staatsvertrage* III 505.
26. Polybios 5.10 6.6 – 8; Plutarch, *Aratos*, 41.5
27. Listed by Holbl, *Ptolemaic Empire*, p 52.
28. 64 Plutarch, *Life of Kleomenes*, to 2.4–10.
29. Holbl, *Ptolemaic Empire*, p 52.
30. Richard A. Billows, *Kings and Colonists, Aspects of Macedonian Imperialism* (Leiden, 1995), pp 94–96.
31. F.W. Walbank, *Philip V of Macedon* (Cambridge, 1940), reprinted by Archon Books (USA, 1967), pp 12–13.
32. This was his mint and a city he clearly favoured; he also controlled Sardis, the traditional government centre of western Asia Minor.
33. Polybios 5.74.4; Justin 27.3.11.
34. Polybios 5.71.1 – 2, stating that the 'free population' was just 6,000 in 219 BC, and there were numerous exiles from the city in other parts of Syria.
35. Porphyry, *FGrH* 269 F 32.8.
36. *P. Haun* 6, Fr 1, 14 and 28–31; W. Huss, 'Eine ptolemaische Expedition nach Kleinasien', *Ancient Society*, 8 (1977), pp 187–193; C. Habicht, 'Bemerkungen zur P. Haun 6', *ZPE* 39 (1980), pp 1–5.

Chapter 3
1. There is no record of the marriage ceremony, but she was already married when Ptolemy III went to Syria in mid-246 BC.
2. Justin 27.2.5.
3. *C. Ord. Ptoli.*, no 22.
4. These births are recorded, curiously enough, on the monument at Aitolian Thermos: *IG* IX 1(2) I 56.
5. Aelian, *Varia Historia* 14.43.
6. Hyginus, *Astronomia*. 2.24; cf. Clayman, *Berenice II*, 124.
7. A useful brief biography is by Christian Jacob, in Christian Jacob and Francois de Polignac, *Alexandria Third Century BC, the Knowledge of the World in a Single City* (Alexandria, 2000), pp 101–113.
8. The poem only survives in a Latin translation by Catullus:, *Catullus, the Poems*, trans. Peter Whigley (London, 1966), nos 65 and 66.
9. Apollonius of Rhodes, *Argonautica*, ed. and trans. Peter Green (Berkeley and Los Angeles, 1997); the introduction is especially informative on his life.
10. G.M. Cohen, *The Hellenistic Settlements in Syria, the Red Sea Basin and North Africa* (Berkeley and Los Angeles, 2006), pp 310, 313, 315.
11. *OGIS* 54 = Austin 268.
12. Johstono, *Army*, p 209.
13. Quoted by Johstono, *Army*, p 208 and note 16.
14. W. Clarysse and G. Van der Veken, *Eponymous Priests of Ptolemaic Egypt* (Leiden, 1983).

15. Judith McKenzie, *The Architecture of Alexandria and Egypt, 300 BC–A.D. 700* (New Haven, 2007), pp 61–67; Roger S. Bagnall and Dominic W. Rathbone (eds), *Egypt from Alexander to the Copts, an Archaeological and Historical Guide* (Cairo and New York, 2017).
16. Athenaios 5.204d - 206c; interpreted as architecture rather than a ship in McKenzie, *Architecture*, p 61.
17. Eusebius, *Chronographia*, 1.251.
18. Polybios 5.70.1–71.12.
19. The following section owes much to Johstono, *Army*, chapter 8, and is essentially a summary of his findings. The condition of the Ptolemaic army is rarely considered except in relation to a battle, or to the settlements of the soldiers as cleruchs; Johstono's treatment is thus extremely useful; I refer interested readers to his account with its references; reforms are also discussed by Christelle Fischer-Bovet, *Army and Society in Ptolemaic Egypt* (Cambridge, 2014), pp 132–148.
20. *P. Haun*, p 6.

Chapter 4
1. For the details of these succession problems, see volume 1 in this series.
2. *IG* IX 1(2) I 56; Clayman, *Berenice II*, 171.
3. Polybios 5.34.1 and 36.1; 15.25.1–2.
4. Polybios 5.34.1.
5. Clayman, *Berenice II*, p 183.
6. Polybios 5.34.10.
7. Polybios 5.35.1–36.2.
8. Polybios 5.36.4–5.
9. *P. Haun* 6; Ps-Plutarch, *Proverbs of Alexander* 13.
10. Polybios 5.37.1 – 38.7.
11. Polybios 5.38 – 39; Plutarch, *Kleomenesi* 36 -37; Walbank, *Commentary*, 1.565–567.
12. ZenoBios 3.94; Clayman, *Berenice II*, 172–172 and 183–184.
13. *P. Haun* 6.
14. Polybios 5.45.7 - 46.5.
15. Polybios 5.61.3.
16. Holbl, *Ptolemaic Empire*, 127; E. Lanciers, 'Die Vergottlichung und die Ehe des Ptolemaios IV und Arsinoe III', *Archiv fur Papyrusforschung* 34 (1988), pp 405–433.
17. Polybios 5.43.1 – 4.
18. Polybios 14.11.1; Plutarch, Kleomenes 33; Justin 30.2.3; Clayman, *Berenice II*, pp 175–176; Ogden.

Chapter 5
1. The attack on Seleukeia is at Polybios 5.58.3–61.2.
2. The most elaborate discussion of the war is by W. Huss, *Untersuchungen zuro Aussenpolitik Ptolemaios IV* (Munich, 1976), pp 20–87.
3. Polybios 5.61.3–6.
4. Polybios 5.61.7–62.2.
5. Polybios 5.62.4.
6. Polybios 5.63.7.
7. Polybios 5.66.1–2.
8. Polybios 5.66.3.
9. Polybios 5.66.4–6.
10. Polybios 5.67.1–13.
11. Polybios 5.62.2–3.
12. Polybios 5.68.3–5.
13. Polybios 5.68.3–4.

224 The Ptolemies, Apogee and Collapse

14. Polybios 5.68.6–69.11; B. Bar-Kochva, *The Seleukid Army, Organisation and Tactics in the Great Campaigns* (Cambridge, 1970), pp 124–127.
15. Polybios 5.70.1–10.
16. Polybios 5.70.10–71.11.
17. Polybios 5.71.12.
18. Polybios 5.71.12.
19. The Seleukid army is detailed at Polybios 5.79.3–12, and the Ptolemaic at 5.82.3–7; see also Bar-Kochva, *Seleukid Army*, pp 128–145, and M. Roberts and B. Bennett, *Twilight of the Hellenistic World* (Barnsley, 2012), pp 80–108; Johstono, *Ptolemaic Army*, pp 5–17 and 258–262, all of which deal with the armies of the battle, and have good references.
20. Johstono, *Ptolemaic Army*, p 262.
21. *SEG* 38, 1571; Hassan Salame-Sarkis, 'Inscription au Nom de Ptolemee IV Philopator trouvee dans le Nord de la Beqa', *Berytus*, 34 (1986), pp 207–209.
22. Polybios 5.87.1.
23. Austin 276.
24. The terms have to be deduced from later events and references.
25. Holbl, *Ptolemaic Empire*, p 131; he details the peace terms.

Chapter 6
1. Willy Clarysse, 'The Ptolemies visiting the Egyptian Chora', in L. Mooren (ed), *Politics, Administration, and Society in the Hellenistic and Roman World*, *Studia Hellenistica* 36 (Leuven, 2000), pp 29–50.
2. Polybios 5.34 and 14.12.
3. Polybios 5.34.10.
4. Walbank, *Commentary*, 1.564; 'from Polybios onwards the tradition is hostile to Philopator', and one might add, to Sosibios as well.
5. Polybios 5.107, and the Raphia Decree, lines 26–28; see McGing, 'Revolt Egyptian Style', at pp 278–283; it has to be said the issue is still unclear.
6. Austin 276; Fischer-Bovet, *Army and Society*, pp 87–89; also J.K. Winniki, 'Die letzten Erengenisses des vierten syrischen Krieges. Eine Neudeutung des Raphiadecretes', *Journal of Juristic Papyri*, 31, pp 133–145.
7. Athenaios, *Deipnosophistai*, 5.203e – 204d.
8. *Ibid*, 204d-206c.
9. For these ships see Dorothy J. Thompson, 'Ptolemaic State Barges' in Costas Buraselis et al. (eds), *The Ptolemies, the Sea, and the Nile, Studies in Waterborne Power* (Cambridge, 2013), pp 185–196, which contains full references.
10. Jean MacIntosh Turfa and Alwin G. Steinmayer Jr, 'The *Syracusia* year as a giant cargo vessel', *International Journal of Nautical Archaeology*, 28 (1999), pp 105–125.
11. Fischer-Bovet, *Army and Society*, pp 73–75.
12. Raphia Decree = Austin 276.
13. Sitta von Reden, *Money in Ptolemaic Egypt from the Macedonian Conquest to the End of the Third Century BC* (Cambridge, 2007).
14. At the Porphyrion fight; Antiochos captured forty ships at Tyre and Ptolemies-Ake when Theodotos and Panaitolos mutinied (Polybios 5.61.3–63.3)
15. Clarysse, 'Ptolemies Visiting'.
16. Polybios 5.34.10.
17. *P. Tebtunis* 3.2.860 (at least 1,000 *arouras*, where discharged Egyptians received 10 *auroras*); *BGU* 6.1415, *O. Wilb* 2, *O. Strasb* 294 (Agathokles' gift).
18. Athenaios, 5.206d-209e.
19. Polybios 7.2.2; Livy 24.26
20. Polybios 7.2.2.
21. Polybios 8.15.1–21.11; Holbl, *Ptolemaic Empire*, p 132.

Notes 225

22. Polybios 5.100.9–11.
23. Polybios 5.24.11.
24. F.W. Walbank, *Philip V of Macedon* (Cambridge, 1940, reprinted 1967), pp 64–65, for Philip's reaction to the news of the Roman defeat at Trasimene; the Aitolian Agelaus' speech at the conference at Naupaktos in 217 BC demonstrated Aitolian concerns as well (Polybios 5.103.7–104 = Austin 73).
25. *IG* VII, 298 (a statue of Ptolemy and Arsinoe).
26. *IG* VII, 3166.
27. *IG* VII 507.
28. M. Feyel, *Continuation a l'epigraphie beotienne* (Le Puy, 1942), pp 94–96; P.M. Fraser, *Ptolemaic Alexandria* (Oxford, 1972), 1.313 and 316 and note 55.
29. *IG* XII.1.37.
30. Polybios 7.11.9; Strabo 10.4.1; Walbank, *Philip V*, p 67.
31. Livy 27.30.1–5.
32. Livy 28.7 .14; Walbank, *Philip V*, p 94, note 7.
33. Polybios 11.4.1; Appian, *Macedonian Wars*, 3.
34. Appian, *Macedonian Wars*, 3; Walbank, *Philip V*, p 99, note 9.
35. Livy 27.4.10; Polybios 9.11a; Walbank, *Commentary* 2.137.
36. Livy to 3.10.3–13.
37. Silenus 15.672–673.

Chapter 7
1. Polybios 14.12.
2. Walbank, *Commentary*, 2.439, says his account is lost, though the war 'fascinated' Polybios. If so, it is a great pity he was so dismissive; one may doubt if he was any more informative in his 'lost' section.
3. The basic collection of sources is by P.W. Pestman, 'Haronnophris and Chaonnophris, two Indigenous Pharaohs in Ptolemaic Egypt' in S.P. Vleeming (ed), *Hundred-Gated Thebes* (Leuven, 1995), pp 101–138; they are referred in the following notes by their letters as awarded by Pestman.
4. Modern accounts of the war of the rebellion include, above all, Anne-Emmanuelle Veisse, *Les 'revoltes egyptiennes', Recherches sur les troubles interieure en Egypte du regne de Ptolemy III a la conquete romain, Studia Hellenistica* 41 (2004); see also McGing, 'Revolt Egyptian Style'; a brief account is by Willy Clarysse 'The Great Revolt of the Egyptians (204–186 BCE)' on the Berkeley website, 2004; Holbl, *Ptolemaic Empire*, has a chapter on the revolt entitled 'Domestic Resistance and the Pharaonic State in Thebes (206–186), pp 153–159.
5. Pestman, 'Haronnophris and Chaonnophris', d.
6. Pestman, 'Haronnophris and Charonnophris', e.
7. Pestman, 'Haronnophris and Charonnophris', kk; S. Cauville and D. Devonchelle, 'Le temple d'Edfou, etappes de la construction, nouvelle donnees historique', *Revue Egyptien* 35 (1984), pp 31–55 and 36; Clarysse, 'Great Revolt', p 2.
8. McGing, 'Revolt Egyptian Style', p 285; *P. Gr. Choachiti*, 12, V, 28–29.
9. Suggested by the movement of the plaintiff's father, a soldier, recorded in Hermeias' court case (note 8).
10. *O. Cairo* 38.258.
11. G. Casanova, 'Una datazione tardiva de Tolomeo IV e it banchiere Portos de Crocodilopolis', *Aegyptus*, 68 (1988), pp 13–18; Karlhans Abel, 'Det Tod des Ptolemaios IV Philopator bei Polybios; Eine historisch-textgeschichte Studie', *Hermes*, 95 (1967), pp 72–90.
12. Justin 30.2.6; F.W. Walbank, 'The Accession of Ptolemy Epiphanes; a Problem in chronology', *JEA* (1936), pp 20–34, together with discussions and references in addendas

in his *Commentary on Polybius*, vols II and III; also T.C. Skeat, *The Reigns of the Ptolemies* (Munich, 1969).
13. Eratosthenes, *FGrH* 241 F 16; Polybios 15.25.2.
14. Polybios 15.25.3 – 5.
15. John Ma, *Antiochos III and the Cities of Western Asia Minor* (Oxford, 1999), pp 65–73.
16. McGing, 'Revolt Egyptian Style', p 9.
17. P.M. Pestman et al, *Receuil des textes demotique et bilingue* (Leiden, 1977), p 11; Clarysse, 'Great Revolt', pp 3–4.
18. A comment noted in McGing, 'Revolt Egyptian Style', p 287, from W. Clarysse.
19. *SB* VI 9367; Clarysse, 'Great Revolt', p 7.
20. Clarysse, 'Great Revolt', p 12.
21. Sosibios' death is implied by Polybios 15.25.11.
22. Polybios 15.25.12–24.
23. Livy 27.4 .10; Polybios 9.11a.
24. Polybios 15.20.1.
25. Polybios 3.2.8, 15.20; 16.1.9, and 12.1; Livy 31.14.5; Appian, *Macedonian Wars*, 4.1; Justin 30.2.8; modern discussions include Walbank, *Commentary*, 2.471–473; Edouard Will, *Histoire Politique du monde Hellenistique* (Nancy, 1982), 2.114–118; Schmitt, *Staatsvertrage*, 3.237–261; E.S. Gruen, *The Hellenistic World and the Rise of Rome* (Berkeley and Los Angeles, 1984).
26. Polybios 15.25.7.
27. Polybios 15.25.20–24.
28. Polybios 15.25.26.
29. Polybios 15.25.34–36.
30. Polybios 15.26.10.
31. *P. Tor. Choachiti* 12 V 27 and *SB* VIII 9681; Pestman, 'Haronnophris and Chaonnophris', document aaa, a complaint about official sale of property which had been declared ownerless sometime after the revolt.
32. Polybios 15.27.1–2.
33. Polybios 15.29.8–14 (Oenanthe); 27.6–29.1 (Moeragenes).
34. Polybios 15.30.5–32.8.
35. Polybios 15.25.10–33.13.
36. Polybios 15.3 3.1–12.
37. On this see Fischer-Bovet, *Army and Society*, pp 95–96.
38. Polybios 16.21–22.
39. Abydos, see note 27.
40. *SB* VI 9367; Clarysse, 'Great Revolt', p 7.
41. Stanley M. Burstein, *Agatharchides of Cnidos, 'On the Eryithraean Sea'* (Hakluyt Society, London 1989), preface.

Chapter 8
1. Justin 30.3.3; Polybios 15.20.1; for a discussion on the purpose of the war, cf M. Holleaux, 'Etudes d'Histoire Hellenistique; la chronologie de la cinquieme Guerre de Syrie', *Klio* 8 (1908), pp 267–280.
2. The road is now the main Syrian route from Damascus to the north, the Bekaa now being Lebanese territory; there is a regular bus service along the road.
3. Polyainos 4.15.
4. Polybios 16.22a.
5. It features in several of the Zenon papyri – P. Cairo Zen I 59001, 59006, 59009, 59093: Cohen, Hellenistic Settlements/Syria, 286 – 288.
6. Polybios 16.18.2 and 22a.
7. Polybios 18.53.5–6.

8. Livy 31.16.4–6; Polybios 16.29.3.
9. Appian, *Macedonian Wars*, 4.1; Polybios 3.2.8, 16.2.4, 2.9 and 7.6; Livy 31.31.4.
10. Polybios 15.25a.11.
11. Polybios 13.2.1 (his exile); 15.25.16–18 (return to recruit).
12. Livy 31.43.5–7, 345–346 and 354–355.
13. D. Gera, 'Ptolemy son of Thraseas and the Fifth Syrian War', *Ancient Society*, 18 (1987), pp 63–73; C.P. Jones and C. Habicht, 'A Hellenistic Inscription from Arsinoe in Cilicia', *Phoenix*, 43 (1989), 317–345; Y.H. Landau, 'A Greek Inscription found near Hefzibah', *Israel Exploration Journal*, 16 (1966), pp 54–70, is a dossier of Ptolemais' correspondence between 201 and 195 BC.
14. Polybios 16.39.1; Josephus, *Antiquities Judaiae* 12.3.3; Porphyry *FGrH* 269 F 45–46.
15. Appian, *Syrian Wars*, 1.
16. Polybios 5.104.
17. Anssi Lampela, *Rome and the Ptolemies of Egypt, The Development of their Political Relations, 273–80 BC* (Helsinki, 1998), pp 63–75.
18. Livy 31.1 6.4; Philip certainly controlled both cities in 196 BC.
19. Appian, *Macedonian Wars*, 4.2; Justin 30.3; discussed in detail by Walbank, *Philip V*, pp 311–317, and at greater length by Lampela, *Rome and the Ptolemies*, pp 76–83.
20. Polybios 16.3 4.1–7.
21. Justin 30.2.8.
22. Polybios 16.34.3.
23. Polybios 16.18.1–19.15; Bar Kochva, *Seleukid Army*, pp 146–157.
24. Josephus, *Antiquities Judaiae* 12.3.3 (quoted from Polybios 16.39.1–2).
25. This is 'The First Greek offensive' in Pestman, 'Haronnophris and Chaonnophris'.
26. *P. dem. Berl Kaufv* 3142 and 3144 (Haronnophris) and 3146 (Chaonnophris).
27. W. Clarysse, 'Ptolemaic Papyri from Lycopolis', *Actes du XVe Congres Internationale de Papyrologie* (Brussels, 1979), pp 101–106; A.F. Shore and H.S. Smith, 'Two Unpublished Demotic Documents from the Asyut Archive', *JEA* 46 (1959), pp 52–60.
28. Strabo 17.1.19, places it in the Sebennytis nome; on the Rosetta Stone (*OGIS* 90 = Austin 283) it is placed in the Busirite nome. It may be that there were two towns called Lykopolis in the Delta, but it is more likely that Strabo got it wrong; one of these may have been the scene of fighting, but the city in Middle Egypt was the more important in military terms, and there was certainly fighting there.
29. Holbl, *Ptolemaic Empire*, pp 154 and 166.
30. Clarysse, 'Ptolemaic papyri from Lycopolis'.
31. Polybios 22.17.1.
32. Jerome, *In Danielam*, 11.15–16.
33. Josephus, *Antiquites Judaiae*, 12.3.3, quoting Polybios.
34. John D. Grainger, *The Syrian Wars* (Leiden, 2010), pp 261–262.
35. Livy 31.43.5–7.
36. Livy 31.19.10.
37. John D. Grainger, *The Roman War of Antiochos the Great* (Leiden, 2001), ch 2; Jerome, *In Danielam*, 11.15 (= Porphyry *FGrH* 260 F 46).
38. Livy 33.19.9–11.
39. Livy 33.20.1 – 2, with a very Livian misinterpretation of what happened and why.
40. Polybios 18.53.4–6.
41. Polybios 18.55.3–6.
42. Polybios 18.55.1 – 2; on Charimortos, Strabo 16.774, and *OGIS* 86.
43. Polybios 18.53.5–54.6.
44. Polybios 18.54.7–12.
45. Polybios 18.54.1.
46. Diodoros 28.14.

47. Polybios 18.55.7.
48. Livy 33.4.1; Appian, *Syrian Wars*.
49. Polybios 28.49–52; Livy 33.39.1–41.2; Appian, *Syrian Wars*, 3.
50. Direct evidence of the peace treaty and its terms does not exist: cf Will, *Histoire Politique*, 2.190–191.
51. Livy 35.13.4; Porphyry *FGrH* 260 F 47; John Whitehorne, *Cleopatras* (London, 1994), pp 80–83.

Chapter 9
1. A figure suggested by Fischer-Bovet, *Army and Society*, pp 67–69, 75; every source, ancient and modern, suggests a different estimate.
2. John D. Grainger, *The Roman War of Antiochos the Great* (Leiden, 2002).
3. John D. Grainger, 'The Campaign of C. Manlius Vulso in Asia Minor', *Anatolian Studies*, 45 (1995), pp 23–42.
4. Livy 36.4.1–3.
5. Livy 37.3.9–10; on all this diplomacy, see Lampela, *Rome and the Ptolemies*, pp 106–107.
6. John D. Grainger, *Diplomacy in the Hellenistic World* (London, 2020), on the diplomatic unimportance of the 'marriage alliance' notion.
7. Diodoros 28.14; Plutarch, *Moralia*, 71c-d.
8. Polybios 17.6; Walbank, *Commentary* 3.205.
9. Polybios 17.1–5.
10. Polybios 18.55.7.
11. Some light is thrown on internal conditions in Egypt by a set of papyri concerning a noble Egyptian family, published in two sets: A. Hanson and P.J. Sijperstein, 'The Dossier of Euphron: three Ptolemaic Letters from Princeton University Collection', *Ancient History*, 20 (1989), pp 133–147, and W. Clarysse, 'Hakoris, an Egyptian Nobleman and his Family', *Ancient History*, 22 (1991), pp 235–243.
12. Polybios 43.1–27; Appian, *Syrian War*, 39; Diodoros 29.10; Livy 38.38.2–18; Walbank, *Commentary*, 3.156–164 and references to discussions there listed.
13. This is noted in two copies of a Ptolemaic decree published by G. Daressy 'Un decret de l'an XXIII de Ptolemee Epiphane', *Receuil de Travaux relatifs a la philologie et a l'archeologie egyptienne et assyrien*, 32 (1911), pp 1–8, and 'Un second exemplair du decret de l'an XXIII de Ptolemee Epiphane', *ibid* 38 (1916/1917), pp 175–179; year XXIII is equivalent to 184/183 or 183/182 BC.
14. This was the 'Second Greek Offensive' of Pestman, 'Haronnophris and Chaonnophris'.
15. *Ibid*.
16. Clarysse, 'Great Revolt', p 7.
17. *Ibid*, pp 8–9.
18. M. Alliott, 'La fin de la resistance Egyptienne dans le Sud sous Epiphane', *REA* (1952), pp 18–26.
19. Clarysse, 'Ptolemaic Papyri from Lycopolis'.
20. *P. Koln* VII 313.
21. *I. Philae* II (the Amnesty decree), and *OGIS* 90 (the Rosetta Stone; Austin 283); John Ray, *The Rosetta Stone and the Rebirth of Ancient Egypt* (London, 2004).
22. L. Mooren, 'The Governors General of the Thebais in the Second Century A.D.', *Ancient Society*, 4 (1973), pp 115–132, and *Ancient Society*, 5 (1974), pp 137–152.
23. *P. Tebt* I 62 and 63; IV 1108–1115; Pestman, 'Haronnophris and Chaonnophris'.
24. Fischer-Bouvet, *Army and Society*, p 93 and note 152, and p 97.
25. Polybios 2.3.5–9 and 23.9.
26. Diodoros 28.14.
27. Diodoros 29.29.
28. Porphyry *FGrH* 260 F 46.

Chapter 10
1. Polybios 22.3.8–9.
2. Holbl, *Ptolemaic Empire*, p 141, calls him 'a weak king', presumably because he did not go to war – but keeping the peace can be seen as strength.
3. Polybios 28.2 1.1–5.
4. O. Morkholm, 'Eulaeus and Lenaeus', *Classica at Medievalia*, 22 (1961), 32–45, is a, rather limited, discussion of their rule.
5. Morkholm, 'Eulaeus and Lenaeus', pp 40–41.
6. *Ibid*, pp 37–39; Mooren, 'Governors-General of the Thebaid', pp 118–123.
7. *Pros. Ptol.* , III.5104.
8. *Pros. Ptol.* , I.270.
9. Polybios 27.13; Walbank, *Commentary*, 3.311–312.
10. Morkholm, 'Eulaios and Lenaios', p 37, for instance.
11. Holbl, *Ptolemaic Empire*, p 143; *I. Philae* I.11; Walbank, *Commentary*, 3.323.
12. Holbl does this, *Ptolemaic Empire*, pp 143–144.
13. J.W. Swain, 'Antiochus Epiphanes and Egypt', *Classical Philology* 34 (1944), pp 73–94, based in part on Polybios 28.21, followed by Diodoros 30.15–17, and Livy 42.29.5–7.
14. Tony Reekmans, 'Economic and Social Repercussions of the Ptolemaic Copper Inflation', *Chronique d'Egypte*, 24 (1949), pp 324–342, in which earlier studies are summarized.
15. O. Morkholm, *Antiochos IV of Syria* (Copenhagen, 1966), ch 2.
16. *Ibid*, Ch. 3.
17. Austin, no 205, clause 13 (annual payments), 14 (payments to Eumenes II), 15 (hostages).
18. Livy 42.6.6.
19. Polybios 31.1 3.2–3; *II Maccabees* 4.4 and 21.
20. *II Maccabees* 4.21–22.
21. Morkholm, *Antiochos* IV, pp 44–47.
22. The name of this hostage-prince, Demetrios, is the first time it was used in the Seleukid dynasty; it links with Seleukos' daughter's marriage to King Perseus to suggest a deliberate aim of developing an Antigonid-Seleukid alliance; Antiochos IV's courtship of Rome therefore indicates a decisive shift of Seleukid foreign policy.
23. Morkholm, *Antiochos IV*, pp 36–37.
24. Appian, *Syrian Wars*, 45.
25. Livy 42.26.7 – 8; Appian, *Macedonian Wars*, 114; Lampela, *Rome and the Ptolemies*, pp 115.
26. *II Maccabees* 4.20–22.
27. This is not attested in any source, but was the obvious place.
28. Diodoros 30.16.
29. 'Ptolemy VII' is the son of Ptolemy VI, who was later killed by 'VIII'; the numbers are, of course, only a modern convention.
30. Polybios 28.12.8–9.
31. Polybios 28.1.1; Walbank, *Commentary*, 3.321–324.
32. Polybios 28.1.7.

Chapter 11
1. Appian, *Syrian Wars*, 2.
2. Porphyry *FGrH* 260 F 49a.
3. J.D. Ray, *The Archive of Hor* (Leiden, 1976), p 126 – Hrynys in Egyptian; ib., 'Observations on the Archive of Hor', *Journal of Egyptian Archaeology*, 64 (1978), pp 113–120.
4. Diodoros 30.16.
5. Porphyry *FGrH* 260 F 49a.
6. *I Maccabees* 1.17.
7. Eg: Polybios 28.1.2.

8. Diodoros 30.8; Morkholm, *Antiochos IV*, p 74.
9. Diodoros 30.18.2.
10. *Ibid*; Diodoros seems uncertain about the accusation; also Polybios 28.18.
11. Polybios 28.21; Diodoros 30.17; Samothrace had Ptolemaic connections; Arsinoe II had taken refuge there when she was threatened by Ptolemy Keraunos, and had paid for the building of the rotunda; such connections would predispose Ptolemy to go there and the Samothracians to be generous.
12. *I Maccabees* 1.18.
13. *Pros. Ptol.*, I 270; Morkholm, 'Eulaeus and Lenaeus', pp 40–41.
14. *Pros. Ptol.*, II 926 and III 5169; Morkkolm, 'Eulaeus and Lenaeus', pp 39–40.
15. Diodoros 30.16.
16. T.C. Skeat, 'Notes on Ptolemaic Chronology: II, The Twelfth Year which is also the First: The Invasion of Egypt by Antiochos Epiphanes', *Journal of Egyptian Archaeology*, 47 (1971), pp 107–112.
17. Polybios 28.19.1.
18. Livy 44.19.9 – but this may probably refer to Antiochos' second invasion.
19. *I Maccabees* 1.19.
20. Polybios 29.19.1.
21. Polybios 28.19.2–6; Walbank, *Commentary*, 3.354–355.
22. Sais: Otto, *Ptolemaeer*, p 50; Naukratis: Walbank, *Commentary*, 3.355.
23. Morkholm, *Antiochus IV*, p 77.
24. Polybios 28.20.3–5.
25. Polybios 28.20.6–9.
26. Polybios 28.20.10.
27. Polybios 28.20.10–13.
28. Porphyry *FGrH* 260 F 49a includes the notion that Antiochos had himself crowned as Egyptian king, but this event would destroy his influence with Ptolemy, and is best placed a year later.
29. Livy 44.19.6–8.
30. T.C. Skeat, 'Notes on Ptolemaic Chronology'.
31. Polybios 30.26.9; Diodoros 30.18.2.
32. Livy 44.19.6–12.
33. Polybios 28.22.1; Livy 45.11.1.
34. Polybios 28.17.4–9.
35. Polybios 28.23.23.
36. Livy 45.11.4.
37. Morkholm, *Antiochus IV*, p 87.
38. Polybios 29.25.3–4; Lampela, *Roman and the Ptolemies*, pp 123–124; Gruen, *Hellenistic World*, pp 655–657.
39. Livy 44.19.6–12; Lampela, *Roman and the Ptolemies*, p 125.
40. Ray, *Archive of Hor*, p 26.
41. Polybios 29.13.4; Livy 45.11.2–7.
42. Morkholm, *Antiochus IV*, p 83, suggests that Antiochos had a 'legal basis' for a new expedition; there is, however, no evidence for the status of the agreement.
43. *I Maccabees* 1.20–28.
44. Justin 34.2.8–3.1.
45. *OGIS* 761.
46. Polybios 29.25.
47. Polybios 29.23.8–25.7; A. Aymard, *Les Assemblees de la confederatin achaienne* (Paris, 1938), p 271; Morkholm, *Antiochos IV*, pp 89–90.
48. Livy 44.19.13–14; Lampela, *Roman and the Ptolemies*, pp 126–128; Gruen, *Hellenistic World*, pp 657–658.

49. Polybios 29.4.8–10; Livy 44.24.1–7.
50. As by Morkholm, *Antiochus IV*, p 91 – but Antiochos welcomed and accepted his service, an unlikely reaction if he had been ineptly defeated.
51. Sir George Hill, *History of Cyprus*, vol. I, (Cambridge, 1940), p 188, note 5; *II Maccabees* 10.19.
52. Livy 44.19.9.
53. Livy 44.11.10.
54. Livy 45.11.10–11.
55. Livy 45.12.1–2.
56. Holbl, *Ptolemaic Empire*, pp 147 and 181.
57. *C. Ord. Ptol.*, 32; *P. Tebt.* III, 698.
58. C. Thiers, 'Civils et Militaires dans les temples. Occupation illicite et expulsion', *BIAO*, 99, pp 493–516, document 6.
59. Ray, *Archive of Hor*, pp 125–129.
60. Porphyry, *FGrH* 260, F 49a; Dorothy J. Thompson, *Memphis under the Ptolemies*, 2nd ed (Princeton NJ, 2012), p 140.
61. Livy 45.12.2.
62. Livy 44.29.1–5.
63. Accounts of the events at Eleusis include: Gruen, *Hellenistic World*, pp 658–660; Lampela, *Rome and the Ptolemies*, pp 124–138; W. Gwyn Morgan, 'The Perils of Schematism: Polybius, Antiochus Epiphanes, and the "Day of Eleusis"', *Historia*, 39 (1990), pp 37–76; Morkholm, *Antiochos IV*, pp 94–96; Walbank, *Commentary*, 3.403–406; Holbl, *Ptolemaic Empire*, pp 146–148.
64. Livy 45.10.1–2.
65. Livy 44.45.1–46.11; Perseus had time to address his assembly, negotiate with the Bisaltai, and travel to Samothrace; we must allow weeks at least for all this.
66. Livy 45.10.8–9.
67. Livy 45.10.5.
68. Walbank, *Commentary*, 3.403–404 calculated a similar date for the meeting ('early July 168') based on the supposed predictions made by the Egyptian priest Hor: Ray, *Archive of Hor*, pp 14–29; everyone's calculations are, of course, only approximate.
69. Livy 45.12; Polybios 29.27.1–13; Diodoros 31.2; Appian, *Syrian Wars*, 66: Justin 34.3; Porphyry, *FGrH* 260 F 50; and others. Unfortunately the frequency of the incident's appearance in the record hardly brings clarity.
70. E. Paltiel, 'Antiochos Epiphanes and Roman Politics', *Latomus*, 41 (1982), pp 229–254.
71. Ray, *Archive of Hor*, pp 14–29 (if a *post facto* dream can be accepted as indicating accurate dating).
72. Polybios 29.27.9-10; Livy 45.12.7–8.

Chapter 12
1. Polybios 29.29.9; Livy 45.32.7.
2. Polyaratos: Polybios 29.2 7.9 and 30.12; Menalkidas: Polybios 38.16.2; Lampela, *Rome and the Ptolemies*, p 136; Gruen, *Hellenistic World*, p 693.
3. For the explication of Hor and his records, see Ray, *Archive of Hor*, 'Historical Information', pp 124–130.
4. Ray, *Archive of Hor*, p 128, makes this suggestion.
5. Polybios 30.16.1; Livy 45.13.4–8; Mooren, 'Governors-General', pp 121–122; *Pros. Ptol.*, II 1919, III 5155, and others.
6. Ray, *Archive of Hor*, p 128; Livy 45.11.7.
7. *UPZ* 59 and 60.
8. Diodoros 31.15a.1–4, is the only source for this episode.

9. McGing, 'Revolt Egyptian Style', pp 273–314, at 289–295; Veisse, *Les revoltes Egyptiennes*, pp 28–32.
10. *P. Tebtunis* III 781; Veisse, *Revoltes egyptiens*, p 136; Fischer-Bovet, *Army and Society*, p 267.
11. K. Goudriaan, *Ethnicity in Ptolemaic Egypt* (Amsterdam, 1988), doc. 115.
12. *P. Gen.* III 128; McGing, 'Revolt Egyptian Style', p 240.
13. *UPZ* I 781; McGing, 'Revolt Egyptian Style', p 241.
14. Diodoros 31.17b; Clarysse, 'Ptolemies visiting the Egyptian Chora', p 48.
15. Diodoros 31.15a.4.
16. *UPZ* I 42.
17. Thompson, *Memphis*, p 270.
18. *Ibid*, p 113.
19. The date was derived from papyri: Holbl, *Ptolemaic Empire*, p 214, note 16.
20. *SB* 12821; see M.I. Roztovtzeff, *Social and Economic History of the Hellenistic World*, volume II (Oxford, 1941), pp 719–723; Holbl, *Ptolemaic Empire*, p 182.
21. *UPZ* I 110; *C. Ord. Ptol.*, 39; Thompson, *Memphis*, pp 236–237.
22. *P. Haun* 4.70; Thorolf Christensen, Dorothy J. Thomson, and Katelijn Vandorpe, *Land and Taxes in Ptolemaic Egypt, an Edition, Translation and Commentary for the Edfu Land Survey* (Cambridge, 2017).
23. Diodoros 31.18.1–2; Livy, *Epitome*, 46.
24. Diodoros 31.18.1.
25. Valerius Maximus 5.1.1.
26. Walbank, *Commentary*, 2.468.
27. Holbl, *Ptolemaic Empire*, p 183.
28. Diodoros 31.17c; Polybios 31.18.14.
29. Holbl, *Ptolemaic Empire*, pp 194–196.
30. Polybios 31.10.

Chapter 13
1. *UPZ* 1.111; the date was stated in the decree, and so it was presumably the date of the decree itself.
2. *C. Ord. Ptol.*, 35.
3. *UPZ* 1.6 and 3.111.
4. Thompson, *Memphis*, pp 199–200; Holbl, *Ptolemaic Empire*, pp 184–185.
5. Polybios 31.10.1–5; Walbank, *Commentary*, 3.474–476.
6. Polybius 31.2.9–11.
7. Polybios 31.18.
8. Polybios 31.17–18.
9. *Pros. Ptol.* VI, 5071.
10. Polybios 31.18.6–16; Walbank, *Commentary*, 3.486–488, including a map to locate the 'great slope'.
11. Polybios 31.20.5–6.
12. M. Hengel, *Judaism and Hellenism* (London, 1980).
13. *II Maccabees* 4.21–30.
14. J.D. Grainger, *The Wars of the Maccabees* (Barnsley, 2012), ch 5.
15. *I Maccabees* 1.54.
16. Josephus, *Bellum Judaicum* 7.427–430; *Antiquities Judaiae* 13.65–71.
17. Josephus, *Antiquities Judaiae* 12.387.
18. Robert Hayward, 'The Jewish Temple at Leontopolis: A Reconsideration, *Journal of Jewish Studies* 33 (1982), pp 429–443.
19. *P. Tebtunis* 3.781.
20. C. de Witt, *Les Inscriptions du temple d'Opet a Karnak* (Brussels, 1958–1968).

21. E. Lanciers, 'Die Agyptische Tempelbauten zur Zeit des Ptolemaios Epiphanes (204–180 B.C.)', *Mitteilungern Deutschen Archeologischen Instituts, Ableitung Kairo*, 53 (1986), pp 81–99; and 43 (1987), pp 173–182.
22. B. Porter and R.L.B. Moss, *Topographical Bibliography of Ancient Egyptian Hieroglyphic Texts* (Oxford, 1927–1952), p 224.
23. De Witt, *Inscriptions*, p 402.
24. Holbl, *Ptolemaic Empire*, p 337.
25. G. Haery, 'A Short Architectural History of Philae', *BIFAO*, 86 (1985), pp 197–233.
26. *Ibid*, p 220.
27. Listed briefly in Holbl, *Ptolemaic Empire*, p 339.
28. Laszlo Torok, 'To the History of the Dodekaschoenos between c.250 BC and 298 AD', *ZAS*, 107 (1980), pp 76–86.
29. Derek A. Welsby, The Kingdom of Kush, London 1996, 66 – 67; Holbl, Ptolemaic Empire, 162.
30. Adel Farid, 'The Stela of Andikhalamani found at Philai', *Mitteilungern Deutschen Archeologischen Instituts, Ableitung Kairo*, 34 (1978), pp 53–56.
31. For Berenike Panchrysos, cf G.M. Cohen, *The Hellenistic Settlements in Syria, the Red Sea Basin, and North Africa* (Berkeley and Los Angeles, 2006), pp 316–320.
32. Holbl, *Ptolemaic Empire*, p 189, and references there.
33. Cohen, *Hellenistic Settlements/Africa*, pp 349–350.
34. The evidence for the attack lies in the will he composed, and in Ptolemy's allegations in the Senate later.
35. R.K. Sherk (ed and trans), *Rome and the Greek East to the Death of Augustus*, Translated Documents of Greece and Rome (Cambridge, 1984), no 31, republished in Lampela, *Rome and the Ptolemies*, as appendix 4.
36. Holbl, *Ptolemaic Empire*, pp 187–188; Lampela, *Rome and the Ptolemies*, pp 166–173.
37. Polybios 33.11.1–3.
38. Polybios 33.1.4–7; Walbank, *Commentary* 3.553–555.
39. Diodoros 31.18.1.
40. Polybios 39.7.6; Diodoros 31.33.
41. *OGIS* 116, a record of Cretan recruits for Ptolemy VI.
42. Polybios 39.7.6.
43. Philip Hendrick, *Libya Architectural Guide, Cyrenaica* (London, 2013), pp 100–101.

Chapter 14
1. *OGIS*, 125–127, statue bases from Paphos and Korion in Cyprus.
2. *I Maccabees* 3.4–49; A. Aymard, 'Autour de l'avenement d'Antiochos IV', *Historia*, 2 (1993), pp 49–73; O. Morkholm, 'The Accession of Antiochos IV of Syria', *ASMNM*, 11 (1964), pp 63–70, and *Antiochos IV of Syria* (Copenhagen, 1996), pp 41–47.
3. Sachs and Wiseman, *Babylonian Chronicles*, -170; recorded explicitly as 'at the command of Antiochos the king'.
4. Polybios 31.1.2–10.
5. Polybios 31.11.1–15.8; Polybios was active in helping Demetrios plan his escape.
6. *I Maccabees* 7.10
7. *II Maccabees* 4.30; D. Ogden, *Polygamy, Prostitution and Death* (London, 1999), pp 143–144, argues for the paternity of the two by Antiochos IV.
8. *II Maccabees* 4.30.
9. Polybios 33.15 and 18.6.
10. Herakleides had escorted Alexander and Laodike to Rome: Polybios 33.18.6–14.
11. Diodoros 31.32a.
12. *I Maccabees* 10.6 – 8.

13. E.T. Newell, *Late Seleucid Mints at Ptolemais-Ake and Damascus* (New York, 1939); H. Seyrig, *Tresors du Levant, anciens et nouveaux* (Paris, 1973).
14. Justin 35.1.10 (probably inaccurate); Josephus, *Antiquities Judaiae* 13.58–61.
15. Justin 35.2.1.
16. Holbl, *Ptolemaic Empire*, p 192.
17. Livy, *Periochae* 50; Justin 35.2.2; Diodoros 32.9c.
18. *I Maccabees* 10.6 – 7; Josephus *Antiquities Judaiae*, 13.86.
19. *I Maccabees* 10.19.
20. Josephus *Antiquities Judaiae*, 13.88.
21. I Maccabees 10.74–76; Josephus, *Antiquities Judaiae* 13.91–92.
22. *I Maccabees* 10.83 – 85; Josephus, *Antiquities Judaiae*, 13.98–100.
23. *I Maccabees* 11.3–7; Josephus, *Antiquities Judaiae*, 13.105.
24. *I Maccabees* 10.89.
25. See note 12.
26. *I Maccabees* 11.6–7.
27. *I Maccabees* 10.86.
28. Josephus, *Antiquities Judaiae*, 13.106.
29. *I Maccabees* 11.9–10.
30. *Ibid.*
31. Diodoros 32.27.9d.
32. Diodoros 32.27.10.2.
33. 'Who was king, who was not king?' – a cry uttered by a poet of Sumerian Mesopotamia 2,000 years before this war, but which fits the situation precisely.
34. *I Maccabees* 11.13; Josephus, *Antiquities Judaiae* 13.108 and 113.
35. Diodoros 32.27.9.6.
36. *Ibid.*
37. For the diadems: Josephus *Antiquities Judaiae*, 13.13; *I Maccabees* 2.13.
38. M. Chauveux, 'Un Ete 145', *BIFAO*, 90 (1990), pp 135–168, and 91 (1991), pp 129–134.
39. Luigi Santi Amantini, 'Tolemei VI Filometore re di Siria?', *Istituto Lombardo (Rend. Lett.) Storia Antico*, 108 (1974) pp 511–529.
40. Diodoros 32.9a; Livy, *periochae*, 50; Orosius 9.22.9.
41. Polybios 5.
42. Josephus, *Antiquities Judaiae*, 13.114.
43. Josephus, Antiquities Judaiae, 13.113–114; Chauveau, 'Un ete 145'.
44. Diodoros 32.9d.
45. Diodoros 32.10.1.
46. Livy, *periochae*, 52.

Index

Abila, 67
Abydos (Egypt), 90, 96, 108
Abydos (Greece), 105, 144
Adulis, 23
Aegean Sea, vii, x, 1–2, 14, 98, 100, 210
Aemilius Lepidus, M., 105–106, 144
Aemilius Paullus, M., 155, 156, 160
Aeropos, 110
Africa, 7, 92
Agelaos, 1
Agatharchides of Knidos, 23
Agathokles, Syracusan king, 21, 24, 58, 79
Agathokles, son of Theogenes, 2, 63, 72, 77, 78, 79, 87, 88, 89, 90–1, 104, 113, 117, 179
 overthrow, 93–5, 96, 100, 101
Agis IV, Spartan king, 25
Ainos, 12, 13, 14, 18, 30, 100, 105
Aitolian League, 25, 29, 33, 53, 70, 81–2, 105, 110, 118, 120, 135
Akhaian League, 14, 25, 26, 29, 33, 53, 127, 137, 149, 154, 159
Akhaios, Seleukid pretender, 32, 33, 47, 55–9, 65, 69, 79–81, 89
Akoris, 126
Alexander the Great, vii, xi, 29, 132
Alexander I Balas, Seleukid king, 196–9, 200–202, 204–206, 211
Alexander II Zabeinas, Seleukid king, 201
Alexander, priesthood of, 3, 21, 22–3, 39
Alexander of Corinth, x, 1, 49
Alexandria, viii, ix, xiv, 1, 4, 8, 10, 19, 22, 23, 37, 39, 40, 47, 52, 56–8, 63, 71–83, 87, 92, 106, 113–14, 129, 134, 144–6, 151–2, 158–60, 179, 187
 library of, 37–8
 and overthrow of Agathokles, 93–5
Alexandria Troas, 30
Alexandria (ship, ex-*Syracusa*), 74
Alinda, 28
Ammonios, 200, 204, 205, 207
anachoresis, 98, 126
Andikhelamani, Nubian king, 189
Andragoras, 17
Andriskos, 4, 5
Andriskos, Macedonian pretender, 197, 201, 210
Andromachos, 39
Andronikos, murderer, 143
Andros, battle, 1–2, 12–13, 14, 47
Ankyra, battle, 32

Antaeopolis, 188
Antigonos I, vii, 29, 41, 63, 208
Antigonos II Gonatas, Macedonian king, vii, ix, x, 1, 13, 14, 19, 25, 29, 132
Antigonos III Doson, Macedonian king, 25–6, 28, 32, 141
Antigonos, son of Demetrios I, 200
Antilebanon Mountains, 31, 41, 43, 98
Antioch, 2, 3, 5–6, 13–14, 15, 19, 34, 35, 55, 56, 144, 199, 201, 204, 208
Antiochis, concubine of Antiochos IV, 197, 200
Antiochos I, king, viii, 31, 42, 47
Antiochos II, king, x, 2, 7, 8, 9, 12, 15, 16, 18, 47, 131
Antiochos III, king ix, 16, 31, 33, 41, 43, 47, 55–70, 79, 84, 86, 89, 91–3, 101–103, 104, 106, 111–12, 115, 164
 and Rome, 118–19, 123, 131, 132, 137
Antiochos IV, king, 136–7, 139–42, 145–50, 151–66, 168, 179, 195
Antiochos V, king, 195, 196
Antiochos VII, king, 200
Antiochos, governor of Kilikia, 8, 10
Antiochos Hierax, Seleukid usurper, 2, 8, 17, 24, 30, 31–2, 34
Antiochos, son of Alexander I Balas, 201, 206
Antiochos, son of Berenike I, 2, 3, 5, 6, 7, 10, 15, 23
Antiochos, son of Seleukos IV, 195
Apama, wife of Magas, x, 50
Apameia, Syria, 7, 42, 56, 123, 157
Apameia-Kelainai, 123
Apollonios, *dioiketes*, 9–10, 20, 23, 36
Apollonios, poet, 37, 38
Apollonios of Miletos, 133, 145
Apollonios Taos, 197, 201–203
Arabia, xi, 97
Arabs, xii
Arados, 16, 123–4, 128, 133
Arameans, xii
Aratos of Sikyon, xi, 14, 25, 26
Archagathos, son of Agathokles, 21
Archelaos, son of Damas, 23
Archias, governor of Cyprus, 193, 197
Archimedes, 74
Ardys, Seleukid commander, 61
Argolid, x
Argos, 26
Aribazos, governor of Kilikia, 4

Aristonikos, son of Aristonikos, 121, 122, 123–4, 125, 127, 128
army, Ptolemaic, 68, 70, 76, 89, 122
  recruits for, ix–x, 11, 41
  reform of, 40–1, 43–6
army, Seleukid, 68, 103
Arsakes, Parthian king, 17
Arsinoe I, 9, 22
Arsinoe II, 8, 9, 36
Arsinoe III, sister and wife of Ptolemy IV, 50, 58, 81, 83
  murdered, 88, 89, 93, 95
Ashkelon, 200, 203
Asia Minor, vii, x, xii, 9, 12, 17, 30, 32–3, 34, 42, 55, 79, 89, 103, 111, 118, 119, 137, 139, 198
Assyrians, xii, 1
Athens, 25–7, 37, 45, 81, 82, 105, 106, 111, 137, 139, 140, 149, 211
Attika, 1, 14, 26, 106
Azotos, 202

Bab el-Mandeb, 39
Babylon, 13, 55, 142
Babylonia, Babylonians, x, xii, 7, 8, 10, 11, 142, 213
Baktria, 7, 17, 55
Balikh River, 14
Banyas River, 107
Barada River, 31, 98
Bargylia, 101, 102
Bekaa Valley, 23, 30, 41, 56, 57, 59, 98, 102
Berenike, wife of Ptolemy I, 21
Berenike I, wife of Antiochos II, 2–4, 5–6, 7–9, 10, 11, 15, 18
Berenike II, wife of Ptolemy III, vii ix, x, 8, 19, 20, 21, 34, 36, 37, 49, 50, 95
  murdered, 52, 54–5, 56
Berenike Panchrysos, 189
Beroia, 143
Berytos, 62, 66, 200
Bithynia, 32
Boethos, *strategos*, 190, 193
Boiotia, 81, 82
Brochoi, 30, 42, 62
Bruttium, 92
Bubastis, 66, 71
Buhen, 190
Byzantion, 80, 82

Caligula, Emperor, 74
Capua, 83
Carthage, 24, 79, 81, 83, 92, 104, 111, 120, 192, 210
Chalkis, Euboia, 154, 160
Chalkis, lines of, 23, 31, 42–3, 98–9
  see also Gerrha-Brochoi lines
Chaonnophris (Ankh-wenefer), Pharaoh, 108–109, 110, 111, 115, 125, 189
Charimortos, 113
Chios, 80, 82

chora, viii, 71–2, 77, 171
Claudius Nero, C., 105
Coinage, Ptolemaic, 75–6, 136
Corinth, x, 1, 13, 14, 112, 210
Cornelius, L., 180
Cornelius Merula, Cn., 184
Cornelius Scipio Africanus, P., 92
Crete, x, 2, 28, 29, 80, 81, 82
Cyprus, xiii, 4, 7, 10, 72, 91, 112, 115, 117, 121, 135, 156–7, 163, 165, 180, 181, 183, 191–2, 196, 197
Cyrenaica, vi, viii, xi, 2, 10, 34, 37, 38, 41, 91, 95, 98, 112, 117, 118, 181, 183, 185, 191
Cyrene, ix, 21, 35, 60, 95, 184–5, 191–2

Dabod, 189
el-Dakka (Pselchis), 189
Damascus, 16–17, 31, 41, 43, 98–9, 101, 102–103, 107
Damasippos, 184
Damophilos, ix
Danae, 94
Daphne, 5
Dardanelles, 117
Decimus, C., 155
Decius Magnus, 83
Deinias (Tynys), 168
Deir el-Medina, 188
Delos, 156, 160–2
Delphi, 135
Demetrios I, Seleukid king, vii, 179–80, 192, 196, 197, 199, 200–201
Demetrios II, Macedonian king, 25, 32
Demetrios II, Seleukid king, 200, 201, 204–206, 209, 212
Demetrios the Fair, ix, 25, 34, 54
Demoxenos, 110
Dendera (Tentyra), 108
Dikaiarchos, 114
Diodotos I, Baktrian governor, 17
Diodotos II, Baktrian governor, 17
Diodotos of Kasiana, 207, 211
Diodotos (Totytts), 169
Diogenes, commander in Athens, 25
Diognetos, Seleukid Admiral, 60–1, 65
dioiketes, 9, 20, 36, 134, 136, 150, 177
Dionysios, *strategos*, 182
Dionysios Petosarapis, 171–5, 176
Dodekaschoenos, 189–90
Dora, 43, 64, 66
Dushares, xii

Edfu, 40, 72, 86, 87–8, 96, 187
Egypt, vii, viii, xiii
  building in, 39–40
  government system, 73
  population, xiii–xiv
  and *passim*
Eirenaios, *strategos*, 145, 147, 148, 149, 169
Ekdelos, viii
Ekron, 203

Index   237

Elephantine, 87, 88, 91, 125, 158, 159, 165, 168, 188
Elephants, Indian, xi, 24, 96, 107
    African, xi, 23–4, 76, 107
Eleusis, Egypt, 159, 160–3, 167, 169, 173, 179
Eleuthera, 28
Eleutheros River, xii, 16, 41, 42, 69, 123, 203
Epeiros, 50, 105, 106
Ephesos, vii, 2, 3, 12
Eulaios, Ptolemaic regent, 134, 135, 139, 145, 149, 151
Eumenes II, king, 137, 164, 196, 201
Euphrates River, 7, 8, 9, 10, 14

Fayum, 158, 174, 178

Gadara, 67
Galatians, 5, 31, 32
Galilee, Sea of, 67
Gallipoli Peninsula, 14
Gaza, xii, 42, 43, 63, 66–8, 97, 98, 100, 102, 110, 143, 145–6, 203, 204
    battle, 21, 44
Gennaios, 5, 6
Gerrha, 30, 42, 62
Gerrha-Brochoi Lines, 30–1, 42, 56, 59–60, 62, 67, 98–9
    see also Lines of Chalkis
Gethros, 67
Gortyn, 81
Greece, ix, 25–7, 79

Hakoris, 96
Hannibal, 81, 83, 92, 104
Hasdrubal, 105
Heliodoros, 136, 140, 195
Hellespont, 14, 15, 30, 34, 46, 210
Herakleides, 197
Herakleopolis, 174, 177
Hermeias, 57
Hermon, Mount, 99, 103, 107
Heroides, *dioiketes*, 177
Hierapytna, 28
Hierax, 207, 211
Hiero II, Syracusan king, 24, 74, 79
Hieronymos, Syracusan king, 79, 83
Hindu Kush, 89
Hippalos, son of Sos, 135
Hippomedon, 13, 14, 30
Hor, priest, 154, 168, 169
Hostilius, C., 155

Ikadion, 5, 6
India, xi, 7, 9, 80, 89, 97, 104
Ionia, 14, 35, 100, 112
Iran, 17, 59, 103, 104, 179
Island league, xi, 28, 105
Italy, 80
Itanos, x, 2, 29, 81
Ituraeans, xii

Jamneia, 202
Jerusalem, 102–103, 110, 186, 199
Jews, xii, xiv, 186–7
Jonathan Maccabee, 198, 199, 201–202, 203–205, 208–209
Joppa, 43, 69, 110, 143, 202, 203
Jordan River, 6, 143, 154
Judaea, 186–7, 197, 201

Kabul Valley, 89
Kalamos, 66
Kallikrates, 8, 37, 47
Kallikrates, Aitolian politician, 155
Kallimachos, 8, 37, 38
Kallimedes, 100, 101, 105
Kallinikon, 14
Kanopos, 40, 53, 71, 163, 169
Karia, x, 3, 22, 28–9, 96, 98, 100, 101, 112
Karnak, 87
Kaunos, 29
Kildara, 3, 19, 23
Kilikia, 4, 6–7, 8, 9, 17, 46, 111, 197, 201, 204
Kineas, son of Dositheos, 148–50, 151–3
Kleomenes III, Spartan king, 25, 26, 27, 33, 45, 47
    in Alexandria, 40, 53
    murdered, 52–4, 59, 71, 113
Kleopatra I Syra, wife of Ptolemy V, 115–16, 118–19, 121
    regent, 130–3, 134, 125, 138, 150, 187, 194, 199
Kleopatra II, 127, 135–6, 144, 148, 151–2, 154, 170–1, 176, 179, 181, 182, 198, 208, 212
Kleopatra III, 199
Kleopatra Thea, 198, 201, 205
Kleopatra (Nubia), 190
Klazomenai, 150
Kleon, governor of Memphis, 158, 169, 170
Knidos, 201
Komanos, 125, 126, 134, 148–50, 151–3, 170
Kom Ombo, 188
Koptos, 22, 96, 108
Korakesion, 111
Kyklades, xi
Kynoskephalai, battle, 112
Kypsela, 15
Kyrrhestai, 57, 59

Laodike, daughter of Antiochos II, 8
Laodike, wife of Demetrios I, 196–7, 200
Laodike, wife of Seleukos IV, 140, 195
Laodikeia, 4
Laodikeia-ad-Mare, 19, 25, 30, 56
Lapethos, 192
Lasthenes, 201
Lebanon Mountains, 16, 31, 42, 62
Lenaios, *dioiketes* and regent, 134–6, 139, 145, 148
Leontios, commander in Seleukeia, 61
Leontopolis, 186, 187
Lesbos, 14

Libya, Libyans, xi, xii, xiv, 22
Lykia, x, 14, 23, 112
Lykopolis (Asyut), 109, 121, 124–5
Lykopolis (Delta), 72, 110, 125, 127
Lykortas, 154–5
Lysias, 196
Lysimacheia, conference at, 115
Lysimachos, king, iii, x
Lysimachos, son of Ptolemy II, 21, 50
   killed, 51, 54
Lyttos, 29

Macedon, Macedonians, ix, x, xii, 1, 19, 25, 26, 104, 117, 164, 210
machimoi, 11, 64, 177–8, 214
Magas, Cyrenaican king, viii, ix, x, xi, 21–2, 41, 49–50
Magas, son of Ptolemy III, 21, 33, 46, 48, 50, 55
   killed, 51–2, 54
Magnesia, 31
Manlius Torquatus, T., 184
Marcius, Q., 180
Marcius Philippus, Q., 152, 153, 155–6
Maroneia, 13, 14, 30, 100, 105
Masinissa, Numidian king, 120
Mediterranean Sea, xii
Megalopolis, 81
Memphis, 64, 71, 72, 113, 127, 151–3, 157–9, 162, 169, 170, 176, 181, 182–3
Menalkidas of Sparta, 167
Menekles, 110
Menyllos, 183, 196
Meroe, 189
mercenaries, Ptolemaic, 11, 75, 81, 101, 110, 123
   detachments, 63–4
   Thracian, 12
Mesopotamia, 8, 11, 14, 17
Methana, x
Miletos, 14, 150
Mithradates V, King of Pontos, 131, 200
Moeragenes, 94, 95
Moeris, 158, 174, 187
Molon, Seleukid pretender, 56–7, 58, 59
Mount Kasios, battle, 145, 147, 149
Mytilene, 82

Nabataeans, xii, xiv
Nag el-Medamad, 188
Napata, 189
Naukratis, 72, 151
Navy, Ptolemaic, xiii, 11, 46–7, 66, 76, 118
   Seleukid, 3, 65–6, 111
Nikaia, lady of Corinth, 1, 14, 49
Nikolaos, 62, 63, 66
Nile River, xi, 9, 23, 36
Noumenios, son of Noumenios, 135, 169–70
Nubia, Nubians, viii, xiv, 125, 189
Numisius Tarquiniensis, T., 153–4

Octavius, C., 161, 183–4
Oenanthe, wife of Agathokles, 22, 56, 88, 95
Oenoparos River, battle, 211
Olympichos, 28, 29, 32
Onias III, Jewish high priest, 143, 186
Onias IV, 187
Orchomenos, 81
Orontes River, 43
Oropos, 81
Orthosia, 16, 17, 41, 43
Ostia, 179

Palestine, 31, 63, 71, 99, 101, 103, 106, 199
Pamphylia, 102, 112, 184
Panaitolos, 61–2, 81
Panion, battle, 107–108, 118
Panopolis (Akhmin), siege of, 175
Parni, 17
Parthia, Parthians, 17, 55, 89, 204
Patroklos, 44
Pella, 67
Peloponnese, 14
Pelops, son of Pelops, 71
Pelusion, 62, 63, 64, 68, 71, 93, 99, 143, 145–7, 149, 153, 157, 159–69
Pergamon, 30, 32, 33, 48, 55, 81
Perigenes, 66
Perseus, Macedonian king, 136, 138, 140, 141, 156, 159, 160
Persians, xii, 11
Phakoussa, 71
Phalara, 81
Philai, 39, 40, 126, 188, 189–90
Philammon, 91, 94
Philip V, Macedonian king, 25–6, 29, 47, 79, 80–2, 91–2, 100, 104, 105, 106, 108, 114, 118, 120, 176, 191
Philip, son of Agemachos, 91
Philistines, xii, 67
Philokles of Sidon, 47
Philometoris, 190
Phoenicia, Phoenicians, xiii, xiv, 4, 31, 56, 71, 99, 111, 143, 145, 199
Phylarchos, 12
Polybios, 51, 54, 57, 61, 64, 72–3, 85, 92, 107, 127, 151, 154–5, 196
Polykrates, 100, 112–13, 114–15, 120–1, 122, 126, 135
Pontos, 32, 58
Popilius Laenas, C., 155–6, 160–5, 167–8, 179, 208
Poseideion, 4, 6
Ptolemais, Cyrenaica, 192
Ptolemaios, recluse, 174
Ptolemaios, son of Thraseas, 102, 110
Ptolemais, Egypt, 96, 108, 135, 187
Ptolemais-Ake, Palestine, 43, 57, 60, 61–2, 63–6, 69, 110, 197, 198, 200, 201, 203, 206
Ptolemy I Soter, viii, xi, xii, xiii, 11, 15, 20, 22, 31, 42, 44, 49, 65, 79

Ptolemy II Philadelphos, vii, viii, x–xi, xii, xiv, 2, 8, 9, 11, 14, 20, 22, 35, 41, 42, 49, 50–1, 73, 104
Ptolemy III Euergetes, vii, viii, ix–xi, xiii, 2–3, 4–5, 7, 8, 14, 15, 17–19, 21, 24, 26–8, 30–1, 33, 34–48 42, 58, 72, 85, 212
   army reforms, 43–6
   death, 47, 49
Ptolemy IV Philometor, 20, 21, 40, 50, 71–8, 79, 104
   death, 89
   fratricide, 51–2, 55
   his great ship, 173–4, 212
   the great revolt, 86, 92
Ptolemy V, 88, 93–5, 105, 113, 117–29, 133, 134, 138, 148, 194
   murder of, 129, 130–1
Ptolemy VI, 86, 127, 130, 134, 135, 144, 148–9, 151–2, 167, 171–2
   land reform, 176–92, 196–212, 214
Ptolemy VIII, 127, 144, 148, 151–2, 167, 171, 172–3, 176, 179, 180, 181–5, 191, 194, 196, 208, 214
Ptolemy Andromachou, 1, 12, 13, 50
Ptolemy Eupator, 194, 198
Ptolemy Keraunos, 49, 50
Ptolemy Makron, 135, 156–7
Ptolemy, son of Agemachos, 135
Ptolemy, son of Lysimachos, xiii
Ptolemy, son of Sosibios, 91
Ptolemy Sympetesis, 184
Ptolemy 'the Son', vii, 49
Puteoli, 179
Pydna, battle, 156, 160–1
Pythangelos, 39

Qasr Ibrim, 190
Quinctius Flamininus, T., 110, 112

Rabbatamana, 67
Raphia, battle, 44, 68–72, 75, 76, 80, 87, 122, 210, 213
   decree of, 69, 73
   peace treaty at, 115–16
Ras Ibn Hani, 25
Rebellion in Egypt, 9–10, 24, 39, 72–3
   in the Delta, 92
   the great revolt, 76, 85, 108, 117–18, 124–6, 213
Red Sea, viii, xi, 23, 96, 117
   expeditions to, 38–9
Revenue Laws, 9, 35
Rhinokoloura, 157
Rhodes, x, xi, 28, 29, 37, 80, 81, 93, 100, 105, 114, 152, 153, 161–2
Rome, 23, 24, 38, 91, 93, 104, 119, 154, 155, 189–95
   and Antiochos III, 119–20, 123, 137
   and Antiochos IV, 137, 140, 135–65
   and Philip V, 81–4
   and Ptolemy VI, 144, 167, 179–80, 183–5

and Seleukos IV, 10, 133, 138
   wars of, 194–5, 209
Rosetta Stone, 107, 126

Sais, 150
Samos, x, 14, 47, 100, 101, 105, 118
Samothrake, 14, 148, 151, 161
Sardinia, 24
Sardis, 80, 81, 101, 111
Seleukeia-in-Pieria, 3, 4, 6, 13, 15, 17, 18, 19, 23, 24, 30, 34, 35, 42, 56, 111, 203–204, 207
   conference at, 65, 69
   recapture, 60–1, 63
Seleukid kingdom, x, 10, 19, 194
Seleukis, 13–14
Seleukos I, king, vii, x, 6, 15, 42, 65
Seleukos II, king, 2–4, 5, 8, 10, 13, 14, 16–17, 24, 30, 31, 32, 33, 41, 42, 43, 47
Seleukos III, king, 32, 33, 43, 47–8
Seleukos IV, king, 123–4, 131, 132, 133, 136, 138, 195
Sellasia, battle, 27
Sempronius Tuditanus, P., 105
Sicily, 79
Side, 184
Sidon, 41, 47, 62, 66–7, 69, 107–108, 110, 111, 113, 200
Sikyon, 159
Simmias, 23
Simmias of Rhodes, 161
Simon Maccabee, 202
Sinai, 63, 99, 143, 145, 157, 202
Siwah oasis, 83
Skopas, 101, 102–103, 106, 107–108, 111, 113–14, 115
Skythopolis, 67
Smyrna, 13
Soknopaiou Nesos, 194
Sollum, 184
Soloi, 4, 11
Sophron, naval commander, 1, 12
Sosibios, son of Dioskorides, 21, 22, 36, 46, 55, 56, 62, 69, 71–3, 77–8, 80, 86, 89, 90, 100, 113, 117
   and killing of Ptolemy IV's siblings and mother, 52–4
Sosibios, son of Sosibios, 94–6
Syracuse, 21, 22, 24, 79, 83, 104, 111
Syracusia (ship), 74, 79
Syria, Syrians, x, xii, xiv 6–7, 8–9, 14–15, 17, 34, 55, 72, 133, 139, 142, 146
   frontier of, xii
Syria-and-Phoenicia, vii, xii, 10, 15–16, 18, 30, 33, 41, 53, 64, 89, 98, 100, 117, 128, 206–207
'Syro-Macedonian Pact', 92–3, 98, 100, 108, 111

Tanagra, 81
Taras, 21, 113
Taurus Mountains, 6, 9, 13, 109

Tenis-Akoris, 96
Tentyra (Dendera), 188
Termessos, xiii
Thebaid, 73, 97, 126, 134–5, 148, 169, 174–6, 178, 186, 190
Thebes, 76–7, 86–9, 91, 96, 108–109, 111, 169, 188
Theodorides of Sikyon, 154
Theodotos of Aitolia, 53, 56, 57
    defection of, 57, 59, 61–2, 64, 66, 81, 102
Theodotos Hemiolios, 57, 60, 62
Theodotos/Theogis, murderer, 52
Theogenes, 22
Theoxene, daughter of Agathokles, 22
Theoxene, wife of Agathokles, 21, 51
Thera, x, xi
Thermos, 25
Thesmophoreion, 94
Thespiai, 81
Thessaly, 29, 81, 108, 110, 160
Thrace, 12–13, 14, 15, 30, 34, 100, 112, 137
Tigris River, 8
Timarchos, 14, 197, 199
Tlepolemos, son of Atrapates, 3, 22–3, 93, 95–6
    overthrown, 99, 100
Triakontoschoenos, 189, 190
Trieres, 66
Tyre, 43, 57, 61–2, 65, 66, 69, 110, 200

Wadi Allaqi, 189
Wars, Fraternal (Seleukid), 14, 30, 32
    Kremonidean, x, 11, 45
    Mercenary (Carthage), 24
    Macedonian, First, 104–105
        Second, 82, 106
        Third, 137, 141–2, 155
    'of the Allies', 80, 81
    Punic, First, 24
        Second, 79, 82, 92
        Third, 192
    Syrian, Second, x, 11, 42
        Third, 1–19, 23, 33, 37, 41, 46, 204
        Fourth, 55–70, 74, 92
        Fifth, x, 98–108, 137, 139
        Sixth, 137–66, 181
        Seventh, 194–211

Xanthippos, 8, 10, 14
Xenon, 57

Yahweh, xii, 187

Zabdiel, 206, 211
Zagros Mountains, 8
Zeno of Rhodes, 107
Zenophanes, 199
Zephyrion, 8, 37
Zeuxis, 57, 101
Ziaelas, Bithynian king, 32